Windows on a New World

Recent Titles in
Contributions in Economics and Economic History

Bridging the Gap Between Rich and Poor: American Economic Development Policy
Toward the Arab East, 1942–1949
Nathan Godfried

Rethinking the Nineteenth Century: Contradictions and Movements
Francisco O. Ramirez, editor

Textiles in Transition: Technology, Wages, and Industry Relocation in the U.S.
Textile Industry, 1880–1930
Nancy Frances Kane

Threats of Quotas in International Trade: Their Effect on the Exporting Country
Gerard Lawrence Stockhausen

A Slippery Slope: The Long Road to the Breakup of AT&T
Fred W. Henck and Bernard Strassburg

The Suppression of the Automobile: Skulduggery at the Crossroads
David Beasley

New Perspectives on Social Class and Socioeconomic Development in the Periphery
Nelson W. Keith and Novella Zett Keith, editors

World Population Trends and Their Impact on Economic Development
Dominick Salvatore, editor

Racism, Sexism, and the World-System
Joan Smith, Jane Collins, Terence K. Hopkins, and Akbar Muḥammad, editors

Electricity in Economic Development: The Experience of Northeast Asia
Yoon Hyung Kim and Kirk R. Smith, editors

Liberalization and the Turkish Economy
Tevfik Nas and Mehmet Odekon, editors

☐ *Windows on a*
☐ *New World*

The Third Industrial Revolution

Edited by
Joseph Finkelstein

Contributions in Economics and Economic History
Number 88

Greenwood Press
New York · Westport, Connecticut · London

Allen County Public Library
Ft. Wayne, Indiana

Library of Congress Cataloging-in-Publication Data

Windows on a new world : the third industrial revolution / edited by
    Joseph Finkelstein.
        p. cm.—(Contributions in economics and economic history,
ISSN 0084-9235 ; no. 88)
    Bibliography: p.
    Includes index.
    Contents: Microelectronics / R. A. Powell — Materials and modern
technology / J. E. Burke — Lasers / Joseph W. Haus and John
Schroeder — Biotechnology / Arnold E. S. Gussin — Frontiers in
biophysics / Jay Newman — The grand system / Alan J. Scrime — The
revolution in manufacturing / I. M. Hymes — Management during the
third industrial revolution / Allan Doyle — The third industrial
revolution / Joseph Finkelstein and David Newman.
    ISBN 0-313-26321-3 (lib. bdg. : alk. paper)
    1. Technological innovations—Economic aspects—History.
2. Information technology—History. 3. Microelectronics—History.
4. Telecommunication—History. I. Finkelstein, Joseph, 1926–   .
II. Series.
HC79.T4W47 1989
338'.06—dc19   88-25094

British Library Cataloguing in Publication Data is available.

Library of Congress Catalog Card Number: 88-25094
ISBN: 0-313-26321-3
ISSN: 0084-9235

First published in 1989

Greenwood Press, Inc.
88 Post Road West, Westport, Connecticut 06881

Printed in the United States of America

The paper used in this book complies with the
Permanent Paper Standard issued by the National
Information Standards Organization (Z39.48-1984).

10 9 8 7 6 5 4 3 2 1

To all who work for a better world in the future

Contents

Contents

Contributors

J. E. Burke, Ph.D.
Consultant
Materials Science and Engineering
Burnt Hills, NY

Allan Doyle
Vice Chairman of the Board
Kollmorgen
10 Mill Pond Lane
Simsbury, CT

Joseph Finkelstein, Ph.D.
Professor of History and Economics and of
    Administration and Management
Union College
Graduate Management Institute
Schenectady, NY

Arnold E. S. Gussin, Ph.D.
Dean, Graduate and Continuing Studies
Union College
Schenectady, NY

Joseph W. Haus, Ph.D.
Department of Physics
Rensselaer Polytechnic Institute
Troy, NY

I. M. Hymes
Program Director
Technology Assessment
IBM
Purchase, NY

David Newman
Assistant Professor of Business Policy in
  the Faculty of Business
McMaster University
Hamilton, Ontario

Jay Newman, Ph.D.
Associate Professor of Physics
Union College
Schenectady, NY

R. A. Powell, Ph.D.
Director, Materials and Equipment Laboratory
Varian Research Center
Palo Alto, CA

John Schroeder, Ph.D.
Department of Physics
Rensselaer Polytechnic Institute
Troy, NY

Alan J. Scrime
Corporate Director—R&D Program Management in
  NYNEX Science and Technology
White Plains, NY

Acknowledgments

Many colleagues and conference participants have heard these themes in Switzerland, England, Japan, South Korea, and the United States. I have learned from these experiences as I have benefited from the professional knowledge of the contributors to this volume.

Special thanks must be paid to Judy Peck, administrative assistant in the Graduate Management Institute, Union College, for her great help in producing this volume. I am convinced that behind each of the contributors is a person of similar talents without whose help this book would not have been completed. I would like to thank the staff of Schaffer Library, Union College, for helping me—always with professional skill, courtesy, and empathy.

My wife, Nadia Ehrlich Finkelstein, has been a constant supporter and help throughout; I am deeply indebted to her judgment and clarity during the many critical periods of this project.

Cynthia Harris of Greenwood Press, my editor, never failed to solve my problems, and earns our gratitude.

Introduction

We are, I believe, at the beginning of a Third Industrial Revolution that will reshape not only our industrial processes, but also bring with it great changes that will affect us all. The First Industrial Revolution of the eighteenth century brought fundamental but primitive changes in the allocation of people, resources, and energy. In the Second Industrial Revolution, the revolutionary impact of automobiles, photography, electric power, and industrial chemicals made the United States a foremost industrial world power. However, what is happening in microprocessors, communications, biogenetics, bioagriculture, lasers, fiber optics, robotics, CAD/CAM (computer-aided design/computer-aided manufacturing), the office of the future, energy, and other areas is greater by far than the changes that occurred in the eighteenth and nineteenth centuries.

Although the United States reaped the largest benefits from the Second Industrial Revolution that shaped our consumer society—from industries pioneered by men like Edison, Ford, and Eastman—a great many indicators point to Japan and other East Asian countries as most likely to succeed in this new revolution. As Americans we need to stop and examine why we have lost our preeminence.

The history of this Third Industrial Revolution begins with the information revolution brought about by the computer and made effective as a revolutionary device in the microprocessor which continues to drive the expansion and diffusion of the new knowledge-based processes. The diffusion and influence of the chip is incalculable as R. A. Powell's chapter "Microelectronics: Welcome to Lilliput" points out. But the Third Industrial Revolution goes far beyond the computer and the microprocessor. Each decade since the second world war has brought crucial developments in related areas of CAD/CAM, fiber optics, lasers, holography, biogenetics, bioagriculture, and telecommunications. The synergy of these new scientific/industrial areas will change our way of life for the next half-century and beyond.

Windows on a New World: The Third Industrial Revolution attempts to integrate some of these outstanding changes. In the main, my colleagues and I have tried to cover a broad and representative selection of major areas. Nine chapters deal with the most important topics relevant to the theme: microprocessors, materials, lasers, telecommunications, manufacturing, management, biotechnology, biophysics, and an overview of some consequences of these changes. Each contribution by a specialist in the field shapes the basic science of the subject and then goes beyond to raise pertinent questions and suggest reverberations. Throughout this volume other important areas are mentioned such as holography, bioagriculture, ceramics, and superconductors, but we have been deliberately frugal in the topics that have been given major treatment. We have tried to make these areas understandable within the framework of larger developments. We are certainly aware that our list of topics is not exhaustive.

We have chosen to treat these subjects broadly but with attention to their complexity because we believe that a simplified treatment would not be appropriate, relevant, or helpful to our readers. We have avoided the use of jargon, but have not avoided equations and mathematics. Though these devices should enhance the understanding of those with a scientific disposition, the discussion alone is meaningful, accurate, and sufficient.

If we have a deliberate thesis it is that the United States, richly endowed by nature, fashioned through its history and people the most successful economy the world has known. At the end of the nineteenth century, we rapidly put into place both a private and an academic structure, such as the Bell Labs and the Massachusetts Institute of Technology (MIT), which gave us preeminence in the world of industrial product development. Although flawed, this combination of private industrial and public academic excellence enabled the United States to become an outstanding scientific and industrial leader. That world is changing. It is being rebuilt and restructured by new and incredibly important breakthroughs. To this end, change and uncertainty will be our constant companions. For those, however, who see all of this as negative and frightening, we would argue that the industrial revolutions of the past lifted the world from poverty and offered new opportunities for millions of people. If this is the end of an era, it is also the beginning of a new one.

The areas of most rapid and radical change in the 1980s are already largely in evidence: microchips, fiber optics and lasers, biogenetics and bioagriculture, computer-integrated manufacturing, robotic devices, revolutionary telecommunications, and, perhaps at a distance, solar energy and superconductivity. Almost daily, the list grows. Approximately twenty-five years ago, Intel incorporated the entire central processing unit of a computer on a single silicon chip. By 1980 VSLIs, very large-scale integrated circuits, were in use with millions of components fabricated and interconnected on a single silicon chip about one-tenth the size of a postage stamp. In the industry, one speaks today of one billion calculations per second as being technologically available by the end of the decade. The microprocessor heralds the advent of a new age of intelligence. Its potential uses are virtually unlimited. Like the biblical sands of the sea, we will continue to proliferate its applications. No one today can even vaguely grasp the enormous potentials of the microcomputer. Sensors, artificial intelligence, new software, and the like point to a world changed beyond our perceptual boundaries.

Even a few years ago the industrial applications of CAD/CAM were still primitive. This process was a great step forward in economizing the time-design-manufacturing cycle as David Newman suggests. Then the computer could easily refer the design on the screen to the shop floor where machines would carry out the instructions. Instead of the crowded, hurried environment of Charlie Chaplin's *Modern Times,* a few operators manipulated software programs on their own consoles. Instructed by the computer, plates of steel a half-ton or more would move into position and be automatically cut by acetylene torches. The manufacturer of the tools, the ordering and inventory of raw materials, the programming of robots, the scheduling of production runs—all these belong to the past. As I. M. Hymes points out in "The Revolution in Manufacturing," the future has already incorporated these simple changes and is lunging forward into an unknown way of making products. For ten thousand years we had an orthodox understanding of the process of manufacturing—whether the product was a shovel or a 747. Hymes points out that we no longer have the luxury of a known path but have moved into an era of order inversion that we still barely comprehend.

Telecommunication changes of all kinds are commonplace. My colleague talks to his colleague at Indiana through Bus Net and transmits articles not by post but by FAX. Even the Justice Department has paid its due to the revolution in our midst by freeing AT&T to enter these new fields. Alan Scrime's "Telecommunications and Technology" takes us through some of these exciting changes and brings us to the shore of the continuing revolution in telecommunications. No one can really do more than guess at the future of these changes in telecommunications at home and throughout the world. The costs of ultra-technology will be enormous, estimated by some at a trillion dollars, and historically comparable to the building of railroads and the electrification of the globe. Everywhere there will continue to be conflict between national interests and international suppliers. The pace and process of deregulation will be different in Japan and West Germany than it is in the United States. Telecommunications is bringing new urgency into our thinking. "If present trends continue," Bruce Wooley of JTECH (Japanese Technology Evaluation Program) warns, "the component technologies on which the information age depends will be dominated by Japan. It may then follow that Japanese companies will ultimately dominate the design and manufacturing of the telecommunication systems based on these technologies. In that case world economic leadership in the information age will belong to Japan." Much of what we will have to do if this is not to occur concerns the development of new materials and the central role of lasers. In his chapter J. E. Burke discusses broadly but critically the theme of "Materials and the Third Industrial Revolution," and Joseph Haus and John Schroeder mark out the special role of lasers in ''Lasers: Now the Age of Light.'' Just a few years ago, I watched a small high-tech company go bankrupt because it did not know what to do with the laser its scientists had developed. The board of directors was awed by a machine that could put a hole in a slug of metal one-fifth the diameter of a strand of hair. But nobody had any industrial applications for this marvelous machine. Today lasers have so many uses that page after page of technical journals are filled with commercial blandishments. We all know that most detached retinas are welded back together by laser. The guidance system of the Exorcet missile is laser-determined. Lasers are already cutting a wide swath through many traditional industries and processes, like printing and tunnel construction, as well as becoming the workhorse of microsurgery. Its half-cousin, holography, not only adorns my credit card, but is a growing field in its own right. Science fiction has turned into fact. What will try our every imagination now is the speed with which these new changes are applied and diffused.

My students know more about biogenetics than I do, and their children will take for granted the benefits which this revolution in knowledge technology and basic science is already bringing. We are at the threshold of a new kind of scientific awareness that has happened before only once or twice in history. The miracle of understanding the structure of DNA which Arnold Gussin explains in ''Biotechnology'' is the basis for a vast range of technological innovations, ranging from medicines to waste disposal treatment. Genetic engineering in plants and animals is already happening at an incredible rate. The vastness of this biological cosmos is cause for both fear and hope; genetic-dominated drugs have been approved and large numbers of them are already being clinically tested. By the end of the century, more than half of all therapeutic drugs will have come from these labs. Already we are manufacturing purer strains of Interferon, bacteria that will eat sludge, human growth hormone, tissue plasminogen activase, and artificial insulin. For fifty years, Eli Lilly bought and gathered pancreas tissue from slaughtered animals all over the United States. The slaughterhouse in Cohoes, N.Y., trucked pancreases to Indianapolis, almost two thousand miles away. Because Lilly had a virtual monopoly in insulin production, and because insulin is a life-support drug for more than two million Americans, Lilly stocked a year's supply in a rolling inventory in the event of a nationwide disaster that might put out of action its manufacturing facilities in Indianapolis and cause the death of millions of people who might needlessly die for want of medication. Artificial insulin licensed to Lilly by Genentech is only one example, a forerunner, of what we may expect.

New genetically inspired drugs will develop more slowly, more because of the problems of clinical testing than genetic changes in agriculture. For the billions of hungry masses, no change was more important than the Green Revolution of the 1960s. In villages all over the world, new strains of traditional grains have brought some relief. What the Green Revolution was to the sixties, the biogenetic revolution in agriculture will be to the eighties and nineties. In place of nature's slow changes, and man's acceleration of these changes, bioagriculture has already moved inside the laboratories where plant biologists can produce desired genetic changes.

In his chapter, "Today's Science for Tomorrow's Technology," Jay Newman shows the dizzying pace at which we are learning and applying this emerging knowledge of biophysics.

Will the Luddites rise again—smashing the microchips, the computers, the numerically controlled machine tools, the gene-splicing devices, the robots? A new Luddite explosion is possible, but not likely. Technologies such as we have described are not the things that people rise up to destroy. The beneficence and opportunities that these "intelligent" devices offer will far outweigh the substantial difficulties they entail. It will be impossible to repress the new knowledge behind this change. For thousands of years, most people have been chain-bound to scarcity. Only over the past two centuries for a small portion of the world's population has industrialization, new knowledge, and democratic government brought a measure of previously denied well-being. Even so, we know the enclaves of poverty and distress that remain in the United States; most of the world is still not far removed from the struggle for mere survival.

In the decades to come, we will have to redefine work and management. What will work consist of? How will work be organized? Will this new "work" be distributed equitably; what of its returns? One European labor leader expressed his concern that we will create two permanent proletariats: an internal one and one in the poorer nations. If the rich of Silicon Valley do not know the poor of Youngstown, what of those who produce the superfluous supplies of sugar, jute, or coffee? Western Europe alone may have a semiproletariat of ten million who are permanently unemployed. In the short run, high rates of unemployment may be commonplace, as traditional modes of economic production become permanently outmoded. New information processes in the service sector may dislocate but not displace thirty million members of the labor force. Office practices are going to be radically changed. Temporarily displaced workers may pose problems for society as serious as the unemployed. While those outside the new ways of doing things could lead nasty, brutish, and long lives, others who work in new industries or in revolutionized old industries may fly to London or Paris for a long weekend. Within the centers of industrial production, management will be summarily modified. As Allan Doyle points out in "Management During the Third Industrial Revolution," many middle managers with their six-figure income and their ingrained orthodoxies will bite the dust, as superfluous as hand-loom weavers became in the eighteenth century. "Top managers" will also disappear as many ultra-tech companies take on patterns of collaborative or academic management. A biogenetic company management might look, and act, more like Cray Computers or Union College than General Motors or USX.

In "The Third Industrial Revolution," we point out that not much is stable. New technologies are springing up, long-established businesses fall on hard times or fail, the economic order is threatened, and society itself faces challenges to leadership values and standards of behavior. This pace of change and the condition of uncertainty are facts of our lives. As this revolution gathers intensity, it must cause serious problems of disruption and dislocation over the entire globe. More than a century ago, the most prescient of social critics, Karl Marx, commented that the bourgeois mode of production had produced more change and goods than all of human history preceding it; we are repeating in the Third Industrial Revolution a sequence as fundamental as that which occurred in the nineteenth century. The outpouring of goods and with it the fall in price of these goods will provide the base for a new surge in the material standard of living and the quality of life. But not without cost.

Since the second world war, we have witnessed U.S. management establishing peace with U.S. labor unions by compromising on soft contracts. The advent of global competition from the Pacific rim has ended this arrangement, only adding to our growing lack of competitiveness in world markets. Labor union leaders are already facing even more cruel problems as the future unfolds. It would be unthinkable for us to believe, and for them to accept, these changes without major challenges. In every avenue and in every way, union leadership will fight to maintain the gains that they have fought to win for their members over the past half-century. And as union membership declines, unions too will become highly politicized and political, with consequences that we in the United States with a largely apolitical labor movement have never known.

For the first time since the founding of the republic our basic political forms may be questioned. So massive a series of changes in so short a time period will raise issues of national planning and control over these technologies (as they already have over DNA research), questions of centralization versus decentralization that will make the new federalism a Parker game. Freedom, liberty, rights of women, minorities, young, and old may all require some kind of umpire.

Social institutions already greatly strained will be called on to bear additional stress. Cultural values and religious fundamentals may be tested anew in even fiercer crucibles. If we do not now know when human life begins, we may twenty years from now not know what life is. Personal and interpersonal relations will change, and cities and civilizations will alter. Art, music, literature, fun, and love may be something else in the twenty-first and twenty-second centuries.

The fundamental problem that will test our civilization will be our ability to handle people here and in the larger world. A decade ago we were afraid that we could not produce enough food; today, of course, we are overwhelmed by food surpluses. By the end of our century more than six billion people will inherit our planet. Our technological capacity to feed these numbers will be easily attainable but to provide a humane global environment for the species will test all our imagination and talents. For hundreds of years we have tried to find some equilibrium for the market societies of the West with only partial success; now we will have to include the four-fifths of the world's population that must be brought quickly into the era of the Third Industrial Revolution. I wish I were as optimistic as Norman Macrae in *2025 Report: A Concise History of the Future* who argues that beginning in 1988 the corner has been turned. I am reasonably confident, however, that we will manage all these challenges and opportunities as a nation, a humanity, and a specie. I am confident because there is no other choice.

1

Microelectronics

R. A. Powell

WELCOME TO LILLIPUT

On July 1, 1948, in the "News of Radio" section, the *New York Times* reported the demonstration of a small, low-power solid-state amplifier that could be used to replace vacuum tubes for certain radio applications.[1] The physicists at Bell Laboratories who developed this curious device called it a "transfer resistor" or "transistor." The replacement of vacuum tubes by transistors was almost, but not quite, considered as important as the summer replacement of the CBS "Radio Theatre" by the "Our Miss Brooks" show.

Thirty-five years later, on October 14, 1983, the *Peninsula Times Tribune* (Palo Alto, Calif.) reported the introduction by National Semiconductor Corporation of a hot, new computer chip that allowed a million pieces of information to be processed in one second.[2] The computer chip was an exquisitely patterned, one-inch square piece of wafer-thin silicon, crammed with transistors the size of a bacterium. It was to become the heart of a typewriter-sized personal computer.

The enormous improvements in miniaturized electronics that made possible the second press release are nothing short of amazing, considering that they were achieved in a little over one human generation.[3] These same thirty-five years, however, span several electronic generations. As a result of such rapid technical evolution, today's younger generation of microelectronics—integrated circuits (ICs)—are the most sophisticated products ever manufactured. They are also one of the most ubiquitous. Not so very long ago, chips were merely something to eat with dip, but today, whether encased in a digital watch, personal computer, television set, video game, missile-guidance control system, or medical diagnostic system, the silicon chip is having a revolutionary impact on our individual lives and society at large.

This chapter presents a current overview of microelectronics and the problems which the IC industry must overcome as it builds increasingly more complex chips. It is also a preview of things to come for participants in the microelectronics revolution.

Microelectronics and Computer Technology

Progress in microelectronics and computer technology have gone hand in hand, with the result that today's computers possess many of the same attributes as their constituent microelectronic components: low cost, high speed, and compact design. In the 1950s, a typical computer took up over 500 cubic feet, and contained 4,000 tubes, 6 miles of wire, and 100,000 soldered joints.[4] It cost $500,000 and consumed nearly 30,000 watts of power. A silicon chip of today, with equivalent performance, is 1/4–inch square and 15–thousandths of an inch thick, costs $50, and consumes 5 million times less power!

Such advanced ICs have allowed us to construct incredibly powerful supercomputers with speeds measured in millions of mathematical operations per second and memories holding tens of millions of words.[5] These machines can perform prodigious mathematical feats. For example, a Cray X-MP supercomputer is able to factor a 71–digit number consisting entirely of ones (11,111, . . .) into its only two factors in 9.5 hours.[6] (For the curious, one need only multiply 241,573,142,393,627,673,576,957,439,049 by 45,994,811,347,886,846,310, 221,728,895,223,034,301,839 to get the 71 "ones.") Next-generation supercomputers will have peak speeds approaching one billion calculations per second. In the time it takes such a computer to add two numbers, a light beam has hardly enough time to travel one foot.

Basically, the reason that computers are so fast is that their circuits are so small. In a computer, the time required to perform a mathematical calculation is closely related to the time required to move electrical signals through the machine. By building more components onto a chip, the signals do not have to travel so far and the time for a given calculation goes down. With a personal computer today, one can perform a calculation a million times faster than by using a mechanical hand calculator.

This millionfold advantage in performance should be compared with the leverage afforded man by other technologies, such as jet airplane travel or nuclear weapons, which have also been developed over the last thirty-five years.[7] A jet airplane allows a man to travel perhaps three hundred times faster than by foot. Loading this plane with hydrogen bombs instead of conventional explosives allows one to destroy an area perhaps one hundred times greater in size. Although these hundredfold increases in speed and destructive power are significant, they do not approach the degree to which the modern IC on a silicon chip has amplified man's computing power.

The Development of Microelectronics

Progress in microelectronics has resulted from making the size of electronic devices ever smaller, so that more and more transistors, resistors, and capacitors could be "integrated" on a given piece of silicon. Initially, transistors were used as discrete electronic components soldered piecemeal onto circuit boards containing other discrete devices such as capacitors and resistors. Then, in the late 1950s, Jack Kilby at Texas Instruments and Jean Heorni and Robert Noyce at Fairchild Semiconductor developed a completely new way to fabricate a solid-state circuit, in which all the components of the circuit would be directly created in the surface of a single slice of semiconducting material such as germanium or silicon to become an integrated, working circuit on a chip.

The Integrated Circuit. That the IC was a significant departure from conventional electronic technology is not surprising. To build a vehicle that moves considerably faster than a horse, what is needed is not simply a mechanical horse, but, rather, a new concept in transportation. In a similar vein, the discrete solid-state circuits found in early transistor radios could not be miniaturized much further by shortening the copper wires connecting the transistors or by using finer soldering irons to connect them.

What made the IC a radical departure from the solid-state electronics of the 1950s was that the separation and interconnection of the various circuit elements were accomplished electrically from within the semiconductor surface, rather than manually from without. The semiconductor crystal of the transistor would now become, in effect, its own circuit board. This approach saved labor and materials costs and made possible the rapid reduction in circuit element, or feature, size and rapid increase in device performance that has characterized the industry ever since.

Small Is Beautiful. Since the early 1960s, ICs have been built with larger and larger numbers of smaller and smaller transistors integrated onto a tiny square piece of silicon which today measures about ¼ inch by ¼ inch. Like walking through ever smaller doorways, the semiconductor industry has successfully passed through the eras of small-scale integration (SSI), medium-scale integration (MSI), large-scale integration (LSI), and into very-large-scale integration (VLSI) with feature sizes in production for the most advanced devices now being about one micron (i.e., one-millionth of a meter or about forty–millionths of an inch).

Next-generation devices will be ultra-large-scale integrated (ULSI) circuits, in which the minimum feature size will be below one micron. Crossing this so-called "one-micron barrier" between VLSI and ULSI technology is a formidable task, and will involve solving a host of interrelated problems in semiconductor manufacturing, materials science, circuit and systems design, and packaging and testing.

Scaling circuit geometries down in size not only increases the number of devices that can be packed together on a chip (packing density), but also increases device speed and reduces the power consumed per device. In this regard, it is useful to consider the "speed-power product," obtained by multiplying the power consumed by a device and its speed. This provides a figure-of-merit for digital circuit performance. For example, a 100 percent improvement each in speed and power consumed results in a circuit that operates twice as fast at half the power consumption. Its speed-power product has been reduced by a factor of $2 \times 2 = 4$, so it "performs" four times better. Considering that the speed-power product for digital devices has decreased by a factor of over 10,000 since 1960, it becomes apparent just how rapidly the IC has evolved!

Silicon—The Basis of Microelectronic Life. An integrated circuit is fabricated in the surface of a thin wafer, or substrate, of a semiconducting material such as silicon. In fact, silicon is the major raw material of the microelectronics revolution in much the same way iron was during the Industrial Revolution.[8] Fortunately, silicon is the second most abundant element in the earth's crust—a common ingredient in rocks and sand, and, therefore, relatively inexpensive. (One course on IC fabrication has even been titled "From Sand to Circuit.")

The same is true to a large extent for many other materials used in wafer processing, such as silicon dioxide and silicon nitride, which are simple compounds of silicon and gases common to our atmosphere, and metals such as aluminum, which are relatively easy to obtain and refine.

The silicon used for IC production is orders of magnitude more refined than nature provides. Today's silicon substrates can be produced with such purity that less than one part per billion of impurity is present. Put more impressively, one part per billion represents a single red golf ball in a stack of white ones stretching from here to the moon.[9]

Not only can a silicon wafer be made very pure, but its electrical properties can be precisely altered for specific device applications by the addition of trace amounts of elements such as boron and phosphorus. In the same vein, the structural properties of iron can be altered by the addition of elements such as carbon and chromium to produce special-purpose steels.

Silicon wafers can be grown, sliced, and polished to have a flat surface with a much larger area than an individual chip. This means that each wafer can carry on its surface hundreds of identical ICs. Each of these ICs, with its hundreds of thousands of transistors, will only be separated from its neighbors at the end of the fabrication process when the wafer is scribed and diced into individual chips.

Not only is handling a large round wafer easier than handling the much smaller individual chips, but hundreds of chips can be processed identically at the same time. To compound the advantage, many process steps can be carried out on a large batch of wafers. For example, when growing silicon dioxide on silicon in a furnace, fifty to one hundred wafers are loaded into the same quartz furnace tube and oxidized simultaneously. Assuming two hundred chips per wafer, this single process step oxidizes as many as twenty thousand chips at one time. Such "batch processing" is mass production on an enormous scale and represents a considerable cost savings.

Bigger Wafers for Better Devices. Industry has been moving steadily to larger wafer sizes, with the dominant diameters currently 75 mm (3 inches) to 150 mm (6 inches), since larger wafers are viewed as a means of raising the production yield of ICs.[10] While a number of companies have discussed their ultimate intention to use 200–mm (8–inch) diameter silicon wafers, none are in production at the moment.[11] Producing such large single-crystal silicon substrates of the exceptional purity and flatness needed for ULSI devices is a significant materials challenge, and the uniform processing and automatic handling of such platelike wafers is expected to be a considerable headache to process equipment vendors.

Not only has the diameter of silicon wafers increased (about 10 percent per year since 1960), so too has the size of the individual IC chips.[12] The ratio of chip length to wafer diameter has maintained a constant value of about 20, with the result that chip size in 1980 (¼ inch × ¼ inch) was several times greater than it was in 1960 (¹⁄₁₆ inch × ¹⁄₁₆ inch). A quantum jump in this trend may be the result of Wafer Scale Integration (WSI).[13] The goal of WSI is to produce a chip 100 times larger than a conventional IC. One advantage of a wafer-scale IC is that there is room to build in multiple copies of critical circuits. This means that chip performance is not degraded by processing defects which may destroy some of these redundant circuits. In addition, greater reliability is possible, since the large chip area simplifies the difficult job of connecting a large number of transistors. In spite of its potential, commercial development of WSI has been limited, and many of its early proponents (e.g., Trilogy Systems) have directed their efforts elsewhere.

Microelectronics—An Affordable Revolution

In the early part of this century, U.S. transportation was revolutionized by high technology in the form of mass-produced automobiles; and we are still feeling the social and ecological effects. The automobile might have remained a sophisticated, costly plaything with limited impact, but instead was brought within the reach of the average worker by assembly-line economics.

Similarly, an important reason why microelectronics has had such a far-ranging impact on society is that it is an affordable technology. For example, in 1969, when the first digital watch was introduced by Seiko, it sold for $1250.[14] Today, even after the inflationary 1970s, digital watches can be bought for $5. (It has been pointed out[15] that if this pricing trend were followed by automobile manufacturers, a Rolls Royce would today cost less than $100.) The first consumer device to incorporate IC technology, Texas Instrument's Pocketronic Calculator, sold for $150 in 1971 when it was introduced. Today, a comparable four-function, hand-held calculator is 30 times less expensive. Such dramatic declines in price have enabled the early fruits of this information revolution to be consumed by average-income Americans on a large scale, thus amplifying and accelerating the impact on society. By 1984, according to one estimate, more chips had been sold than McDonald's hamburgers.[16]

MANUFACTURING IN MINIATURE

Each year since the first ICs were introduced in 1959, the number of components per circuit has nearly doubled.[17] Gordon E. Moore (then at Fairchild Semiconductor and now Board Chairman and CEO of Intel Corporation) first noted this trend in 1964 and predicted it would continue.

Trends in Integration

Today, in accordance with "Moore's Law," we have circuits in production with about $2^{20} = 1,048,000$, components. This level of integration has made possible 256K and 1M memory chips. (In microelectronics, the symbol K does not stand for 1000 as in the metric system, but rather for $1024 = 2^{10}$.) Four megabit memories (4M) are just now becoming available—an astonishing bit of engineering, since the number of nerve cells, or neurons, in the human brain is only about a thousand times greater.

Certainly, this trend will not keep up indefinitely, and the steadily increasing level of integration we have seen on chips since 1959 cannot keep pace with a simple yearly doubling curve. Recent progress suggests that a doubling time of two years is more appropriate for the semiconductor industry of the 1980s. At some point, however, it will cease to be advantageous, in terms of both performance and cost, to reduce the size of silicon devices.[18] At sufficiently small dimensions, thermodynamic and quantum mechanical effects will limit device performance. In addition, the economics of building and maintaining manufacturing facilities for, say, 0.1–micron ULSI devices may price them out of the marketplace.

It is still an open issue among industry gurus at what point the usable size of silicon devices will bottom out. One panel of experts, who in 1983 addressed the question of practical versus theoretical limits of VLSI, generally agreed that at much below 0.5–micron feature size, device technology would become unproductive.[19] Others, however, have argued that 0.2–micron feature size is not yet at the fundamental limits of the technology. Indeed, in 1987 workers at IBM announced the fabrication of experimental logic circuits based on 0.1–micron technology with transistors having features only a few hundred atoms wide.[20] It is important to realize that even 0.5 micron is about as long as one wavelength of visible light and is smaller than many bacteria. It is a remarkable feat of manufacturing skill to build working devices that small.

While the semiconductor industry is not yet at the 0.5 micron level in production, an advanced silicon IC chip is undeniably the most intricately manufactured product ever produced by the human race, having over a million electrically functional, microscopic transistors precisely controlling the flow of current through a complex pattern of interconnections—all this on the surface of a polished, wafer-thin piece of silicon less than ¼ inch on a side.

Viewed through a low-power optical microscope, the intricate pattern of interconnected components on a chip looks much like the streets of a city as seen from the air.[21] In this case, of course, electrons rather than cars move along the avenues. Using this city-streets analogy, we can appreciate the complexity of today's VLSI circuits by imagining that the space between conducting interconnects is the length of a city block.[22] In the MSI chips of the mid-1960s (about twenty-five microns), chip complexity was comparable to that of a small town. A microprocessor today, using 5–micron LSI technology, is as complex as the entire Los Angeles basin. Designing the 1–micron geometry chips needed for VLSI is as complex a task as designing an interconnected grid of streets covering all of California and Nevada. Quarter-micron geometry chips, possibly the smallest we can expect after considerations of silicon device performance and manufacturing cost, would represent as complex a network as an urban sprawl of streets covering the total surface of North America! Reliably and economically producing such an electronically functional microcircuit is an awesome technological challenge.

Ironically, in order to fabricate smaller, less expensive, microcircuits processing equipment has become larger and more expensive. Unit costs of production-worthy semiconductor equipment are often $500,000 or more, and sophisticated electron-beam lithography systems for directly writing submicron patterns on wafers can cost upward of $2 million.

The rising price of this equipment reflects the complexity of today's microchips as well as the tight process tolerances and control needed to produce them. To attain this level of performance, advanced process equipment is more and more dependent on the very chips it is designed to improve; one generation of microprocessors and memory chips is exploited to produce the next. This symbiotic relationship has allowed equipment and chip technology to feed on one another for the mutual benefit of both market segments.

The First Step

The circuit design and layout of a new IC must be completed before any new product is committed to pilot or full-scale production. This requirement means that designers must prepare a detailed map showing the size and location of each of the IC's myriad transistors, capacitors, and resistors, as well as the functional characteristics of each of the circuit elements and how they are to be interconnected.

Early ICs could be designed and laid out manually, but the complexity of next-generation ICs, such as 4–megabit memories and 32–bit microprocessors, demand the use of digital computers, which are themselves the products of an earlier generation of ICs. The rapid and positive feedback inherent in this relationship between manufacturing tool (computer) and manufactured product (IC) is a distinguishing characteristic of microelectronics and has led to ever more complex chips and higher-speed computers. It is as if some bizarre silicon-based evolution is operating where one generation of computer technology gives birth to a more advanced microchip, which rapidly takes macroscopic form as the next generation of computer.

The complexity of IC design requires the extensive use of CAD and computer simulation of how the circuit will perform before it is actually built.[23] Computer simulation allows rapid fine tuning of the design by observation of the ways in which changes in circuit elements modify the electrical behavior of the finished integrated circuit.

Even with CAD, however, the design and layout of new VLSI chips is a time-consuming process—demanding as much as several years for difficult microprocessors. As an added complication, the finished IC has three-dimensional architecture and may be composed of as many as ten individual layers of circuitry stacked one on top of another. The CAD process must then generate the separate layout of each of these layers, the geometric patterns that define the physical structure of each circuit component.

Considering the expense and effort that go into chip design, it is no surprise that design piracy is of growing concern. Until recently, proprietary semiconductor chip layouts and design work were covered only by conventional copyright law, which provided little protection and relatively little penalty ($10,000) for infringement. Under the Semiconductor Chip Protection Act, chip masks are protected for ten years from pirated copies, with penalties of up to $250,000 for infringement.[24] Interestingly enough, the act allows for "reverse engineering" of chip design, in which competitors can analyze an innovative design and improve on it. Using modern analytical techniques, chips can be, in effect, peeled back layer by layer to deduce the original fabrication sequence.

Once a new circuit is designed and laid out, the detailed fabrication steps needed to manufacture it must be developed. As with the layout phase, this phase also benefits from computer technology. Although circuit modeling by computer is established as part of microelectronics, process modeling is much more recent. Now available are computer software packages with names such as SUPREM-IV, which allow the process engineer to predict the structure of devices resulting from a proposed sequence of process steps.

Reliable process simulation promises to make process development less empirical in the future—with considerable cost savings. As a specific example of process modeling, a process engineer might want to simulate how the distribution of dopant atoms of arsenic introduced into the silicon surface region is altered by the growth of a subsequent oxide overlayer. Empirically, this involves a great deal of effort. Large numbers of wafers must be cleaned in solvents and placed in oxidation furnaces for various times and temperatures, and the arsenic distribution measured using costly, surface-sensitive analytical techniques. In addition, development time spent on a fabrication or "fab" line means that there is less time to get proven, saleable products out the door. In contrast, computer simulation allows the effect of different oxidation processes to be rapidly observed on a computer terminal, guiding the process engineer to the optimum process.

Of course, no process simulation is better than the underlying physical models, and unfortunately, our basic understanding of the physics and chemistry of many IC process steps is still rudimentary. Nevertheless, since the cost of both IC fabrication equipment and the ultraclean environment required for this fabrication is increasing, we can expect to see more and more new product wafers "carried down" simulated fab lines in the future.

The Bottom Line

Once the circuit is laid out and the necessary process steps specified, the IC is built in theory. In practice, of course, life is not so simple and the bottom line issue is usually one of yield. "Yield" may sound like a freeway road sign, but it is the most important process parameter of all. Yield refers to the percentage of devices on a wafer that successfully pass a given process step. One hundred percent survival is a rarely achieved goal. Some simple processes, like cleaning the wafer of any surface oxide by a dip in a hydrofluoric acid bath, have a very high yield. Others, like etching a submicron pattern into aluminum, have a much lower yield. Ultimately, the yield of usable, saleable devices at the end of the fab line is the product of yields at each process step (assuming that bad chips occur randomly on the wafer)—and fabrication of a sophisticated chip may require hundreds of separate steps.

Herein lies a major problem with sequential microelectronic fabrication. To assume, for example, that each step in a hundred-step fab line process has a yield of 98 percent may seem like very good performance—only two chips out of 100 on a wafer failed a given process step. After 100 process steps, however, the yield is only $0.98 \times 0.98 \ldots \times 0.98 = 0.13$, and 87 percent of the chips do not perform well enough to sell. And knowing which chips perform properly and which must be rejected is not as simple as it may seem, because test equipment tends to lag behind the state-of-the-art chips it must test. Since the test equipment can operate only as fast as its own components, it may be inadequate to test next-generation, ultrafast ICs.[25]

To obtain high yield, devices must be fabricated in areas of extraordinary cleanliness. In our everyday experience, a hospital surgery room is probably the cleanest area we are likely to visit. When all those present are properly gowned and masked, this room represents a suitably clean environment for state-of-the-art surgery. However, such an area contains hundreds of times more airborne particles than the contamination-free areas required for successful IC processing.

In semiconductor parlance, clean rooms are designated as Class 10, Class 100, and so on, depending on the size and quantity of particles per cubic foot of air. For example, a Class 100 clean room must have no more than 100 particles of 0.3–micron diameter or greater per cubic foot of air.

The lower the class designation, the better, since even a single minute particle that is present on the silicon wafer during a key process step can cause a defect in the equally minute microchip, making it useless. Even parts per million amounts of impurities such as sodium, a common element in human sweat, can alter the electrical performance of transistors and reduce the percentage of usable chips to uneconomically low levels. As a result, enormous effort must be taken to insure that the artificial microclimate in which wafer fabrication occurs is as clean as possible, with air being continuously filtered and recirculated.

Since clean room space is prohibitively expensive ($500 a square foot for Class 10, or about ten times the cost of an oriental rug), today's process equipment is designed to have as small a ''footprint'' as possible. This sometimes means that only the operator controls and wafer load/unload stations are in the clean room, while the bulk of the machine takes up space in an adjoining, less costly area having higher particle counts.

In the IC business, cleanliness is indeed next to godliness. It is also next to impossible. One reason is that many chemicals used in processing themselves contain particles—although efforts to produce exceptionally clean, filtered VLSI-grade solvents are underway.

A more important problem is that people, by their very presence, generate huge numbers of particulates. A Class 10 clean room becomes hundreds of times ''dirtier'' when a person enters in street clothes. As a result, special over-clothing, known as ''bunny suits,'' must be worn to reduce particle generation. (One study has found that wearing sandals on the fab line can reduce airborne particulates.[26]) People have even been known to inadvertently transmit contaminants contained in their underarm deodorants down their coat sleeves and onto the surface of wafers. As device geometries shrink to the submicron level, it may be necessary to exclude persons from the process line altogether. It is said that increasing factory automation made possible by advances in microelectronics will cost jobs. The irony is that some of the people who manufacture today's chips may themselves be replaced in the future by automated VLSI fabrication lines.

Wafer Fab

There are many excellent reviews of microelectronics for the nonspecialist which describe how a modern IC is fabricated out of a silicon wafer and to which the lay reader is referred.[9,12,27–30] Basically, a larger number (in fact, hundreds) of process steps are carried out sequentially on each wafer either to alter the electrical properties of the silicon or to create circuit patterns in thin films of materials such as silicon dioxide or aluminum deposited on a wafer surface. The insulating oxide might be patterned so as to electrically "isolate" neighboring transistors from one another; the conducting aluminum might be fashioned into the complex grid work of interconnect lines which define the path of electric current on the chip, or made into contact pads so that electrical contact can be between the chip and the outside world.

Layer upon layer, the three-dimensional architecture comprising the microchip takes form as the wafers move down a modern IC assembly line. Wafers are subjected to a variety of physical and chemical processes during this journey—heated to high temperatures (400–1200°C) in oxidizing or inert gases, cleaned in organic solvents and etched in acid baths, metallized, coated with evaporated films of metals in chambers having extremely low pressure (about one-billionth of atmospheric pressure), bombarded with energetic ions of materials such as arsenic and boron, and so on. Viewed in cross-section, the finished semiconductor device resembles an intricate layer cake, where metal, silicon dioxide, doped single crystal and polycrystalline silicon and so on are carefully stacked and interconnected to make a functional transistor.

Since the process chain connecting the starting silicon substrate and the finished chip is no stronger than its weakest link, manufacturing high-performance VLSI chips has required advances in many areas of process technology: lithography, etching, oxidation, metallization, testing, packaging, and so on.[12,31-33] This situation, in turn, has encouraged equipment vendors to work more closely with process engineers in developing next-generation hardware for micromanufacturing. In addition, workers in a variety of scientific disciplines—solid-state physics, electrical engineering, materials science, chemistry—have been brought together by the needs of creating microstructures.

In the housing industry, the development and use of new structural materials such as particle board have lowered building costs. New construction techniques such as prefabrication have saved on labor, while new architectural concepts such as cluster housing have reduced the need for costly real estate. So, too, in the semiconductor industry, the challenge of building better ICs will require new materials, improved fabrication techniques, and more efficient circuit architecture. Following are examples of some of the challenges facing the IC industry in wafer fab, as device geometries go below the one-micron size required by next-generation ULSI devices.

Lithography. A good example of the kind of challenge facing VLSI process technology as the semiconductor industry enters the ULSI era is lithography. Optical or photolithography lies at the heart of the IC manufacturing sequence and is the process by which visible light is used to define the desired microscopic circuit pattern at the chip surface. In much the same way, illumination of a negative in a photographic darkroom is used to produce a photographic print.

The problem with light is that, being a wave, it fans out, or diffracts, as it passes through an opening. These diffraction effects become more of a problem as the width of the opening becomes comparable to the wavelength of the light, which in turn adversely affects the quality of the resulting image on the wafer.

Unfortunately for ULSI, the device dimensions are fast approaching the submicron wavelength of visible light. Since the use of shorter wavelength radiation reduces diffraction effects, there is current interest in developing lithography systems using higher energy ultraviolet light or X-rays. Another approach being actively developed is the use of finely focused charged-particle beams of electrons or ions to create a microscopic pattern directly on the wafer. The electron beam (e-beam) acts like a microscopic pencil, which by way of sophisticated computer control, writes the desired pattern.

The ultimate demonstration of direct-write lithography is probably the use of a finely focused electron beam to write the initials of the National Research and Resource Facility for Submicron Structures (located at Cornell University) on a grain of common table salt.[34] Not so common is the fact that the letters thus machined were only about as wide as the DNA double helix. Were it practical, this level of microminiaturization would allow us to store a photographic quality print of every page of every book in the U.S. Library of Congress on a single postcard![35]

Interconnects. Another challenge to the IC industry is developing suitable conducting materials for ULSI metallization and patterning these conductors so as to interconnect the hundreds of thousands of devices on advanced chips. One problem is that the interconnects take up a large percentage of the silicon "real estate" that could otherwise be used to build chips more densely packed with transistors. Already, for memory circuitry, the area required to connect the transistors is greater than the area of the chip itself. How then, does the on-chip wiring fit on the chip? The answer is that several vertical levels of interconnects are used, reducing the density of wiring on each level. This high-rise approach has its limits, however, and even with twelve levels, the interconnects can account for nearly half the area of a 16K memory chip.

Another interconnect issue concerns the material chosen for metallization. As device geometries are scaled down, so too is the cross-sectional area, with the result that the electrical resistance of the current-carrying interconnect lines increases. This increased resistance can lead to unacceptably large time delays for electrical signals moving throughout the chip, in effect "retarding" the ability of a microprocessor chip to calculate quickly. The fact that larger chip sizes are being used further compounds this problem, since longer interconnect lines are needed. High-power dissipation in resistive lines can also overheat the chip and degrade performance. Furthermore, the tiny metal lines in ULSI circuits will be required to carry enormous densities of current, about one million amperes/cm^2. In aluminum, such densities lead to so-called "electromigration," whereby individual atoms are in effect pushed along by the current of electrons, which leads to actual open-circuit breaks in the conductor and reduced device lifetime. To get around these and other problems, new conducting materials are aggressively being developed for ULSI applications. The list of candidates already includes alloys of aluminum with materials such as copper or titanium, and compounds of silicon with tungsten, tantalum, molybdenum, or titanium (so-called refractory metal silicides). Nevertheless, the process engineer must be able to reliably pattern these materials, and compatibility with other process steps is of some concern.

Silicon Dioxide. One of the most important materials in the IC industry is silicon dioxide. Thin films (about 200 Å) of thermally grown silicon dioxide are an integral part of metal-oxide-semiconductor (MOS) devices, one of the two major families of semiconductor devices manufactured today. (To deal with today's super-thin oxides, thickness is measured in Ångstroms [Å], where 10,000 Å = 1 micron.) However, ULSI devices require certain oxides that are even thinner—about 100 Å or less in thickness. Growing such films uniformly over the surface of large six–inch wafers with mechanical and electrical properties suitable for submicron MOS devices is an area of intense, and often proprietary, activity.

Probably no two electronic materials have been as extensively studied as silicon and silicon dioxide. Yet there is still much that is not understood about the growth of ultrathin oxide films on a silicon surface, and the thin boundary region between the substrate and its oxide. In the development of ULSI-compatible processes, ignorance is not bliss.

SEMICONDUCTOR TECHNOLOGIES

To store information or to perform mathematical operations on a semiconductor chip, the basic transistors can be connected in a variety of ways. In some cases, it is desirable to use semiconductors other than silicon or to develop entirely different technologies. A number of nonsilicon approaches to fabricate both mathematical and memory circuits are under development today. These include technologies based on compound semiconductors such as gallium arsenide (GaAs),[36–38] on diamond-thin films,[39–40] and, for the ultimate in speed (below ten–trillionths of a second), on superconducting Josephson junctions, which must be cooled to very low temperatures in order to function.[41] Although silicon-based technology is more mature than these approaches, the "best" technology for ULSI is not decided, and it is useful to keep an open mind.

Silicon

Basically the ways of realizing mathematical or memory functions on an IC chip using silicon technology can be divided into two major families: MOS and bipolar. In MOS transistors, charge carriers of only one sign (+ or −) are involved in transistor operation, while in bipolar transistors, both charges are involved. Within both families, a bewildering alphabet soup of individual technologies is possible. For MOS, there are NMOS (N-channel metal oxide semiconductors), PMOS (P-channel metal oxide semiconductors), and CMOS (complimentary metal oxide semiconductors); for bipolar, there are TTL (transistor-transistor logic), ECL (emitter-coupled logic), I^{2}L (integrated-injection logic), linear, and so on.

A detailed discussion of these technologies is beyond the scope of this chapter, but in general, bipolar devices tend to consume more power than MOS, and this has prevented bipolar integration from reaching the levels needed for ULSI. It is generally agreed that by 1990 MOS technology will dominate the VLSI market and account for the major portion (perhaps 70 percent) of all IC sales.

The rising star of silicon technology is complementary-MOS, or CMOS, in which NMOS and PMOS transistors are paired to form integrated circuits which consume very little power when operating.[42-43] On the negative side, CMOS circuits require more components for a given circuit function and consequently take up more area on the silicon chip. Their processing is more complex than NMOS or PMOS, which increases production costs and reduces yield. Nevertheless, CMOS is rapidly becoming the favored approach for ULSI chips because of the performance advantage it offers. It has also made substantial inroads in both consumer electronics (watches, games, and toys) and military applications.

A silicon IC is usually thought of as being built in the surface of a wafer-thin substrate. Relative to the three-dimensional architecture of a microchip, however, the substrate is incredibly thick. The maximum vertical dimension of a ULSI circuit (1–2 microns) is hundreds of times smaller than the substrate thickness of about 500 microns, so that in reality, the electrical action in a microchip is confined to a thin crust on top of the wafer—like the biological action on earth (radius about 4,000 miles) which takes place within the 10–mile-thick surface biosphere. In much the same way, the electromagnetic interactions of light waves with an aluminum film on glass allow us to see our reflection in a mirror, though the atomically thin film of reflecting metal is thousands of times thinner than the transparent glass on which it is deposited.

Good electrical isolation of the thin electrically active parts of the IC from the much thicker silicon substrate is necessary for optimum device performance, and new technologies are under development to improve this isolation. One of the best known is referred to as silicon-on-sapphire (SOS). In SOS, devices are built in a thin silicon layer grown on an insulating sapphire wafer. This reduces cross-talk between transistors (known as ''parasitic effects'') and leads to faster speed. Combining the best of both worlds, one can envision a kind of super-silicon technology in which CMOS circuits are built into the silicon layer of an SOS wafer. Natural sapphire is quite expensive (a 3–inch diameter sapphire wafer costs about five times as much a one made of silicon), however, and may not be the best substrate material for silicon-on-insulator technology. For this reason, SOS is sometimes referred to as "silicon-on-something else." For military applications, however, CMOS using SOS technology appears to be a good compromise between high-circuit density and the ability to survive in a nuclear environment.

It has been noted that "silicon is to semiconductor technology what iron and steel have been to modern metallurgy—enormously useful foundations that served well for relatively unsophisticated demands."[44] Reaching the ultimate in device performance may not be simply a matter of scaling silicon-based technology down to the 0.1–0.2 micron level, but may require developing entirely new microelectronic technologies. Four such approaches are gallium arsenide ICs, diamond ICs, Josephson junctions and, in a futuristic vein, organic computers.

Gallium Arsenide

In many people's minds, microelectronics and the silicon chip are one and the same. But this is not strictly true. Silicon is simply one of several dozen materials that exhibit semiconducting properties and which can be used to make microelectronic devices. For example, the earliest transistors were built out of germanium, not silicon, as was the first integrated circuit from Texas Instruments.

Although silicon-based ICs represent over 95 percent of the market today, alternative materials are being developed. One, based on the use of the compound semiconductor gallium arsenide, is particularly promising.[36-38] Unlike silicon, which is in group IV of the periodic table of the elements, gallium and arsenic come from the neighboring groups, III and V, respectively, making GaAs a III-V ("three-five") semiconductor. Current sales of GaAs ICs are about $100 million, but by some estimates, could reach as much as $1 billion by 1990. By comparison, worldwide production of silicon ICs in 1990 is expected to be about $50 billion.[45]

In terms of both speed and power consumption, devices based on GaAs offer advantages over silicon. For applications requiring extremely high frequencies, GaAs is expected to outperform silicon. For example, current silicon devices cannot be practically operated much above about 6 Gigahertz (GHz)—6 billion cycles per second—while GaAs amplifiers above 90 GHz have already been built.[46]

GaAs discrete transitors are well suited for application in microwave communications and radar, where high-quality signal amplification is needed. Because electrons in GaAs travel several times faster than in silicon, very fast signal processing can be achieved. Hewlett-Packard reportedly has developed a 5-GHz GaAs chip that could transmit the entire contents of the Encyclopedia Britannica in under a second.[47] In fiber optic communication systems, GaAs circuits may permit as many as 100,000 individual telephone conversations to be carried over a single pair of optical fibers. A number of supercomputer makers, such as Cray Research and Fujitsu, plan to use GaAs selectively in machines to boost performance. Microelectronic memories, however, still favor silicon, since the levels of integration in GaAs (16K) do not approach those of the more mature silicon technology (4M).

Although GaAs discrete devices have been on the open market for many years, GaAs integrated circuits are relatively new. (In early 1983, Harris Microwave Semiconductor introduced the first commercially available digital IC based on GaAs.[48]) GaAs ICs are particularly attractive for military and space systems because they operate over a wider temperature range than silicon, have ultra-high speed, and excellent radiation hardness.

GaAs is not without its problems, however. Principally, these are the relatively high cost of obtaining GaAs wafers and the complexity of their processing, which could lead to low yield. It has sometimes been said facetiously that "GaAs is the semiconductor of the future—and always will be." The current view seems to be that GaAs will not challenge the dominance of silicon IC technology in the near term. However, where speed is an overriding concern, it will have significant impact. Mention should be made of companies, such as Los Angeles-based GigaBit Logic, who are beginning to commercialize GaAs-based ICs. Only time will tell whether such companies can achieve for the GaAs chip in the 1980s what Fairchild did for the silicon chip in the 1960s.

Diamond

In the periodic table of the elements, the second and third elements in column IV are the well-known semiconductors silicon and germanium. On closer inspection, one finds that the first element in the column is carbon. Crystalline carbon (diamond) turns out to be a semiconductor with potentially outstanding properties—particularly for military applications. Diamond-based transistors are highly resistant to radiation damage, faster conductors of electricity than silicon, and, because diamonds conduct heat better even than copper, able to operate at high power with little cooling. The hardness of diamond is legendary. Workers in the Soviet Union, Japan, and the United States have fabricated diodes and transistors in the lab based on artificial diamond-thin films and Sumitomo expects to have a diamond transistor on the market by 1988. At the moment, however, the principal hurdle to a "diamond age" of microelectronics seems to be producing artificial thin films of diamond which have the necessary crystalline perfection and chemical purity for demanding IC applications.[39–40]

Josephson Junctions

Josephson junction (JJ) technology offers another alternative to silicon.[41] The junction created by Nobel prize-winning physicist Brian Josephson, has potentially the shortest switching speed (1 trillionth of a second or 1 picosecond) of all devices, but must be operated at very low temperatures. Typically, the junction is composed of a fifty Å-wide barrier between two superconductors made from lead alloys rather than silicon. Since the barrier width must be rigorously controlled to obtain reproducible device performance, processing is incredibly demanding (5 percent of fifty Å represents the size of a single atom). Other complexities with this technology involve packaging the device so that signal propagation delays caused by the connections themselves do not negate the fast response of the devices, and design of a cooling system to achieve and maintain operating temperatures which can be near −450°F when lead alloy superconductors are used.

Josephson junctions aside, it has long been recognized that the performance advantage offered by superconducting microelectronics is often offset by the practical problems and costs associated with maintaining chips at such ultra-low temperatures. In this regard, a major step forward was made in 1986 with the discovery by two researchers at the IBM Zurich Laboratory of a new class of high-temperature superconducting materials—materials that have no electrical resistance to DC current flow when cooled to temperatures near that of liquid nitrogen (−330°F).[49–51] By comparison, pre−1986 superconductors required operating temperatures near that of liquid helium (−450°F). The practical consequences are clear when one considers that costs of liquid helium and liquid nitrogen are about the same, respectively, as scotch whiskey and bottled water.

The discovery of high-temperature superconductors—which won the 1987 Nobel Prize in physics for K. A. Muller and J. Georg Bednorz—could have an enormous long-term impact on microelectronics once the problems of depositing and processing high-quality thin films of these materials are overcome. These new materials may be used to provide interconnections with extremely low power dissipation for supercomputer systems. With regard to ultrafast devices, we can expect to see renewed development on Josephson junction devices, work which has been more or less on hold in the United States since 1983 when IBM abandoned a fourteen-year effort to base a mainframe computer on JJ technology. Since Nippon Telegraph & Telephone (NTT) and other Japanese companies have continued to work on Josephson junction-based computers, they are particularly well positioned to take advantage of the new high-temperature superconductors.

While the search for a room-temperature superconductor goes on, today's high-temperature superconductors still require cryogenic temperatures (−330°F) to operate. If these new materials are to be incorporated with conventional silicon electronics on the same microchip, then the semiconducting and superconducting parts of the chip must both operate reliably at this temperature. Unfortunately, our understanding of the combined use of semiconductors and high-temperature superconductors is rudimentary, and more documentation on the performance of advanced silicon microelectronic circuits at low temperature will be needed to capitalize fully on semisuper hybrid technology.

Organic Computers

Even more futuristic than the ultracool, ultrafast Josephson junction is the concept of a molecular computer or biochip in which microchips are made of proteins and manufactured by *E. coli* bacteria which themselves were genetically engineered for the job.[52–55] Since the density of molecular packing is so great, one can in theory build a computer the size of a cube of sugar with ten million times the memory of today's machines. Chemical computers will not really be "electronic," since the current flow is expected to be by movement of atomic nuclei rather than by electrons. Also, they will be based on carbon rather than silicon.

Even given the highly creative standards of microelectronics, the organic IC is visionary and is probably not going to appear anytime soon. But researchers have taken some preliminary steps toward both a simple molecular switch and a molecule that could store a single bit of information. These organic structures could become the basic building blocks of mathematical and memory devices for a future biochip. (For developments in this futuristic field, readers may wish to consult the *Journal of Molecular Electronics* [John Wiley & Sons].[56])

The existence of biochips raises all sorts of intriguing and highly speculative possibilities. For example, imagine an entire molecular computer implanted into the brain, where it could monitor one's bodily systems and indicate if any malfunctions are likely to occur, or an advanced organic computer that could be taught to replicate itself, in essence becoming its own wafer fab line. With circuit elements as small as organic molecules, a biochip would rival the human brain itself for information storage density. It has been established that the brain contains enough room to store approximately ten trillion (10^{13}) bits of memory. Since the volume of the brain is not very large, an enormous amount of information is packed into a small space—over 10 billion bits per cubic centimeter. How does this figure compare with what inorganic microelectronic memories will offer over the next decade?

By the year 2000, memory chips with 64 megabit capacity should be available. Plugging such packaged chips as closely as possible into both sides of a 10 cm × 10 cm printed circuit board will then allow us to pack 8 billion bits of memory within a physical volume of about 100 cubic centimeters. While this density of information storage will be an amazing achievement of modern technology, it will still be hundreds of times less than that promised by the biochip.

THE IMPACT OF MICROELECTRONICS ON DEFENSE

In 1978, Braun and MacDonald noted that ''the transistor was not simply a new sort of amplifier, but the harbinger of an entirely new sort of electronics with the capacity not just to influence an industry or a scientific discipline, but to change a culture.''[57] It is difficult not to be involved in this revolution, since the technology has become so pervasive in U.S. society, both civilian and military.[58-59] Every time people use modern telephones, they are inadvertently making use of the computer on a chip. Microprocessors are in televisions, automobiles, watches, and appliances; minicomputers are more and more frequently found in homes, offices, and classrooms; ICs are in weapons and playthings. This chapter and the next examine some of the ways in which chips have already changed the way we work, play, communicate, and defend our boundaries.

Defense Electronics

It is no accident of design that the most popular of today's video games appear to be compact weapons systems, since the entertainment value of conflict and simulated destruction is well known. On the electronic battlefield of the video arcade, eye-hand coordination can be developed by blasting space invaders out of existence or gobbling up enemies piecemeal.

But the electronic battlefield is not confined to the civilian sector. Since the earliest days of the transistor, the U.S. military has invested heavily in solid-state electronics and is today using IC technology in high-performance armaments to offset the significant numerical advantage of the Soviet Union. These developments have created a kind of cybernetic cold war in which the United States enjoys perhaps a 5-year lead over the Soviet Union in electronics for military weapons and communication. Basically, it is a question of quality versus quantity, of cost-effective force multiplication. Launching one Smart missile that always hits its target is equivalent to a number of unguided missiles, only one of which will statistically be on target. The ability to detect Soviet submarines electronically when the United States is out of the more limited Soviet range could offset the 2 : 1 Soviet numerical superiority. As a result of this increasing commitment to microelectronics, the U.S. Department of Defense now spends roughly 50 percent of its budget on electronics for military weapons and communications.

Economically, this policy makes good sense, since the end products have a relatively high value (e.g., $100 million for an aircraft) compared to the chip costs. Such leverage is similar to the high value-added returns from putting microelectronics in expensive consumer products such as automobiles and top-of-the-line stereo systems. There are two notable differences, however, with military products. In the first place, microelectronic chips have a high obsolescence rate (about five years per IC generation) compared to the operational life of the military product (20–30 years for a plane or missile) for which they are destined. Second, although IC cost reductions have been an important market-driving force in consumer electronics, the number of cruise missiles or B-1 bombers needed by the government is relatively firm. Reduced cost of the electronics for such systems would probably not result in the demand for a significantly greater number of such products by the military.

Microelectronics enters the military electronics network in a variety of ways. Specific hardware, such as precision-guided weapons (PGW), makes heavy use of microprocessors. These "fire and forget" Smart weapons, guided by lasers or other directed radiation sources such as microwave beams, are deadly accurate—unless, of course, their sensing and control signals are jammed by enemy electronic countermeasures (ECM). Since Smart weapons are vulnerable to a host of ECMs, the military has directed attention at electronic counter-countermeasures (ECCM) as well. And so it goes, like a microelectronic chess game.

Collectively, the military's piece of the electronic action is known as C^3 (command/control/communications). C^3 (or C^3I if one includes electronic intelligence gathering) comprises collectively the computers, satellites, telephones, and other telecommunications of the U.S. strategic defense network. C^3 links the Pentagon with its worldwide network of 27 major military command centers, which in turn are linked to the military land-sea-air defense triad (missile-silos, submarines, strategic air command, etc.).

Computers in Defense

In the United States, the coupling between microelectronics and the military has always been close because of the pivotal role of computers in the national defense strategy. For example, the primary job of the earliest electronic digital computer, ENIAC (Electronic Numerical Integrator and Computer), was to solve ballistics problems for the Aberdeen Proving Grounds (1947–1955).[60] From 1950 to 1970, the government contracted out $900 million on semiconductor R&D (1965 dollars), and Defense Department and NASA contracts helped fuel the extraordinary growth of the U.S. microelectronics and computer industry.[61]

Transistor-based computers, with better reliability, increased speed, and "number-crunching" ability were well suited to weapons systems which were growing more complex and responsive each year. For example, the IBM STRETCH system capable of a million instructions per second, was built to give the Ballistic Missile Early Warning System near-instantaneous data analysis and computation. Particularly important was the decision by the air force and NASA in 1962 to use ICs in the Apollo space program and in the guidance system of the Minuteman Intercontinental Ballistic Missile (ICBM).

The situation changed during the 1970s as the growing private sector market in microelectronics displaced the federal government, which today accounts for only about 10 percent of total U.S. semiconductor sales. As one example, 60 percent of IBM's total revenue was government-related in the late 1950s, while in 1980 the figure was only 2 percent.[61] This is not to say that the Department of Defense (DOD) has taken a passive role toward an industry in which it has a vested interest. Recent events indicate just the opposite.

The VHSIC Program

To protect its lead in high-performance computer and communications technology, the DOD has embarked on an ambitious R&D funding program to help the IC industry cross the "one-micron barrier" into VLSI technology. Between 1980 and 1990, DOD expects to direct some $1 billion into the private sector for the phased development of very high-speed integrated circuits (VHSIC)—chips faster than any now produced *in a production environment* and which will control next-generation weapons systems. Already DOD has committed nearly $700 million to the program. When "matching" funds invested by VHSIC participants are included, total dollars invested could approach $2 billion by 1990.[62] The VHSIC program (pronounced "vissic") makes the federal government once again a major player in microelectronic development.

What, it may well be asked, is the difference between VHSIC and VLSI? The difference is principally one of application, since very high-speed devices in general have a very high level of integration. Chips destined for VHSIC applications must first and foremost be very fast. For applications in radar, they must be 50 times faster than today's fastest ICs, for targeting of weapons 100 times faster, and for electronic warfare where speed is survival, as much as 200 times faster. In addition, VHSIC chips must be highly resistant to radiation (radiation-hardened), since they may be operating in space where ionizing radiation is more intense, or in the charged particle clouds produced by nuclear bursts. They must withstand temperature fluctuations from about −70 to +260°F.

Clearly, these chips go far beyond the needs of consumer electronics (unless you plan to run your Apple PC on the surface of the moon!), even though much of the advanced processing needed to make them could be used to produce VLSI chips as well. It should be noted that there are several types of ICs needed for future DOD programs which VHSIC does not address at all. Included in this category are digital ICs based on GaAs and integrated optics.

Concerns have been expressed that VHSIC will draw an already limited supply of process engineers and circuit designers from consumer-oriented chip users to better paying defense contractors and that the focus on specialized military applications will push semiconductor R&D in directions that are not in the best long-term interests of the IC business. In addition, since VHSIC chips are intended to be an integral part of specific military hardware, they may not be so easily adapted for use in consumer markets. Nevertheless, many consumer-oriented companies have participated actively in the DOD program in the interest of national defense and because meeting the VHSIC military goals will help them meet private sector goals as well. It should be noted that not only are semiconductor chip houses involved in VHSIC, but semiconductor equipment makers as well, since processing submicron devices demands very sophisticated process hardware.

In addition to its continuing involvement in VHSIC, DOD is likely to play a key financial role in the establishment of "Sematech," a major U.S. consortium of chip makers whose objective is to develop and transfer advanced microelectronic manufacturing technology to its member companies.[63–64] A DOD subsidy on the order of $100M/year is being sought by Sematech, to cover about half its expected yearly costs. Simply stated, the justification for heavy DOD involvement in this private sector initiative is self-preservation. The chain of reasoning put forth by the Defense Science Board in its Task Force Study of Defense Semiconductor Dependency (February 1987) is instructive. The argument goes as follows: (1) U.S. military forces depend heavily on technological superiority to win, and electronics is the technology that can be leveraged most highly; (2) semiconductors are the key to leadership in electronics and require competitive, high-volume production; (3) high-volume production is supported by the commercial market rather than the military market, which today accounts for less than 10 percent of world semiconductor sales in dollars and less than 3 percent in quantity; (4) leadership in commercial volume production of semiconductors is being lost by the United States and will soon reside abroad—in countries such as Japan and, possibly, South Korea. The unacceptable conclusion is that (5) U.S. defense will soon depend on foreign sources for state-of-the-art technology in semiconductors. It is clearly in the national interest to turn this situation around.

The Effect of Radiation on Microelectronic Circuits

Whether such exotic space-wars systems as killer satellites with directed ion or laser beam weapons proliferate or not, the militarization of space has clearly begun. Military surveillance and communications satellites are already in synchronous orbits around earth carrying sophisticated microelectronic chips. Scientists are finding out, however, that advanced ICs can be highly susceptible to charged particles from the earth's Van Allen belts or from cosmic rays.[28,65] As a result, there have been over a dozen cases of U.S. satellite components suddenly turning on or off. A single alpha particle (the nucleus of a helium atom) crossing a single device can cause errors, which can subsequently cause the complete circuit to malfunction.

These errors can be either "soft" or "hard." The soft error upsets the binary information stored as a 1 or 0 in the circuit memory, changing a 1 to a 0, or vice versa. Although the device continues to function, it gives false information. More severe is the hard error in which the radiation damage permanently alters the device, preventing it from properly functioning or possibly burning it out. As transistors shrink in size, they appear to be more prone to these radiation-induced upsets.

One scientist working on this topic, Peter McNulty, has observed that "at the present time, designing an electronic system for use in space involves a tradeoff between the speed and size allowed by LSI and VLSI circuits and increased [single particle upset] rates."[65] This issue has, of course, great military significance, since some fraction of VHSIC chips, whether in communications satellites or ICBMs, must function reliably in space.

Electromagnetic Pulse Effects on Microelectronic Circuits

In addition to being upset by naturally produced cosmic rays, microchips are particularly vulnerable to the electromagnetic pulse (EMP) of radiation produced when a nuclear bomb is detonated at high altitude.[28,66−67] The phenomenon of EMP was known over twenty years ago, but is only recently being discussed in the popular press. On the evening of July 8, 1962, as part of its atmospheric atomic weapons testing program, the United States exploded a high-altitude, 1.4-megaton nuclear bomb (known as Starfish Prime) 250 miles above Johnston Island in the Pacific Ocean. Seconds later, the Hawaiian Islands, nearly 800 miles to the northeast, were plagued by electrical failures. Streetlights, burglar alarms, and power lines went dead or were disrupted. Basically what happened was as follows.

The fission products of the nuclear explosion emitted energetic gamma rays, which in turn knocked the electrons out of atmospheric air molecules. An intense electric current was thereby created which acted like a radio transmitter, producing a short-lived but powerful burst of electromagnetic radiation. This transmitter "broadcasted" in a broadband extending from very low frequencies to 100 MHz—wherein reside the transmission frequencies of power lines (60 Hz), AM radio stations (about 1000 kHz), FM radio stations (about 100 MHz), and some television channels. Intercepted by conducting power lines and aerial or ground-based antennas, the EMP burst created current surges that disrupted or burned out any solid-state equipment at the other end. Moreover, created at such a high elevation, the pulse illuminated wide areas of the earth's surface.

A single 1–megaton explosion, 1,800 km above the Midwest, could affect 50 percent of the United States. The electric fields produced even 1,000 km from the blast would result in disruptively large electric fields (25,000 volts/m). And EMP pulses move fast, going down a conventional lightning rod in 20-billionths of a second—100 times faster than natural lightning. EMP would, however, do no direct harm to humans, provided they were not in close contact with a metal object. In this sense, it is just the opposite of a neutron bomb, which disrupts and destroys personnel but not hardware.

Both commercial electronic grid—radios, telephones, televisions, telecommunications—and military C^3 systems (particularly land-based missiles) are vulnerable to EMP. Semiconductor devices could be burned out, or worse still, malfunction and cause a missile to hit the wrong target. One scenario is that, as a prelude to a massive nuclear attack by an enemy, several high-altitude nuclear explosions would be detonated over the central United States, causing the entire national power and communications grid to fail, blocking out portions of the military C^3 system and causing chaos in the civilian population from coast to coast. This scenario was in fact portrayed in the CBS television movie "The Day After," when freeway traffic in the Kansas City area was brought to a standstill by EMP-induced ignition failures moments before the first nuclear bombs actually fell in their vicinity.[68]

In the 1960s, the effects of EMP would have been minor, since vacuum tubes are millions of times more resistant to EMP than solid-state devices. However, as the Pentagon utilizes ever more sophisticated microchips for military communications and weapons systems, the susceptibility of these systems to EMP increases. Along these lines, one should recall the 1976 defection of a Soviet pilot who delivered his intact, advanced MIG-25 interceptor to the Japanese. Known as a Foxbat, the plane was found to rely heavily on old-fashioned vacuum tubes and was regarded as electronically backward. Based on our current knowledge of EMP, a different view is possible. As Edward Teller said, "That [Foxbat] was designed by a person as crazy as a fox."[66]

For the military, at least, the situation can be dealt with since, at considerable cost, electronic systems can be shielded from EMP, or radiation-hardened ICs can be produced which are less susceptible to disruption. Alternatively, EMP-resistant communications systems based on nonmetallic fiber optic links can be developed.

Unfortunately, the nonmilitary electronic grid remains vulnerable. On a more encouraging note, however, there appears to be a maximum EMP pulse which can be produced by a nuclear blast—50,000 volts/meter—so that shielding for, say 100,000 volts/meter, should provide an adequate margin of equipment safety.

THE IMPACT OF MICROELECTRONICS ON THE CONSUMER

Many people were first introduced to the wonders of microelectronics through consumer electronics, specifically the portable transistor radio which used cool, tiny solid-state devices rather than hot, bulky tubes. Before discussing how microscopic devices have affected our daily lives, it is interesting to consider the fate of the macroscopic device they replaced—the vacuum tube. As Peter Franken wrote in 1981, "some of you are probably too young to know what a vacuum tube is; imagine a sort of glass cylinder with strange prongs at the base, one of which is always slightly bent."[69]

Most people assume that the vacuum tube went the way of the dinosaur once the rapid evolution of solid-state electronics began. But this is not the case. To be sure, integrated circuits have fossilized certain technology such as the slide rule (the sentimental may want to note that Philomath, Oregon, is now home to the Philomath International Slide Rule Society, dedicated to establishing a definitive slide-rule museum).[70] But ironically, 25 years after the first IC, vacuum tubes were a $1.8 billion business compared to only $1.4 billion for computer chips and $0.7 billion for transistors.[71]

Vacuum tubes have continued to make a strong showing because it is more difficult to use semiconductors when excessive heating may occur, such as in high-power/high-frequency applications. In addition, tubes are more robust by nature and are not easily upset by current surges or other electrical transients. As a result, vacuum tubes are used in such places as home microwave ovens, military and airport radar, transmitters, and satellite communications. The picture tube in a television set or computer video monitor continues to provide detailed images at low cost, even though the electronic circuitry in both cases is decidedly solid state.

Digital Watches

Advanced microelectronics entered the U.S. consumer market in the late 1960s, when hand-held, four-function ($+$, $-$, $\div$, $\times$) calculators and then, slightly later, digital watches from Japan began to appear in consumer outlets. By 1978, perhaps 50 percent of all watches sold were electronic (digital or quartz). Today's quartz watches have an accuracy of 1–2 minutes per year, as compared to 1–2 minutes per week for a mechanical watch, and they are far more flexible. For example, it has been possible to integrate several functions into electronic watches, such as calculators, programmable melody-playing alarms and timers, blood pressure monitors, and digital thermometers. (Many readers have probably attended large meetings where they have heard hundreds of digital watches in the audience beep, warble, and chirp on the hour like some startled flock of high-technology birds!) One of the drawbacks of digital time measurement is that the information contained in the relative spatial position of clock hands is lost. This means that the direction of clockwise motion cannot be checked on one's wrist. Second (and speaking for most people raised on analog clocks), the time to wait until, say, lunchtime is more readily "felt" by the angular distance of the minute hand from 12 than by the more precise fact that it is 11:43:08 A.M.

Video Games

The sophistication of video games such as Zaxxon or PacMan, whether viewed in electronic arcades or on less sophisticated home computers, is a far cry from the rudimentary, but microprocessor-controlled, game of Pong designed by Nolan Bushnell in 1972. The importance of Pong is not that it ushered in an age of fabulous electronic toys which today are capable of synthesized speech (e.g., Teddy Ruxpin by Worlds of Wonder). Rather, as Dirk Hanson has pointed out in *The New Alchemists,* Pong was the perfect vehicle for introducing the personal computer to consumers, for bringing the revolution in microelectronics and computer science into the privacy of one's home in a nonthreatening and palatable way.[28]

Cameras

Increasingly, solid-state electronics is being used in photographic equipment to control focus, exposure, and shutter speed, thereby making cameras easier to use, lighter in weight, and more reliable. For example, by making use of 4K LSI technology, Canon was able to eliminate 300 mechanical parts in its AE-1, 35–mm camera.[58] Automatic focusing is available on cameras by Konica, Honeywell, Polaroid (the Sonar SX-70), and others. In regard to photography, the Japanese seem particularly well positioned, since they not only make the chips but dominate the world market share of 35-mm cameras (Nikon, Canon, Olympus, Konica, Minolta) and are strong in photographic film (Fuji) and videocassette technology as well.

Home Appliances

Microprocessors have allowed a number of features to be added to appliances, such as microwave ovens, washing machines, refrigerators, and televisions, increasing control of appliance functions and reducing energy consumption. The textile industry, so important in the first Industrial Revolution, has already benefited from computer-controlled laser cutting of cloth and by the introduction of advanced sewing machines such as the Singer Athena 2000, which has pushbutton control of 24 stitch patterns, optimizes stitch width, length, and density, and has increased reliability, since 350 mechanical parts could be eliminated by its NMOS LSI chip.[58] Microwave ovens and televisions are particularly interesting, since both state-of-the-art IC technology and vacuum tube technology co-exist in the same product. In designing consumer goods, there is a tendency to incorporate microchips simply because they are available and fashionable. In such cases, the major justification is product differentiation, that is, the potential customer perceives company A's refrigerator as a better one because it can talk.

Automobiles

By means of microcomputers and microprocessor chips, a variety of fuel-saving, diagnostic, and convenience functions can now be built into modern automobiles, including electronic fuel injection, solid state ignition, seat belt, low fuel/oil pressure alarms, and tire pressure sensors that operate while the car is in motion.[72] Synthetic-voice synthesizer chips that tell the driver when the headlights have not been turned off (the electronic equivalent of the backseat driver) are becoming commonplace, and future opportunities abound in such areas as active suspension, user-specific driver instructions, and collision avoidance. Microchips, because of their light weight and lower power requirements, are ideally suited to applications in transportation. In addition, by monitoring and controlling engine performance in real time—somewhat like giving the car a tune-up every second—they optimize fuel efficiency and reduce hazardous fuel emissions. Using a $10 chip to leverage the sale of a $10,000 car is also very smart business. Presently, electronics accounts for about 3 percent of a vehicle's cost; however, by 1995 this is expected to rise to above 15 percent. The number of electronic systems in automobiles and trucks is expected to rise even faster—from about 10 million in 1985 to 100 million in 1995.

An automobile is not an ideal environment in which to operate semiconductors because of high levels of electromagnetic interference from the engine's ignition system, mechanical vibration, wide swings in temperatures, and so on. Consequently, some automotive companies have developed their own in-house capability to design and produce the specialized chips they require. For example, Delco Electronics, a division of General Motors, supplies GM with automotive entertainment and engine-control products. Among other things, Delco produces over 400,000 ICs and 20,000 on-board computers daily, 90 percent of which go to GM.[72]

A small taste of things to come is an electronic navigational guidance system from Honda.[73] The ElectroGyro-Cator displays the position of an automobile along a chosen route on any one of a thousand video road maps stored in memory and displayed on a 5 × 6-inch television monitor. Costing over $1000, the system is not yet priced for mass consumption. A similar navigational system under development by Ford is known as the Tripmonitor. By the late 1980s, Ford hopes to use the navy's transit satellite system (tens of thousands of miles above the earth) to feed tracking data to private automobiles or military vehicles equipped with the Tripmonitor. Since digital disks could allow thousands of road maps to be stored, we may never need to ask for directions again. On the other hand, since the tracking satellite "knows" the location of a car at all times, so presumably does the government agency that owns the satellite.

The Office of the Future

Offices of the early twentieth century were changed by the telephone and typewriter. In the late twentieth century, the proliferation of electronic word-processing systems in modern offices, the use of minicomputers for collection and processing of business data, and the advent of electronic mail leave little doubt that microelectronics is changing the traditional 9-to-5 work environment.[74]

In many cases, microchips have enabled the performance of conventional office equipment to be significantly improved without radical change in design. For example, the keyboard of a word processor is similar in appearance to that of a typewriter, even though the processor can store and modify text, justify margins, and even check for misspellings of common words. A digital telephone of today is not all that different in appearance from a 1960s model, but by use of microelectronics, many functions such as automatic dialing and transfer of calls are now possible.

Overall, the office of the future will require advances in several areas of technology: data display and storage, communications, and printing. And, because of the enormous volume of information which modern businesses process, microchips with fast speed and large memories are needed—in short, VLSI chips.

Whether increasing automation is going to cost jobs is open to debate, but as Dirk Hanson has pointed out, "whether the microchip creates jobs or destroys them . . . a growing percentage of the work force will be involved in the ongoing experiment of finding out."[28]

Particularly vulnerable in the office are secretaries, the majority of whom are women. The growing use of word processors and the increased productivity they afford mean that fewer persons are needed to accomplish traditional secretarial tasks. Since a less skilled typist can use the technological leverage of the word processor to compensate for lack of manual skill (e.g., slow typing speed, keystroke mistakes), cheaper labor can be used. On the other hand, automation should permit a select percentage of talented secretaries to move up to more challenging, entry-level management positions. The net effect could be a polarization of office workers into the very skilled and the barely skilled, creating a gap in the middle levels of the office work force and unemployment in the secretarial ranks.

Scientific Research

The birth of the electric utility industry in the late nineteenth and early twentieth centuries and the resulting "electrification" of the country were widely recognized as revolutionary technical changes. Equally important, but not as widely perceived at the time, was the birth of organized research and development—a concept legitimized and popularized largely by the success of Thomas Edison, who employed a team approach to problem solving. The idea that technical inventions could be achieved by logically organizing people and resources was a significant by-product of Edison's primary search to replace gas illumination by the electric light bulb.[28,75]

Similarly, the development of solid-state microelectronics to replace vacuum tubes has had a significant effect on the way scientific research is conducted. One obvious effect is that a computer capable of a million calculations per second has made it possible to analyze statistically large quantities of experimental data or mathematically model extremely complex systems in areas such as hydrodynamics (weather forecasting) and astrophysics. Personal computers now allow individual researchers a "number-crunching" ability only possible in the past on large, less accessible mainframe computers.

In addition, the decision-making powers of microprocessors allow experiments to be controlled and monitored to a degree not possible by human intervention. In many cases, it is even possible to "perform" an experiment by computer simulation. In chemical synthesis, this may allow new reactions to be tested for feasibility and yield before carrying out the procedure in the laboratory.

Finally, the increasing impact of library automation on research should not be ignored. On-line searching of scientific and patent literature by computer database searching makes it possible for researchers (even those without access to a large library) to have prompt access to state-of-the-art results, avoiding duplication of effort and guiding future experiments.

THE SILICON VALLEY

Scientists have often debated whether life based on silicon, rather than carbon, is possible. In fact, life based on silicon has been thriving in a small California community for over thirty years.

The Mecca of Microelectronics

The petri dish containing this growing microelectronic culture is located in the Santa Clara Valley, some thirty miles south of San Francisco. Known as the Silicon Valley (a term popularized by Don Hoefler in 1971), it is not an official name on any map, but holds a place of special importance for the semiconductor industry.[28,30] It was where the first West Coast semiconductor company,

Shockley Semiconductor Laboratories, set up shop in 1955; where some of the earliest silicon ICs were mass produced; where the microprocessor was created; and where an alchemist's dream of turning base silicon into gold became a reality for a number of venture capitalists and high-technology entrepreneurs.[28]

In the early 1950s, the Valley was mainly orchards, with the fledgling electronics industry clustered near Stanford University in Palo Alto to the north. Today, the orchards have been replaced by urban sprawl, traffic congestion, and an enormous proliferation of major semiconductor chip houses and support service companies. SEMI (Semiconductor Equipment and Materials Institute) listed over sixty in its 1983 "Guide to Semiconductor Companies in the Silicon Valley." The list includes Advanced Micro Devices, American Microsystems, Inc., Apple Computer, Atari, Avantek, Data General, Fairchild Semiconductor, Hewlett-Packard, Intel, Intersil, Litronix, Lockheed, Monolithic Memories, National Semiconductor, Raytheon, Signetics, Siliconix, Synertek, Varian, and Zilog. The high-tech glamour of the Valley attracts visitors from the world over, anxious to see firsthand what the revolution in microelectronics and computer technology is all about. Even Queen Elizabeth of England, on her 1983 visit to the United States, found time for a tour of Hewlett-Packard.

Activity in the Valley has been characteristic of the semiconductor industry it represents: "innovative, intensive, rapidly growing, intensely competitive."[28] Corporate life can be fast-paced and unorthodox by past business standards. Historically, new start-up ventures, often led by dynamic inventor-entrepreneurs, have catalyzed the rapid growth of innovative semiconductor technology in the Valley. For example, when Intel spun off from Fairchild Semiconductor in 1968 (Fairchild Semiconductor itself having spun off earlier from the Shockley transistor company), it was only one of thirteen semiconductor company start-ups in Silicon Valley that year. Six years later, Intel itself was to provide the start-up for Zilog. And so it goes, with engineers and marketeers changing partners as frequently as lovers on a daytime soap opera.

Well-paid Silicon Valley has been a mecca for high-technology workers, with high pay and the promise of a California life-style. However, in recent years conditions have changed dramatically. The Silicon Valley has traditionally been subject to a roller-coaster type of economy in which boom times are closely followed by busts. (A typical joke concerns the fab line worker who asks his supervisor if they will be working overtime up until the layoffs.) Nevertheless, the extended downturn in the computer and microelectronics industries surprised most valley observers. The valley is currently coming out of a 3–year slump following a phenomenal expansion of production capacity in 1984. Throughout 1985 and 1986, the mecca of microelectronics was characterized by forced vacations, frozen pay, layoffs, and plant closings; however, by late 1987, there were positive signs that the U.S. semiconductor manufacturing industry had emerged from the worst recession in its history.[76]

Although the close association of microelectronics and Silicon Valley appears to be a geographic anomaly of the West Coast, this is not strictly true. For example, on the East Coast, Boston's Route 128 became home for a number of new high-technology firms after World War II, with Harvard and MIT serving as the academic counterparts of Stanford. Also, because of the escalating cost of Santa Clara County land and shortages of qualified workers, many semiconductor firms have built new plants in other parts of the United States, creating semiconductor-oriented industrial parks in the process—the Silicon Ranch in Texas and Arizona, the Silicon Forest in Oregon, and the Silicon Prairie in Indiana. In other countries as well, industrial "theme parks" designed in the Silicon Valley image exist, such as Scotland's Silicon Glen. And low-cost, off-shore assembly of ICs on the "Silicon Islands" of Hong Kong and Taiwan are well established. These Silicon Valley clones attest to the fact that Northern California is not the only growth medium for the IC culture.

International Developments

Although the Valley began as a distinctly U.S. phenomenon, it has become more international in flavor as foreign buy-ins have occurred. For example Philips (the Netherlands) currently owns Signetics, Siemens A.G. (West Germany) owns Litronix, Robert Bosch (West Germany) owns 25 percent of American Microsystems, and until quite recently, Schlumberger (France) owned Fairchild Semiconductor. The principal foreign presence in microelectronics, however, is not European but Japanese.

It is impossible to speak about the future of microelectronics without touching on the role of Japan, or "Japan, Inc." as that island nation has come to be known in the IC community. Even the annual "New Year's Wish List" of *Electronics* magazine listed the following New Year's wish for 1984: "For U.S. electronics engineers, courses in Japanese as a second language."[77] The Japanese presence can be appreciated by the fact that in 1986 six of the top ten merchant suppliers of semiconductors were Japanese—NEC, Hitachi, Toshiba, Fujitsu, Matsushita, and Mitsubishi, accounting for about $10 billion in semiconductor sales.[78] These figures reflect in large part Japan's dominance in advanced memory chip production—such as the 256K and 1-megabit Dynamic Random Access Memory (DRAM). When the first high density memory chip, the 1K RAM, was introduced by Intel in 1970, the United States had a near 100 percent market share. Each succeeding advance in memory chip sophistication (4K to 16K to 64K to 256K) has seen a decreasing U.S. market share (87 percent to 62 percent to 43 percent to 17 percent, respectively).[79] Currently only about 8 percent of 1M DRAMs sold are made in the United States.

Philosophically, the Japanese strength in memory chips is only fitting. After all, memory plays a major part in Japanese society, where thousands of complex

Chinese pictograms (kanji) must be committed to memory by school-age children and where a hierarchy of social relationships and appropriate levels of verbal politeness must always be kept in mind. One might even ask, does the regular geometric pattern of memory cells in a DRAM appeal on some deep level to the Japanese esthetic—like a Zen rock garden etched in silicon? Yet in spite of their success with memory-based products, the Japanese have not been strong in logic-based products, such as microprocessors. The reason for this may have as much to do with Japanese culture as with microelectronic technology.

Traditionally, the Japanese have neither encouraged nor rewarded great originality. Instead, throughout its 2000–year history, Japan has aggressively imported foreign ideas and then refined and improved upon them. This is true of the written Japanese language (derived from Chinese pictograms), Zen Buddhism (a variation of Indian Buddhism), and, more recently, microelectronics. With few exceptions, such as the Esaki diode from Hitachi, the quantum leaps forward in microelectronics have not come from Japan.

Starting with the invention of the transistor at Bell Laboratories in 1947 and up to the present day, the major breakthroughs in microelectronics such as the integrated circuit (Jack Kilby at Texas Instruments; Bob Noyce at Fairchild Semiconductor) and the microprocessor (Ted Hoff at Intel) have been products of U.S. engineering. Making successful DRAMs, however, does not depend on developing original technology, but on applying the traditional Japanese strengths of product improvement and quality control. More specifically, VLSI memory chips require superior manufacturing technology—the ability to do reliable, ultra-precise microfabrication in mass production. Making small improvements in standard process steps (e.g., depositing a metal with better uniformity) improves device performance and results in a substantial and immediate market advantage. VLSI microprocessor chips, on the other hand, require superior design technology, which in turn relies on creative engineering and the heavy use of computer simulation. The design and layout of an advanced microprocessor can take several years of such sustained, original effort. Until recently, the Japanese have shied away from this kind of activity. Ironically, since a great deal of creative software design time goes into coping with limited storage space in computer memory, the Japanese success in producing higher capacity memory chips may partially compensate for their deficiency in software engineering.

On the other hand, memory chips, because of the regular and repetitive patterns of their circuitry, are inherently less difficult to design than logic chips. As a result, memory devices have historically led all other types of ICs in having the highest density of components per chip. Japanese micromanufacturing skills already developed to produce high-volume, low-priced 1M DRAMS are the same skills which will be needed to produce low-volume, high-priced VLSI microprocessors when their designs have been perfected. Japanese chip makers therefore have the manufacturing base in place to dominate both memory and logic chip production in the future.

While memory chips are physically very small, their economic impact is very large—and getting larger each year. In 1985 alone, over $50 billion worth of 64K and 256K DRAMs will have been sold worldwide—representing enough memory capacity to store the complete contents of 100,000 large encyclopedias. And by 1990, sales of advanced megabit memory chips may well exceed $10 billion.

Like armies marching off to war, chip houses are preparing to fight for possession of this growing market. One foreign alliance has already been formed: the half-billion-dollar "Mega Project" between Philips (the Netherlands) and Siemens (West Germany); while in the United States, Texas Instruments and Motorola are separately tooling up to produce high volumes of VLSI memory chips. Within the last year, IBM has reported substantial progress in bringing advanced memory technology (1–4M DRAMs) out of the laboratory and into the marketplace. While IBM only produces its chips for internal consumption (a "captive" supplier versus a "merchant" supplier), the presence of made-in-America 1M DRAM chips in the IBM mainframe computers indicates the growing strength of U.S. memory chip technology.

Lest the battle for microelectronic supremacy be viewed as a contest between U.S. and Japanese chip makers, it is worth pointing out that South Korean companies such as Gold Star, Daewoo, Samsung, and Hyundai may soon be serious contenders. In the early 1980s, South Korean activity in semiconductors was limited mainly to producing discrete devices and ICs produced overseas. Today, South Korean companies sell over $1 billion in semiconductors annually and are on the verge of introducing 4M DRAMs.[80]

Cooperative Ventures

Recognizing the importance of microelectronics in Japan's present and future economy, the Japanese government's Ministry of International Trade and Industry (MITI) began in the mid-1970s to subsidize the development of VLSI devices in Japan.[28] MITI provided $100 million over a seven-year period to fund a cooperative venture among five private companies: NEC, Mitsubishi, Toshiba, Fujitsu, and Hitachi. Selected workers from the participating companies temporarily joined forces to advance the collective state of the art in Japanese microelectronics. In the process, a pattern for productive cooperation was established which has been adopted by U.S. workers as well.

For example, a number of cooperative research facilities in microelectronics have started to appear across the United States. As joint ventures among industry, universities, and state/regional government agencies, these cooperatives have come together "to pool and leverage resources, both intellectual and financial, to pursue and develop for their common good, both a basic scientific knowledge and technological expertise; and to establish world-class facilities for training the next generation of professionals in the technologies that will be vital to our society."[81]

A partial list of such ventures includes the National Research and Resource Facility for Submicron Structures (Cornell University), Microelectronics Center of North Carolina, Massachusetts Microelectronics Center (under development), Center for Integrated Systems (Stanford University), and the Semiconductor Research Corporation.

In addition, the creation in 1982 of the Microelectronics and Computer Technology Corporation (MCC) in Austin, Texas, is a direct private sector response to cooperative VLSI development.[82] MCC is made up of a consortium of fifteen U.S. electronics companies who will temporarily pool their resources and personnel to develop next-generation computer hardware and software. An annual budget of $100 million was targeted for advanced research and development by four hundred engineers and scientists.

Perhaps the most ambitious cooperative U.S. initiative in microelectronics is Sematech consortium, launched in late 1986.[63-64] The objective of Sematech (Semiconductor Manufacturing Technology Institute) is to regain U.S. leadership in semiconductor manufacturing from the Japanese over the next five years by developing and distributing such technology to its approximately 20–member companies, including such heavyweights as AT&T, Hewlett-Packard, IBM, Intel, Motorola, National Semiconductor, Rockwell, and Texas Instruments. The scope of the venture, which is expected to include a major wafer fabrication unit for 164-Megabit DRAM production in the United States, will be determined in large part by government financing. Fully funded, Sematech is expected to cost about $250 million per year.

LONG-RANGE EFFECTS OF MICROELECTRONICS

One can only speculate on what the long-term cumulative effect on society of changes brought on by microelectronics will be (see table 1.1). One effect is the compression of time and space resulting from worldwide, microelectronic-based satellite communications and high-speed data processing fostering the creation of a global village. Loss of privacy or individuality is likely to be of increasing concern to the residents of this village, since abuses of privacy in this computer age are well documented.

Another issue concerns informational overdose whereby ability to make a decision is hampered by too much rather than too little detailed information. On the other hand, since microprocessors are very good at making programmed decisions, there could be a strong tendency to giving the chip more control over

Table 1.1
Effects of Microelectronics

Areas Impacted	Specific Developments	Possible Effects
Office of the Future	Word-processing systems; self-correcting typewriters with built-in vocabularies of commonly misspelled words; direct speech-to-text transcriptions of letters and reports; direct translation of foreign languages.	Loss of clerical jobs; creation of a work force consisting of highly skilled and barely skilled.
Banking	Automated banking; banking by home computer; instant credit verification.	Emergence of a cashless and checkless society; loss of privacy.
Communication	Home computers linked via telephone lines or satellite by rooftop microwave antennas.	Evolution of the global village.
Appliances	Microprocessor-controlled, energy-efficient products with increased features.	Increased leisure time for the homemaker.
Automobiles	Fuel-efficient, closed-loop electronic engine control; automatic diagnostic techniques; electronic position finders.	Lower use of imported oil; lowered smog emissions.
Supermarket	Check-out automation and real-time inventory control.	Consumer confusion on product costs; more sophisticated marketing studies can be carried out.
Entertainment	Narrow-casting; electronic games; video cassettes; compact disks.	Emergence of home as center of learning and play.
Energy Consumption	Microprocessor control of energy use in home and office; of gasoline consumption in motor vehicles.	Less dependence on imported oil.
Manufacturing	Computer-aided design; numerically-controlled machine tools; automated test/inspection.	Increased quality control; faster development of new products.
Health Care	Electronic prosthesis (implantable cardiac pacemaker); noninvasive diagnostics; computer diagnosis; consumer-oriented fitness gadgetry.	Electronic compensation for the handicapped; more accurate and rapid medical dianosis.
National Defense	Electronic countermeasures; Smart weapons; killer satellites.	U.S. defense more dependent on microelectronics for the competitive edge; more susceptible to electromagnetic pulse disruptions.

our lives. As Frank Oppenheimer has said, "If we are not careful, computers will . . . permit the business of living and learning to proceed even more mindlessly than they have in the past."[7]

There may be a gradual shift of functions now performed separately in the office, classroom, and store to a central location—in all probability, the home. Whether the home re-emerges as the center of society as in preindustrial times remains to be seen; however, a number of activities can already be centralized there. Using a personal computer at home, one can perform a number of business, secretarial, and library functions. Information can be retrieved, analyzed, stored, or produced in hard copy. Banking can be accomplished by phone; certain entertainment (first-run movies, video games) and educational (computer-programmed learning) programs can be carried out by means of video casette or videodisk systems. Not only will information be rapidly available at home from further away (e.g., transmission via satellite to home microwave antennas), but more communication channels will allow programs to be aired that cater to a small audience. For example, an ongoing television series on Slavic history would probably never appear on major network prime-time programming because of its uneconomically limited audience share. If, instead of 20 television channels, however, there were 2,000 channels, special-interest group programs could be economical, leading to narrow-casting instead of broadcasting.

In national defense, our increasing use of microelectronic technology is already changing the way we gather and analyze intelligence data and design and control weapons systems. Many of our fastest, most sophisticated mainframe computers are in fact dedicated to applications such as cryptography, missile targeting, and aerodynamic modeling of next-generation aircraft.

History provides many examples in which the introduction of new military technology has influenced events far removed from the battlefield. A case in point is the Battle of Agincourt, fought in 1415 between feudal English and French armies. The battle soundly demonstrated the supremacy of the rapid-fire, armor-piercing Welch longbow (English technology) over the less advanced crossbow (French technology). Moreover, the English victory shattered the myth of the invincible armored knight on horseback and "turned the medieval social order upside down."[83] More recently, in World War II, we witnessed the development and use of atomic fission weapons—an event having profound political and social fallout forty years later. The increasing application of microelectronics in national defense may be another such "battlefield development" whose full impact on society at large remains to be felt.

Willing or unwilling, we are all participants in the ongoing revolution in microelectronics and computer science. Unlike earlier industrial revolutions, which were energy and material intensive (increasingly in short supply these days), this revolution is information and intellectual effort, resources that are inexhaustible. In the decades ahead, we can expect to see our society affected more and more, and ultimately, transformed by "the power and promise of the silicon chip."[59]

NOTES

1. Theodore H. Geballe, "This Golden Age of Solid-State Physics," *Physics Today* (Nov. 1981), pp. 132–143.

2. Rob Hof, "The Hottest New Computer Chip is Here," *The Peninsula Times Tribune* (Oct. 14, 1983), p. B-8.

3. *Electronics*, 50th Anniversary Issue (April 17, 1980).

4. N. W. Larkin, "Impact of Technology on the Development of VLSI," in *VLSI 81*, ed. John P. Gray (Academic Press, 1981), pp. 313–18.

5. Irwin Goodwin, "Supercomputers: Who'll be the Fastest with the Fastest?" *Physics Today*, (May 1984), pp. 61–64.

6. "Researchers Factor 71-Digit Number in 9.5 Hours," *Research & Development*, (May 1984), p. 50.

7. Frank Oppenheimer, "Chips and Choices," in *The Exploratorium*, Vol. 8, No. 1 (Spring 1984), pp. 2–3.

8. J. D. Meindl, "Theoretical, Practical and Analogical Limits in VLSI," Proceedings of the 1983 International Electron Device Meeting, IEDM (Institute of Electrical & Electronics Engineers, 1983), pp. 8–13.

9. "Wafer Processing," *Circuits Manufacturing*, Vol. 20, No. 7 (July 1980), pp. 21–34.

10. Aaron D. Weiss, "Substrates Review: Silicon, Sapphire and GaAs," *Semiconductor International* (June 1983), pp. 66–71.

11. JEJ, "SEH Grows 8 in. Silicon Ingots," *Semiconductor International* (April 1984), p. 32.

12. S. M. Sze, "VLSI Technology Overview and Trends," *Japanese Journal of Applied Physics* 22, Supplement 22-1, 3–10 (1983).

13. Ron Iscoff, "Wafer Scale Integration: An Appraisal," *Semiconductor International* (Sept. 1984), pp. 62–65.

14. "Timeline," in *The Exploratorium*, ed. P. Murphy, Vol. 8, No. 1 (Spring 1984), p. 15.

15. Erwin A. Frand, "Thoughts and Advertisements-I," *Industrial R&D* (Oct. 1981), p. 25.

16. Colin Covert, "Chip Shots—A Brief History of the Indispensable Silicon Chip," *TWA Ambassador* (Nov. 1983), pp. 102–6.

17. R. N. Noyce, in *Microelectronics*, (San Francisco: W. H. Freeman, 1977) pp. 2–9. [This book reprints eleven articles from the Sept. 1977 *Scientific American*.]

18. James D. Meindl, "Opportunities for Gigascale Integration," *Solid State Technology* (Dec. 1987), pp. 85–89.

19. Pieter Burggraaf, "Lithography Trends," *Semiconductor International* (June 1983), p. 42.

20. John A. Armstrong, "Solid State Technology and the Computer: 40 Years Later, Small is Still Beautiful," *Solid State Technology* (Dec. 1987), pp. 81–83.

21. Pat Murphy, "In the Chips," in *The Exploratorium*, Vol. 8, No. 1 (Spring 1984), pp. 10–14.

22. Carver A. Mead, "VLSI and Technological Innovations," in *VLSI 81*, ed. John P. Gray (London: Academic Press, 1981), pp. 3–11.

23. William Lawson, "CAD/CAM for IC Design and Fabrication," *Microelectronic Manufacturing and Testing* (July 1983), pp. 24–25.

24. "Chip Protection Aids Chemicals," *Chemical Week* (Oct. 24, 1984), p. 20.

25. Peter H. Singer, "Testing Ultrahigh Speed Devices," *Semiconductor International* (Sept. 1984), pp. 50–55.

26. Ron Iscoff, "Sandals Lower Particle Count," *Semiconductor International* (August 1984), p. 36.

27. William G. Oldham, "The Fabrication of Microelectronic Circuits," in *Microelectronics,* (San Francisco: W. H. Freeman, 1977), pp. 40–52.

28. Dirk Hanson, *The New Alchemists* (Boston: Little, Brown & Co., 1982).

29. Dennis W. Hess, "Process Technology of Silicon Integrated Circuits," *ChemTech* (July 1979), pp. 432–45.

30. Allen A. Boraiko, "The Chip," *National Geographic,* Vol. 162, No. 4 (Oct. 1982), pp. 421–57.

31. Jerry Lyman, "Scaling the Barriers to VLSI's Fine Lines," *Electronics* (June 19, 1982), pp. 115–26.

32. Frederic N. Schwettmann and John L. Moll, "IC Process Technology: VLSI and Beyond," *Hewlett-Packard Journal* (Aug. 1982), pp. 3–4.

33. Peter H. Singer, "The Transistor: 40 Years Later," *Semiconductor International* (Jan. 1988), pp. 74–77.

34. Arthur L. Robinson, "Cornell Submicron Facility Dedicated," *Science* 214 (Nov. 1981), pp. 777–78.

35. Edward M. Purcell, "The Back of the Envelope," *American Journal of Physics* 51 (1983), p. 874.

36. Joseph F. Dunphy, "Gallium Arsenide: A Cinderella," *Chemical Week,* (Jan. 7–14, 1987), pp. 13–24.

37. Stephen Solomon, "Gallium Arsenide: The Right Stuff," *Science Digest,* (Nov. 1982), pp. 54–57.

38. Phillip Robinson, "Gallium Arsenide Chips," *BYTE* (Nov. 1984), pp. 211–27.

39. Arthur L. Robinson, "Is Diamond the New Wonder Material?," *Science,* Vol. 234 (Nov. 28, 1986), pp. 1074–76.

40. Malcolm W. Broune, "From Rocket to Razor Blade, Diamond-Coating Era Dawns," *New York Times,* (Sunday, Sept. 14, 1986), p. 1.

41. Hisao Hayakawa, "Josephson Computer Technology," *Physics Today* (March 1986), pp. 46–52.

42. Rick D. Davies, "The Case for CMOS," *IEEE Spectrum* (Oct. 1983), pp. 26–32.

43. "CMOS to Become Dominant IC Technology," *Semiconductor International,* (April 1984), p. 26.

44. "Future Technology," *Electronics* (April 17, 1980), pp. 530–63.

45. Joseph Grenier, "A Five Year Wafer Fabrication Equipment Forecast: Restrained Optimism Prevails," *Solid State Technology,* (Jan. 1987), pp. 34–37.

47. "Fastest Semiconductor Circuit Ever," *Microelectronic Manufacturing and Testing* (Oct. 1984), p. 7.

47. "Data Transfer Boosted to 5 Gbit/sec," *R&D* (April 1984), p. 88.

48. "First Commercial GaAs Integrated Circuits," *Semiconductor International* (April 1984), p. 24.

49. Lawrence Barns, "Superconductors," *Business Week* (April 6, 1987), pp. 94–100.

50. "Superconducting Materials Stimulate Activity in High Speed IC Research," *Semiconductor International* (Sept. 1987), pp. 24–26.

51. Skip Derra, "Special Report: Superconductivity," *Research & Development* (Sept. 1987), pp. 57–64.

52. Irwin Stambler, "Molecular Computers Generate Interest and Skepticism," *IR&D* (Jan. 1984), pp. 56–57.

53. Natalie Angier, "The Organic Computer," *Discover* (May 1982), pp. 76–79.

54. Eric Drexler, "Mightier Machines from Tiny Atoms May Someday Grow," *Smithsonian* (Nov. 1982), pp. 145–55.

55. Joseph Alper and B. J. Spalding, "Molecular Electronics: Carbon Aims to Dethrone Silicon," *Chemical Week* (July 30, 1986), pp. 32–34.

56. "Announcements and Call for Papers, Journal of Electronics," *Physics Today* (May 1984), p. 94.

57. Ernest Braun and Stuart MacDonald, *Revolution in Miniature: The History and Impact of Semiconductor Electronics* (New York: Cambridge University Press, 1978).

58. Saburo Muroga, *VLSI System Design* (New York: John Wiley & Sons, 1982), pp. 1–60.

59. James D. Meindl, "Microchips: The Power and the Promise," *The Stanford Magazine* (Spring/Summer 1980), pp. 10–17.

60. "Computers and Semiconductors," in *Only One Science* (Washington, D.C.: National Science Foundation, 1981), pp. 7–37.

61. James Botkin, Dan Dimancescu, and Ray Stata, *Global Stakes* (Cambridge, Mass.: Bollinger Publishing Co., 1982).

62. John R. Moore, "VHSIC—A User's Perspective," presented at Advanced Defense Preparedness Association's Annual Technical Review, May 1984.

63. Richard Bambrick, "Sematech Gets SIA Go-Ahead: Target Government, Ind. for Funds," *Electronic News* (Nov. 24, 1986), p. 1.

64. Charles H. Ferguson, "Sink or Swim with Semiconductors," *Applied Optics* (November 15, 1987), p. 4703.

65. Peter McNulty, "Charged Particles Cause Microelectronics Malfunction in Space," *Physics Today* (Jan. 1983), pp. 108–9.

66. William J. Broad, "The Chaos Factor," *Science 83* (Jan./Feb. 1983), pp. 41–49.

67. David W. Hafemeister, "Science and Society Test VIII: The Arms Race Revisited," *American Journal of Physics* 51 (Mar. 1983), pp. 215–55.

68. *Time,* December 5, 1983.

69. Peter Franken, "Optics: An Ebullient Revolution," *Physics Today* (Nov. 1981), pp. 160–71.

70. Joe Menosky, "Napier's Bones," *Science 83* (Sept. 1983), pp. 83–84.

71. Roger Rapoport, "Life in a Vacuum," *Science 84* (Mar. 1984), pp. 89–90.

72. Peter H. Singer, "IC Production for Automobiles," *Semiconductor International* (April 1984), pp. 118–20.

73. Patrick Cooke, "Look Homeward (Electronic) Angel," *Science 84* (May 1984), pp. 75–78.

74. E. C. Greanias, "The Effect of VLSI: Prospects for the Office of the Future," in *VLSI Electronics: Microstructure Science,* vol. 4, ed. Norman G. Einspruch (New York: Academic Press, 1983), pp. 243–82.

75. "Creating the Electronic Age," *EPRI Journal,* Vol. 4, No. 2 (Mar. 1979).

76. Donald E. Swanson, "U.S. Semiconductor Materials Strengthen World Leadership," *Semiconductor International,* (Oct. 1987), pp. 100–101.

77. Editorial, "The Annual New Year's Wish List," *Electronics* (Dec. 15, 1983), p. 24.

78. Gene Norrett, "The Formation of USA, Inc.," *Solid State Technology* (Nov. 1987), pp. 33–35.

79. Jim Peterman, Texas Instruments, private communication, June 1987.

80. Myung S. Bae, "The Korean Semiconductor Industry: A Brief History and Perspective," *Solid State Technology* (Oct. 1987), pp. 141–44.

81. "Microelectronics Tech Center News," *Solid State Technology* (Sept. 1984), pp. 101–2.

82. "MCC Appoints Directors of Its R&D Programs," *R&D* (May 1984), pp. 60–62.

83. James Burke, *Connections* (Boston: Little, Brown & Co., 1978).

2

Materials and Modern Technology

J. E. Burke

The word *materials* has become part of the vocabulary of all people who follow the advancement of technology, and articles on materials appear almost as frequently in the business and financial papers as in the technical press. Feature articles extolling the wonders of modern materials are common even in the daily papers. There is good reason for this. Substantially all major technological advances of the past five decades have required development of new materials or important modification of existing ones. The atomic bomb, for example, required the development of techniques for making large quantities of little-known uranium and of the totally new element of plutonium, and for fabricating them into precisely determined shapes. Nuclear energy for civilian use subsequently required development of uranium dioxide for fuel and hafnium-free metallic zirconium for reactor components. The introduction of jet engines was possible only after a whole new class of superalloys was invented for making components to resist the high stresses and corrosive conditions encountered at the high temperatures existing inside gas-turbine engines. The remarkable recent advances in electronics, communications, and computers would have been impossible without the now ubiquitous high-purity silicon and certain other semiconducting single crystals unknown before World War II. Similarly, many other advances in transportation, lighting, communications, and information handling (i.e., the advances of modern technology) have demanded other materials with specific new combinations of properties, and as a result, hundreds of new materials have appeared.

Future technological advances will require yet further developments in materials. Some of them will be achieved by the usual combinations of applied science, serendipity, and discovery. Others will not be achieved because of limitations imposed by nature, because the contemplated product would not be economically viable in the immediate future, or because particular investigators are unable to solve a solvable problem. In any case, for the future it is important that materials continue to be sought and developed to remove barriers to contemplated technological innovation. In most cases, this will have to be done by the potential users of the new materials, because the major profit will come from the new technological device the material makes possible rather than from the manufacture of the new material itself.

Although new materials with special combinations of properties are imperative for technological advance and are the primary subject of this chapter, old established materials such as iron and steel, Portland cement, concrete blocks and bricks, gypsum plaster board, wood and plywood, window glass, polystyrene and polyethylene, and synthetic fibers for clothing are necessary for ordinary modern living, and their manufacture involves an appreciable fraction of the labor force. Economically, they are much more important than high-technology materials.

Materials science deals with the fundamental chemistry and physics of the properties and synthesis of materials. It is an accepted academic discipline though the separate crafts continue independently in their own right. In this chapter, after a brief review of early developments in materials and a discussion of the birth and scope of materials science, each of the subdisciplines will be considered in turn with emphasis on the remarkable new materials they are contributing to today's technology.

EARLY DEVELOPMENT OF MATERIALS

Materials have always been important to human culture as is evident from the use of the terms *Stone Age, Bronze Age,* and *Iron Age* for early periods of civilization. Man readily learned to use naturally occurring materials, and quickly took advantage of the accidental new ones which the use of fire brought about: the hardening of clay into stonelike pottery, and the production of several metals and their alloys by the reduction of their ores with the carbon of firewood. By 1500 to 1200 B.C. not only stone, wood, bone, leather, and animal and vegetable fibers were available, but also pottery, bricks, gold, silver, copper, tin, lead, and iron. The Romans added zinc to this list, and the Chinese learned to make translucent porcelain about A.D. 700 (the Europeans about one thousand years later). Except for these, no new materials were added to technology until the second half of the nineteenth century. At that time, the great advances in chemistry over the previous century, the associated knowledge of the properties of many substances, and the development of techniques for the preparation of many new ones set the stage for the introduction of a host of new materials in technology.

Materials for Artificial Illumination

The first important motivation for the development of new materials was the search for improved artificial illumination that began after the middle of the nineteenth century. The classical light source was the candle flame, in which soot particles are heated to incandescence while they are being burned. The new technology sought materials that could be repeatedly heated to temperatures of 1500°C to 2500°C without degradation, more severe demands than had ever been placed upon materials before. The developments of new materials to make possible the new light-emitting devices introduced before and shortly after the turn of the century were technological achievements of the first order. Even today they would be impressive advances, and for that day they were truly remarkable.

Following Thomas Edison's development of the phonograph and the carbon microphone for the telephone, he turned his attention to the incandescent lamp and began his celebrated search for a good source for a carbon filament to be operated in a vacuum. On New Year's Eve, 1879, he demonstrated his success by lighting his laboratory grounds in Menlo Park. The solution of that materials problem led not only to an improved light source but to the development of the whole electricity-generating industry.

Other approaches followed. Flames had been used for illumination for millennia, and by 1800 coal gas was beginning to be used for illumination, but although the gas flame was larger than a candle flame it was no more efficient in converting chemical energy into light. About 1890 Carl Auer (later Count von Welsbach) found that the then very rare thorium oxide, mixed with about 1 percent of much rarer cerium oxide would glow with a brilliant light when heated in a gas flame. He devised methods of making gauze domes or mantles of this material. When held in a gas flame this "Welsbach Gas Mantle" converted the chemical energy of the flame to light much more efficiently than did candles or a simple gas flame. Auer's mantles are still used today in camping lanterns and in areas of a few cities for nostalgic outdoor lighting.

In 1897, Walther Nernst, a famous German chemist who may well be considered the father of modern physical chemistry, devised and patented the device that came to be known as the Nernst Glower. It was a more efficient light source than the carbon filament lamp, and consisted of a nonmetallic zirconium oxide filament doped with 15 percent yttrium oxide. This remarkable white oxide conducts electricity very well at high temperatures. It was preheated with a small electrically heated platinum spiral to make it conductive, and then heated to incandescence by passing a current directly through the oxide. It was the most efficient light source known until it was displaced, in about 1910, by the ductile tungsten filament, another triumph of materials development which provides the filaments for all domestic incandescent lamps today.

Impact of Photography

Photography took advantage of materials developments, but the coupling between it and the invention of new materials was not as close as with lighting. In 1838 Louis Daguerre discovered a process for making photographs on silver plates fumed with iodine vapor. It created enormous interest but used no negative so copies could not be made. Soon the "wet-plate" process was introduced which did provide negatives. An alcohol-ether solution of cellulose nitrate, called collodian, was coated on a glass plate, sensitized with silver bromoiodide, and exposed in the camera while still wet to make a negative that was printed on sensitized paper coated with egg albumin. At the peak of use, about 1860, 90,000 eggs a day were used for this product. Matthew Brady and his colleagues used this process to photograph the U.S. Civil War.

Dried collodian left a horny, brittle substance which was of little use until Hyatt in 1870 discovered how to plasticize it with camphor, thus producing celluloid, the first synthetic plastic. (He was actually seeking a substitute for ivory for billiard balls!) Hannibal Goodwin filed a patent for a photosensitive emulsion supported on this material in 1887, but George Eastman produced the first commercially successful photographic film in 1890, and Edison used the film to make his kinetiscope in 1894. In this case, except for Daguerre's sensitized material, there was no direct connection between the new materials and the products which depended critically upon them; but had the new materials not existed, the new products would not have been developed.

Early Scientific Metallurgy

Until World War II, metals were the materials whose properties were best understood and most subject to experimental control. Early in the present century, metallurgists began to use the methods of physical chemistry to understand their material, calling their field "physical metallurgy." In particular, the studies of chemical thermodynamics of J. Willard Gibbs permitted the presentation of "phase diagrams" of alloys. Probably even more important was the comprehension that many of the properties of metals, particularly the strength properties, were controlled by the size, shape, and arrangement of the microscopic crystals or constituents of metal; that this "microstructure" could be seen and usefully studied with an optical microscope; and that this microstructure could be greatly altered by changing chemical composition or by mechanical working and heat treatment.

Understanding of the mechanism by which steel is hardened was one of the early achievements of physical metallurgy. It had been known for millennia that when red-hot steel is rapidly cooled by plunging it into water or brine it becomes very strong and hard. However, it was not until 1930 that an outstanding research group under E. C. Bain at the United States Steel Company explained the mechanism of this transformation and measured the precise cooling rates necessary to form "martensite." This work, and other excellent research that produced such products as strong aluminum alloys, stainless steel, and chromium plating, provided the background for what was to become materials science.

MATERIALS SCIENCE AND MATERIALS TECHNOLOGY

An important goal of traditional materials research has been to develop improved or cheaper materials and processes for synthesizing or forming them. There is a large element of craft in such work, and the processes used in the various fields have been quite different. As a result, the technologies of metallurgy, plastics, semiconductor materials, and ceramics have developed quite independently, and these (and other smaller) subdisciplines of materials technology continue to be independent fields. Although many universities have departments of materials science and/or engineering, most graduates of these departments identify themselves as metallurgists, ceramists, or specialists in semiconductors or plastics rather than as materials engineers.

However, there is a body of science applicable to all materials. The properties of all materials are strongly influenced by their structure, where the term *structure* refers to structure at all levels—the crystallographic arrangement of the individual atoms; the size and chemical composition of the microscopic crystals that make up most materials; the molecular weight and degree of crystallinity of the polymer; the size, shape, and location of the tiny flaws that are always present. The observation and description of structure, the relation of structure to the electrical, mechanical, optical, magnetic, or other properties of the material, and the understanding of the movements of atoms and microscopic transformations that occur during processing and that control the final structure of a material are important in all materials and their study is the realm of materials science.

Obtaining knowledge of structure and composition has been facilitated by the enormous development of equipment for observing all kinds of materials and determining their chemical composition on a very small scale. Classically, the optical microscope could see details as small as one-thousandth of a millimeter (one micrometer). Now the electron microscope can see details about one thousand times smaller, and other devices can measure the chemical composition of a speck one micrometer in diameter or a few atoms thick on a surface. Advanced X-ray and neutron diffraction techniques can quickly measure the crystal or even the magnetic structure of crystals. Many other new techniques exist for advanced materials characterization. The existence of a good materials characterization operation that deals with all kinds of materials can be a strong cohering force for a materials research group.

The Beginnings of Materials Science

Materials science began with the development of a science of metals in the period immediately following World War II.

During the war, the national needs for equipment and weapons required the development of a host of new metals and other materials. Examples are uranium and plutonium for the atomic bomb, high-purity graphite for the plutonium-making nuclear "piles" at Hanford, Washington, armor-piercing projectiles and projectile-resistant armor, early superalloys for turbo-superchargers, and special high-purity magnesium oxide crucibles for melting uranium and plutonium. To meet these needs, not only metallurgists were involved but also chemists, physicists, crystallographers, mechanical engineers, and a few ceramists. All worked closely together to solve the materials problems. An important consequence was that this close professional association introduced the nonmetallurgists to the fascinating unsolved problems in metallurgy, and partly because many of the new people brought a more academic background to the field, the idea developed that it should be possible to develop a more scientific understanding of the behavior of metals.

Conditions favored this development. It was generally recognized that the enormous advances in technology made during the war stemmed from basic research in the prewar period, and this created an atmosphere of admiration for basic research. Second, it was clear that the demands of civilian nuclear power, improved electronics, transportation, and other technologies would require improved materials and that basic research on metals might assist in their development. Finally, a great number of poeple were changing jobs during the immediate postwar period, so people were now available to staff new organizations. As a result, several new interdisciplinary groups to work on the science of metals were established and staffed with outstanding people. These groups, notably at MIT, the University of Chicago, the University of California at Berkeley, the General Electric Company in Schenectady, and the Atomic Energy Research Establishment at Harwell in England, involved not only classical metallurgists but also specialists in chemistry, physics, crystallography, and related fields. Similar groups were later formed at other places and there followed an immensely prolific and successful study of the fundamental structure and properties of metals.

Metals Science

The important new concept of metals science was that it would be valuable to study and understand metal properties and behavior in general, with no goal of making an improved product—an approach introduced by the more academic metallurgists. The goal was to avoid the complexity of real metals and to study elementary phenomena in the simplest systems experimentally possible. Single crystals, ultra-high-purity materials, model materials such as alkali halides, and purely mathematical or geometrical models were widely used.

An enormous range of topics was covered in the early work on metals science. Good theoretical understanding of the mechanical, electrical, and magnetic properties of metals was established, as well as understanding of the property-controlling transformations that occur when a metal is deformed, heated, or subjected to a hostile environment. The definition of the theoretical limits of many of these properties was now possible. For example, the maximum possible values of the flow and fracture stresses which metals can withstand were established with assurance, and experimental verification of the conclusions was accomplished.

Crystal Dislocations. One celebrated area was the development of the concept of an atomic scale defect in the crystal structure of metals called a dislocation, and the theoretical calculation of its behavior and the experimental verification of its existence. Metals are composed of a large number of microscopic crystals, usually much less than one-thousandth of an inch in diameter. It has long been known that these crystals deform when the planes of atoms in the crystals slide over each other. It was always observed, however, that the strength of even the strongest metals was only a few percent of the strength theory said it should be. The postulated explanation was that a particular kind of defect, called a dislocation, concentrated the stress, so that only a few atoms moved at a time but their cooperative movement deformed the whole piece. One can visualize the role of a dislocation by considering the problem of moving a large rug spread out smoothly on the floor. One person cannot slide the whole rug at one time because its weight is too great. However, the edge away from the direction of movement can be easily moved a little bit in the desired direction to create a ruck or wrinkle in the rug, then this ruck can be worked along to the front end of the rug, moving the whole rug a few inches.

A dislocation is essentially a crystallographic wrinkle, an extra plane of atoms that can be moved at a stress much lower than that necessary to move the whole plane of atoms. Their presence in nearly all crystals accounts for the fact that metals can be readily deformed. When dislocations were first discussed seriously, belief in them was pretty much a matter of faith. One could draw pictures of what they were supposed to look like and compute how they should reduce the flow stress of a metal, but there was no direct evidence for their existence. Very shortly, however, techniques were developed for observing dislocations directly, both by etching surfaces and more directly by the new technique of electron microscopy. Perhaps more exciting, some tiny crystals, grown from the vapor or under some other special conditions, were found to be dislocation-free, and since they had no defects to facilitate deformation, their strength was very close to the theoretical strength of the material, several million pounds per square inch, or about ten times stronger than had ever been observed before.

These "whiskers," as they were called because of their small dimensions, attracted enormous attention in the 1960s, but led to one of the early disappointments of metals science, and showed that understanding does not necessarily lead to technological improvement. The theoretical strength of crystals and the origin of weakness in metals was well understood and experimentally crystals which had the predicted theoretical strength could be made. Many kinds of extraordinarily light and strong devices were dreamed about. Workers had visions of suspension bridges supported by cables a few inches in diameter. Unfortunately, no means of making important use of the enormous strength of these tiny crystals was ever developed, and they remain a technological curiosity even though they provided direct confirmation of the theoretical properties of a dislocation-free material.

METALLURGY

The development of superalloys presents a fine example of what can be done with a combination of science and good experimental research: making many new alloys, then testing them to determine what is wrong, and finally, making more until the desired properties are attained.

Superalloys

Research on superalloys began during World War II with the development of alloys for turbo-superchargers for piston engines. It continues today with the development of materials for jet engines and other gas turbines.

Piston engines in aircraft operate better at high air pressure than at low pressure. Starting about 1920, small tubines powered by the exhaust gas of the piston engine were used to drive compressors to deliver air at sea-level pressure to engines in high-altitude airplanes. These turbo-superchargers enormously increased the power and efficiency of aircraft piston engines, and permitted them to fly at altitudes where air resistance is less and overall operating efficiency of the aircraft is high. The exhaust temperature of a piston engine can be exceedingly high and high temperature alloys are required for these devices. Providing acceptable alloys greatly challenged metallurgical science at that time, but useful ones were developed.

Starting in 1940 in England and Germany, the first modern turbojet engines for powering aircraft began to be made and tested; initially, they drew heavily on the technology developed for turbo-superchargers. In an aircraft gas turbine the turbine wheel is driven directly by combustion gas at very high temperatures and the turbine shaft drives an air compressor whose sole function is to provide high pressure air for the combustion chamber. The expulsion of the hot exhaust gas through an orifice at the rear of the aircraft engine provides the thrust to propel it.

The components of the combustion chamber, and the blades and wheel of the turbine handle combustion gas at temperatures in excess of 2000°F. Even though they are cooled by the careful direction of some of the combustion air, they may reach temperatures above 1800°F in modern aircraft gas turbines. Some of these alloys show incipient melting at 2200°F and are thus used at a higher fraction of their melting points than any other materials.

The development of the early superalloys was one of the major metallurgical accomplishments of the World War II period, and the development of improved ones continues to be one of the major goals of metallurgical technology today. The first alloys used were similar to the common 18 percent nickel/8 percent chromium stainless steels, which resist corrosion but are not very strong at high temperatures. Next came a group of cobalt-based alloys, similar to the dental alloy vitallium which had been in use for a number of years because of its resistance to corrosion in the oral environment. Requirements grew for alloys that would be stronger and have longer life at even higher temperatures, and metallurgists had to use all the science and technology available to them.

Design of Superalloys. The goals of alloy designers are to make a product that is resistant to oxidation and other causes of corrosion and will not deform beyond a specified amount in either short or long times at the working temperature. To do this they have available to them a number of alloying additions whose effects are generally known and a number of mechanical and heat treatments of the final product. Every trick known to metallurgical science or technology is employed to squeeze out a few more degrees of operating temperature or a few more hours of blade life. Each addition has a primary effect of its own and also influences the behavior of the other additions.

Alloying additions can:

1. Protect against corrosion by forming a more or less impermeable oxide film on the surface of the final part.
2. Strengthen or harden the alloy by dissolving in the matrix metal.
3. Form tiny carbide particles with the carbon always present in these alloys. Dispersed carbide particles interfere with deformation and strengthen the alloy.
4. Form a precipitation hardening phase with proper heat treatment. The nickel aluminide phase, also called gamma prime, is produced in the nickel-based alloys by suitable heat treatment at elevated temperatures. This is the most effective strengthening agent, and great effort is devoted to making it appear in the best possible configuration.

The effect of the most important alloying elements in superalloys is shown in table 2.1 for each of the two major categories of superalloys: those that have cobalt as the major constituent and those that have nickel.[1]

All of these methods of strengthening alloys were known before superalloys, but these combinations are unique. It is not possible to compute the effect of all

Table 2.1
Effects of Alloying Additions on High-Temperature Superalloys

Element	Amount of Addition-Wt.% Ni-Base Alloys	Co-Base Alloys	Effect of Addition
Chromium	5-25	19-30	Oxidation resistance, Carbide former Solution hardening
Molybdenum Tungsten	0-12	0-11	Carbide former, solution hardening
Aluminum	0-6	0-4.5	Precipitation hardening Oxidation resistance
Titanium	0-6	0-4	Precipitation hardening, Carbide former
Cobalt	0-20	---	Affects amount of precipitate
Nickel	---	0-22	Stabilizes Austenite
Niobium	0-5	0-4	Carbide former, solution hardening
Tantalum	0-12	0-9	Carbide former, solution hardening

the different additions because although each has a primary effect, they also interact with each other to modify those effects. As a consequence, the development work can be generally guided by theory, but the final compositions and heat treatments must be optimized by making alloys and then determining their properties, sometimes in very lengthy tests.

One problem has been that when the alloys are given their strengthening heat treatment, phases other than the desired ones may form. Sigma phase is a dreaded compound; it can appear in iron, nickel, and cobalt alloys with other metals in certain composition ranges. This exceedingly brittle phase may form on extended heat treatment, during use at high temperatures, or when the alloys are welded. It may have many different compositions. Mathematical theories, based upon a concept called the electron vacancy number, have been developed, and are included in computer programs such as PHACOMP, to permit the easy calculation of alloy compositions to be avoided. Even so, trial-and-error optimization of new alloy compositions must be done to ensure that sigma phase will not form and embrittle the product.

Superalloy Processing. The properties of materials are controlled not only by the identity of their major chemical components but also by minor alloying, doping, or impurity constituents, and by the size and arrangement of the microscopic crystals that make up their structure. All of these are controlled almost entirely by the procedures used to make the product. Some of the details of processing superalloys will be discussed here. It must be understood that the processing of most advanced materials is as important, complex, and difficult as is the processing of superalloys. The development of suitable processing is always a major step, and frequently *the* major step in the development of a new material. Substantially new metallurgical processing techniques were necessary for making superalloys, and a host of new techniques have been introduced for forming the alloys to the desired intricate shapes, while controlling the microstructure to give desired properties.

Nearly all superalloys are melted in a vacuum to maintain purity and to prevent oxidation of some of the special alloying additions during the melting process. There are a large number of different processes used for vacuum melting and their acronyms sound like a list of government agencies. VIM (vacuum induction melting) is initially used to form the alloy for most superalloys, followed by ESR (electroslag remelting) or VAR (vacuum arc remelting). In some cases EBR (electron beam refining) is used and more recently even better processes such as VADER (vacuum arc double electrode remelting) are used. Some of the alloys are processed to the final shape by conventional metal working at high temperatures, but since everything has been done to make them resistant to deformation under these conditions, they are not easy to process. Many of the strongest ones are formed by investment or lost wax casting, in which a wax model of the final piece is made and then invested or coated with a refractory ceramic. The wax can then be melted out and the molten metal poured in to fill the mold and make the desired shape with high precision. This process is also used by dentists to cast gold alloy replacement teeth.

Most recently another old process, powder metallurgy, has been used to make these high-technology materials. Good properties are attained in alloys which have been very rapidly cooled, but rapid cooling is not possible in larger pieces. Hence RST (rapid solidification technology) is used. The molten metal is blown into tiny droplets in a near vacuum with a high-velocity helium blast, and the final pieces are then assembled from the powder with a pore-free product produced by HIPPING (hot isostatic pressing) the final product. A diametrically opposed process has also been used for many turbine blades. The boundaries between the microscopic crystals or grains that make up the superalloy are a source of weakness, and some workers have eliminated them using a special solidification process that makes the final product a single crystal. The method is very similar to that used to grow single silicon crystals for transistors and other semiconductor devices.

After more than forty years it is still possible to make advances in these very thoroughly researched materials. Perhaps the end of the road is approaching, and they will be replaced by ceramics, but there are enormous problems to be overcome before that substitution is made.

CERAMICS

Ceramic pieces are among the oldest articles made by man, and early specimens are important artifacts recovered on archaeological digs. Their quality and beauty improved over the years, culminating in the high-fired translucent porcelains made by the Chinese after about A.D. 800. These were greatly admired in the courts of Europe, and it is claimed that about 1700, Augustus, Elector of Saxony, gave the king of Prussia a regiment of dragoons in exchange for a set of forty-eight Chinese vases. By about 1710, Boettger, an alchemist in the court of Augustus, was the first to reproduce the Chinese translucent porcelains in Europe, and from this work finally developed the celebrated porcelain factory at Meissen (Dresden).[2]

Until the present century the most advanced work in ceramics was motivated by the desire to make beautiful objects, and the ancient porcelain-making processes continue to this day. The growth of the importance of metals toward the end of the nineteenth century increased the need for heat- and molten metal-resistant ceramic refractories for metal melting. Ceramic refractory development consequently moved to the forefront of technology. These refractories were first made from clay, with certain other mineral additions, but the more modern ones are made from relatively pure magnesium oxide and chromium oxide.

Early Nonsilicate Ceramics

Until the mid-1950s in the United States, and somewhat later in most of the rest of the world, ceramics were considered to be exclusively silicate products, made by firing shaped products made from clay and other minerals.

During and immediately after World War II, some new inorganic, nonmetallic materials that had important combinations of properties were developed. The first of these were the magnetic ferrites, iron oxides similar to the ancient mineral magnetite, Fe_3O_4, except that some of the iron atoms were replaced by other metals such as magnesium, zinc, or cobalt to modify the magnetic properties. These were first made by J. L. Snoek of the Philips Company in Eindhoven, the Netherlands. Most important, these soft magnetic materials are nonconductors of electricity; they can be magnetized and demagnetized very rapidly since eddy currents, which would resist the change in magnetization, cannot flow. As a result they are often used in high-frequency electronic devices. At about the same time the compound barium titanate, which has a variety of important properties, also began to be investigated. First of all, it is piezoelectric: if suitable electrodes are applied to surfaces of the solid and an electrical voltage is applied, the piece changes shape. Conversely, if the piece is subjected to a mechanical force to alter its shape, an electrical potential appears across the faces. This property is used in a variety of ways to make electromechanical transducers. It can create sound waves for sonar gear to measure water depths or to detect the distance of objects under water. In air, it will operate as a buzzer; many modern watches have alarms that utilize small piezoelectric beepers. In reverse, it can convert motion into electrical impulses as in a phonograph pickup head. Finally, this versatile compound has an enormous dielectric constant, so that it is used extensively as the dielectric in capacitors of very large capacitance in all electronic equipment.

These early materials are notable in another respect. Because they were manufactured from powders by processes that somewhat resembled those used for some silicate ceramics (by pressing a powder to a final shape and then heating the compact to consolidate it), the products were called ceramics, though they otherwise had little in common with the silicate materials that had been called ceramics prior to this time. This led to applying the same name to the whole class of nonmetallic, inorganic materials made from powders.

Development of Advanced Ceramic Science

By the mid-1950s it became apparent that there was a variety of other nonmetallic, inorganic materials that might have technologically interesting properties. At that time, the research to "make metallurgy scientific" was at its peak, and the new "ceramics" appeared to be a promising field. As a consequence, over the next fifteen years or so there was an influx of metallurgists into the ceramics discipline, paralleling the influx of chemists and physicists into metallurgy about a decade earlier. This meant that some of the techniques used to study metals were applied to these materials. In particular, the microscopic structure of a number of new ceramics was determined, the mechanical properties of the brittle ceramics and of a variety of glasses were studied, and the kinetics of the structure controlling processing reactions, such as the sintering of powders, were measured.

There are two consequences of this extension of metallurgical techniques. The first is the recognition that there is a central set of scientific principles that can be applied to both metals and ceramics, with the subsequent extension of this idea to other fields of polymer science and semiconducting and electronic materials (materials science). In addition, partly by the application of this science, and partly by more conventional empirical development techniques, the newly broadened field of ceramics developed a whole new category of materials. These materials are all nonmetallic, inorganic substances, mostly oxides; but some of the most interesting recently developed ceramics are silicon carbide and silicon nitride. They have combinations of properties not found in any other materials, and as a consequence, are associated with many potentially important or already important technological developments.

Ceramics for Heat Engines

One of the most talked about potential uses for new ceramics is in heat engines such as small gas turbines for automobile propulsion or adiabatic, uncooled diesel engines operating at high temperatures.

Research toward this goal has been in progress since about 1970. Techniques were developed for making silicon carbide and silicon nitride ceramics. These products retained their strength to temperatures 500 to 1000°F above the maximum use temperatures of the superalloys used in gas turbines. In addition, silicon, carbon, and nitrogen, the elements required to make these magnificent materials, are found in sand, wood, and air, and are cheaply available in endless quantity while the superalloys require cobalt, nickel, and chromium, metals not found in abundant quantities in the United States.

It is true that these materials are "brittle." In technical terminology, this does not mean that they are weak—only that they always fail by fracture without any prior plastic deformation. However, there was reason to hope that with skillful processing it would be possible to make these brittle materials so strong that they could withstand the stresses imposed in use without fracture.

Motivated by this opportunity, an enormous amount of research has been done since 1970 in industry and in universities. In the United States, the government has spent several hundred million dollars over the ensuing years in an attempt to develop these materials and techniques for using them. The Japanese have identified ceramics—in particular, ceramics for heat engines—as an important product to develop. As a result there is at times an almost hysterical excitement about the possibilities for these materials.

At the present time, two major difficulties remain to be overcome, and each is most impressive. Although the raw materials for ceramics are cheap and plentiful, processing costs are extremely high because of the difficulty of fabricating the complex shapes required at extremely high temperatures. As a result, finished ceramic products cost much more than the superalloys they might replace. The other problem is technical and more fundamental. Ceramics are brittle; they do not flow plastically. A flaw initiates a crack at some critical point and the whole piece then fails catastrophically. The strength of a piece depends upon the size of the largest flaw in it; the larger the flaw, the lower the stress at which it will fail—and some flaws are produced in any manufacturing process. In a ductile metal, relatively large flaws can be tolerated because the metal flows plastically, blunting the flaw and making it less effective. In a ceramic, there is no flaw-blunting mechanism available, so the piece can have only very small, safe flaws. Although small strong specimens can be made, if many are produced a certain fraction of them will have flaws large enough to initiate fracture, and will thus be too weak for use. In sufficiently large pieces, every piece will have a flaw large enough to initiate fracture. Work in this area continues, but the difficulty of the problems is shown by the fact that many very competent people have worked on it for more than fifteen years, and as yet have not devised procedures to produce a product strong and cheap enough to make a useful heat engine. In the short term, ceramics may find some use in automobile engines in such components as valve seats, but they will not revolutionize the automobile industry in the foreseeable future.

Pure Aluminum Oxide

When the term *ceramic* is used, the model most technologists have in mind is aluminum oxide. In impure form, with an addition of clay or another silicate to bond it, aluminum oxide (or alumina, following the ancient nomenclature for oxides of a metal) is used extensively in electronics. It first became important in the era of vacuum tube electronics, where insulating ceramics were needed with low "dielectric loss." A high dielectric loss ceramic is one that will heat up in the presence of a high-frequency electrical field, exactly as food is heated in a microwave oven. More recently, a very similar composition has become widely used as a support or carrier for the integrated circuit silicon chips used in computers and other advanced devices. The market for these ceramic devices, which have most intricate circuitry inside them, is about $1.5 billion a year, and it will undoubtedly grow. Most of these so-called substrates and chip-carriers are made by Japanese companies, in particular by Kyoto Ceramics, now called Kyocera. This causes some consternation in the U.S. ceramics community, probably more than is justified, as there is growing manufacture by U.S. companies.

Pore-free Ceramics

Until about 1960, all ceramics made from powders had residual porosity which scattered light and made them white or opaque or at best translucent in very thin sections. Through the extensive study of the mechanism of sintering, approaches were developed, first at the General Electric Company in Schenectady, which permitted ceramics to be sintered from powders to yield a pore-free, highly translucent (even completely transparent) ceramic body. The first such product, lucalox alumina, found immediate application as an envelope for a new type of discharge lamp, the high-pressure sodium vapor lamp with an efficiency of over 100 lumens per watt, more than twice that of the mercury vapor lamps previously used almost exclusively for outdoor lighting. In the approximately twenty years since that development, outdoor lighting in the United States and much of the world has changed from a bluish to a golden color because of the use of this new ceramic as the envelope in which to contain the highly corrosive vapors of high-pressure sodium, which could not be contained in the glasses previously used or in any other known material.

Fuel for Nuclear Reactors

The early nuclear reactors used uranium metal as the fuel. However, uranium reacts vigorously with hot water so modern boiling water or pressurized water reactors require and use inert uranium dioxide ceramic pellets. Hundreds of millions of pounds of these pellets, about ½ inch in diameter and ½ inch long are prepared each year by conventional procedures for high-technology ceramics, and because of the high value of enriched uranium dioxide, these pellets probably have the highest dollar value of any ceramic made. The need to make them with extreme precision and still at reasonable cost has prompted research and development work on the preparation of powders for ceramic processing, which has benefited not only the nuclear industry, but ceramics processing in other areas as well.

Ceramic Electrolytes

A large variety of different combinations of properties is exploited in the new ceramics. Most of the ceramics are good electrical insulators, but some conduct electricity by the motion of charged atoms or ions through the crystals, much as electricity is conducted in the sulfuric acid liquid in an automobile battery except that this electrolyte is solid. Zirconium oxide, doped with another oxide such as yttrium oxide, behaves in this way. It was first used as the filament of the Nernst Glower, a successful incandescent lamp in the period immediately preceding the development of the tungsten filament. The modern use is in a device to measure the air : fuel ratio in automobile exhausts when vehicles are equipped with fuel injection. The measurement is made by constructing a galvanic cell with the doped zirconium oxide as the solid electrolyte. The voltage from this cell is dependent upon the amount of unconsumed oxygen in the exhaust gas, and the resulting signal is fed to an on-board computer that controls the amount of fuel injected. The device looks not unlike a small spark-plug of which the ''insulator'' is the ionically conducting doped zirconium oxide.

Another device utilizing a ceramic electrolyte has attracted considerable attention. It is a high energy density storage battery using beta alumina as a solid electrolyte. In this compound, the sodium ions have exceedingly high mobility at temperatures of a few hundred degrees Celsius, so in this cell it is possible to combine electrolytically metallic sodium and molten sulfur, a reaction that creates a great amount of electrical energy per pound of constituents used. The battery could be used for vehicular propulsion or, on a larger scale, for storage of enormous amounts of electricity to load-level for utilities. It is a most attractive sounding device, and work on it continues at several establishments. If cell life can be lengthened and the cost of preparation of the ceramic tubes used for the electrolyte reduced somewhat, this product may have great economic importance.

ORGANIC POLYMERS AND PLASTICS

The term *plastic* is applied to those synthetic resins or polymers that are molded into useful shapes, and this differentiates them from synthetic fibers which are chemically similar compounds. In addition, many molded plastics have inorganic filler materials to extend them and make them cheaper, or to improve their properties. The presently available plastics have many interesting and useful properties. Volume for volume, they are cheaper than many metals they replace and they can be formed to many shapes much less expensively than metals. They are resistant to atmospheric and aqueous corrosion, they have low specific gravity and strength and toughness adequate for many applications, and may have outstanding properties when combined with high-strength filamentary materials such as the polymer kevlar, or with glass or graphite fibers. On the other hand, they will not resist very high temperatures, their stiffness is much lower than that of competitive metals, and they are soft and scratch more readily. The growth in the use of plastics has been spectacular. In 1979, the total volume of plastics produced exceeded the total volume of steel for the first time. For comparison of usage with metals, the amount of plastic is always given in volume rather than weight; since the density of most metals is several times that of plastics, the weight of the plastic needed to replace a metal may be several times less than that of the metal.

Contrary to metals, ceramics, and electronic materials, new plastics usually do not have properties that lead to technological innovation in other fields, but being a little cheaper, more corrosion-resistant, and easier to fabricate they replace wood, metal, paper, and glass in a host of applications. As a result, the average person may be more aware of the growth in the use of plastics than of the growth in other advanced materials.

The use of natural plastic materials to make useful objects occurred before the era of synthetic polymers. For example, shellac was formed into many useful products, such as Daguerreotype cases and 78 RPM phonograph records. In the period following Daguerreotypes, photographs were made by the wet plate process, which required coating sheets of glass with collodian, a solution of cellulose nitrate in alcohol and ether. When this dried it left a horny brittle substance which many people examined, but which was of little utility until 1870, when John W. Hyatt, in a celebrated development, found that it could be plasticized with the addition of camphor. Hyatt used the product, celluloid, for the manufacture of billiard balls. It subsequently became the material of which men's collars were made and the first flexible support for photographic film. In 1907, Leo Baekeland first made the phenol-formaldehyde synthetic resin which he called bakelite, and the success of that product in many applications marked the real beginning of the present synthetic plastics industry.

Many of the early uses for inexpensive plastics such as polystyrene were ill-advised, and dictated solely by cost. Because of the brittleness of early plastic toys and other products, plastics received something of a bad name. However, since World War II an enormous number of new plastics has been produced with outstanding properties. As a consequence, their use is increasing some 7 percent per year. Very broadly, these new plastics can be divided into two classes: commodity plastics and engineering plastics.

The commodity plastics are the most important economically. Total U.S. production totalled about 54 billion pounds in 1987 and should reach about 75 billion pounds a year by 2000. For many years the annual growth rate has been about 7 percent, but it is expected to fall to about 3 percent.[3] The commodity plastics serve a broad variety of functions, with packaging being the largest and most important (see table 2.2). A potential market not yet penetrated is major household appliances such as refrigerators and washing machines.

Table 2.2
Use of Commodity Plastics

APPLICATION	SHARE OF PLASTICS MARKET		
	1970	1985	2000
Packaging	24%	28%	30%
Building and Construction	21	22	20
Consumer Products	11	8	7
Electrical and Electronic	10	6	7
Adhesives, Inks, Coatings	8	5	5
Furniture and Furnishings	7	5	5
Transportation Equipment	5	5	6
Industrial	1	1	1
Exports	6	8	7
Production, Billions of Lbs.	19.2	47.8	75.6

Engineering plastics have the best mechanical properties and are used in automobiles, electronics, hardware, plumbing appliances, microcomputers, and many other places. Tables 2.3, 2.4, and 2.5 present some statistics about engineering resin use and potential growth.[4] A major application for engineering plastics is in automobiles. In 1950 plastics contributed little to the weight of a car, but by the mid–1950s they had increased to about 9 percent of the weight of a car. This fraction will no doubt continue to grow, partly from quality considerations amd partly from the need for tailoring individual products to small market segments. Fabrication tooling is cheaper for plastic parts than it is for steel parts. It is estimated that by 1990 as many as 1.6 million vehicles per year will be made with bodies entirely of plastic.[5]

Table 2.3
Use of Engineering Plastics (1984)

PLASTIC	MILLIONS OF POUNDS		
	USA	REST OF WORLD	TOTAL
Nylon	403	841	1244
Polyphenylene oxide	175	183	358
Polyacetal	128	374	502
Polytetramethylene Terphthalate	120	142	262
Polysulfone	13	5	18
Polyphenylene sulfide	10	10	20

Table 2.4
Industries Using Engineering Plastics

INDUSTRY	% OF SALES	% ANNUAL CHANGE
Transportation	28%	10%
Construction	13%	6%
Electrical and Electronic	25%	15%
Industrial Machinery	15%	3%
Other	19%	8%

Table 2.5
Estimated Growth for Engineering Plastics

COUNTRY	MILLIONS OF POUNDS		ANNUAL CHANGE
	1984	1989	
USA	1149	1703	8-8.5%
Japan	616	926	8-9%
Western Europe	1028	1343	5-6
Other	255	330	7-7.5

Fibers

Rayon fibers have been made by the regeneration of cellulose for over eighty years, but completely synthetic fibers had their beginning with the small commercial manufacture of nylon by the DuPont Company in 1938. The success of that fiber exceeded all expectations. It was followed by the production of the

Table 2.6
Production of Textile Fibers
(Thousands of Metric Tons)

Year	Cotton	Wool	SYNTHETIC FIBER Filament	Staple	REGENERATED CELLULOSE Filament	Staple
1900	3162	730			1	
1910	4200	803			5	
1920	4629	816			15	
1930	5870	1002			205	3
1940	6902	1134	1	4	542	585
1950	6647	1057	54	15	871	737
1960	10113	1463	417	285	1131	1525
1970	11784	1602	2391	2831	1397	2187
1980	14137	1581	4731	5756	1159	2085

acrylic fiber orlon by the same company in 1945, of polyester fiber by ICI in 1950, and of polypropylene in Italy in 1957. The growth of these materials relative to regenerated cellulose fibers is shown in table 2.6.[6]

COMPOSITE MATERIALS

Composite materials are an important class which is split between low and high technology. The term is usually applied to a product having a relatively low strength, or at least low stiffness matrix material, with a strong fibrous reinforcing agent added. The model for these materials when they were introduced in the mid-1950s was bamboo for fishing rods, and the first application was to make rods of plastic-filled epoxy with long glass fibers that ran the length of the rod. This product had surprising strength and ability to withstand extreme bends. It worked because even if some glass fibers broke, the load they originally bore was shifted to a number of adjacent fibers so the crack did not grow. This technology was next extended to making large shapes such as boats from glass fiber fabrics which were laid up into the desired shape and then impregnated with the unpolymerized plastic. Upon polymerization a very strong body was obtained. Products were next made somewhat more simply by chopping the fibers into relatively short lengths, blending them into the plastic, and forming the whole mixture. If the length of a fiber is ten to twenty times its diameter, the reinforcement obtained is nearly as good as that obtained with a very long fiber. In the form of fiber glass-reinforced epoxy and other polymers, this composite has had enormous success.

A high degree of stiffness is desired in the reinforcing fibers, and even the special glasses used had limited stiffness; soon other fibrous reinforcing agents were developed. For a time, it appeared that very expensive boron fibers would be useful in military applications, but then techniques were developed for making extraordinarily strong carbon fibers by the careful graphitization of rayon and other organic fibers. The carbon-carbon bond in these fibers has many of the characteristics of the bond in diamond, so that these fibers have exceedingly high strength and stiffness. These have found application in sporting equipment such as tennis rackets, fishing rods, and golf club shafts, but they really have greater importance in more demanding applications. To be used most effectively, the reinforcing fibers must be oriented in proper directions to carry directed loads. In aerospace and military applications, the cost of this is acceptable, but for more popular use cost is a limitation at the present time.

Not all the important composites are plastics reinforced with filaments. A very popular one able to withstand relatively high temperatures is the carbon-carbon composite: carbon filaments embedded in a low density amorphous carbon matrix. It has been possible to make perfect crystal whiskers of silicon carbide in an inexpensive way from the silicon and carbon in rice hulls, and this material is being investigated as a reinforcing agent in aluminum, which is otherwise quite soft and of relatively low strength. In addition, there is a most interesting organic polymer, kevlar, which has a strength approaching that of carbon fibers. Combined with a plastic matrix of a material such as a polycarbonate resin, it has the potential of making good bullet-proof armor.

SEMICONDUCTORS AND ELECTRONIC MATERIALS

The field of electronics has been one of the most demanding in requiring new materials for its advance, and a great many of the rewards for developing new materials have appeared as new electronic devices. Many of the new materials developed for electronic devices have been mentioned elsewhere in this chapter, including such ceramics as the ferrites and ferroelectric barium titanate, as well as silicate-bonded aluminum oxide devices used to support semiconductor integrated circuits and glass fibers used in fiber optics. Fundamental to the field are the semiconducting materials, silicon, germanium, and the several compound semiconductors such as gallium arsenide. The brief discussion in this section is confined to them.

The basic impetus to semiconductor development was the invention of the transistor by Bardeen, Brittain, and Shockley at Bell Laboratories in 1948. It was immediately apparent that materials (semiconductor) purity was a major problem in this field, and this drove purification and characterization techniques to previously unknown heights. In a major development in 1952, W. D. Pfann, also at Bell Laboratories, provided a technique for producing single crystals of silicon of extreme purity and perfection of structure, by the technique of zone refining. In its effect on the rest of technology this development outshines all others. Now, large silicon single crystals are commodity items, and the great advances are those of designers and processing people who manage to squeeze ever more circuits onto a tiny silicon chip.

At one time it was hoped that the development of understanding in materials science would make it possible to predict precisely the properties of materials from a knowledge of their chemical composition and microstructure. Unfortunately, the complexity of most materials has made this impossible, but in the semiconductors, the materials are so simple and pure that such predictions are routinely made. Largely because of this simplicity, in no class of materials has our ability to manipulate structure both on an microscopic scale and an atomic scale proceeded as far as it has in semiconducting electronic materials. The attempts now being made to develop cheap silicon cells for solar energy require that some of this perfection be sacrificed, and it is possible that even amorphous silicon will be used to greatly reduce manufacturing cost. These trade-offs have not yet been optimized.

There was an early battle between several potential semiconductor materials (chiefly silicon and germanium) for dominance in device production, and silicon eventually won because of its superior processing and native oxide, which can be used as the insulating layer in device processing. In recent years, other semiconducting materials have challenged silicon for specific applications. For high-speed, high-frequency, and some high-power applications, certain semiconductors composed of the group III and group V elements (chiefly gallium arsenide and its associates) have higher carrier mobilities and can provide about a fivefold increase in the speed of devices. If the difficulties with processing these materials can be overcome, they may replace silicon, at least in part, and current progress is very promising. Other semiconductors of the III–V or II–VI types are being developed for photodetector or photodiode applications where the band gap of silicon is inadequate.

Superconducting Oxides[7]

The announcement in 1986 by Bednorz and Müller[8] of superconductivity at 30K in a mixed oxide phase containing lanthanum, barium, copper, and oxygen not only won the Nobel Prize but started the most intense international study of a class of materials that has ever occurred. The excitement was greatly helped by the discovery in 1987 of the famous 123 compound $YBa_2Cu_3O_7$ which is superconducting at 93K, above the temperature of inexpensive liquid nitrogen. Since then there have been many major international conferences on these materials. The material is particularly exciting not only because it was not predicted by present superconductor theory, but it is also not clear that it can be explained by present theory. Furthermore, there are the tantalizing potential technological applications that have been so much talked about: a truly room-temperature superconductor, loss-free electric power transmission lines, magnetically levitated trains, and other glamorous applications. At the present time, none of these applications is possible. The new compound is brittle and is not easily formed into filaments. More important, it is somewhat unstable chemically, and ways of controlling particularly its surface composition must be developed. Magnetic resonance imaging for medical diagnostics is the largest commercial use for superconductors; the several hundred devices in the United States use the superconducting niobium-titanium alloy which can carry about one hundred thousand amperes per square centimeter, one to several thousand times what the 123 compound can carry, and for most suggested applications, the critical current carrying capacity of the ceramic must be increased. It is certainly probable that such an exciting new discovery will be found to have important technological applications, but it is equally probable that the use will be one that has not yet been thought of.

Fiber Optic Materials

Possibly the most exciting and useful but least advertised recent materials-based technological accomplishment is fiber optics, the long-distance transmission of information by light beams conducted over fine glass filaments of incredible transparency. The glass is so transparent that a one-mile-thick piece can transmit light at least as well as a common windowpane. There are many advantages in transmitting information by photons through glass fibers rather than by electrons through metal cables. First, the much higher carrier frequency, which at 3×10^{14} hertz is some 100,000 times the ultra-high frequencies used for television communications, provides an enormously increased bandwidth or signal-carrying capacity. Second, transmission losses are much lower than for electrons down a wire, requiring far fewer repeaters or amplifiers. Signals can be carried 20 miles or 30 kilometers before amplification is required, at least twice the distance for copper. Third, since optical fibers are electrical insulators, they are not affected by stray (or intentional) electric fields and are essentially immune to electronic spying or magnetic fields that might be created by an atomic bomb blast, so they provide more secure communication. Finally, these fibers are small, which leads to enormous cost savings over conventional cables in transmission lines. The fibers were developed in an exceedingly short time. The first low loss fibers were produced at Corning in 1970, an important improvement in processing was made by the Bell Telephone laboratories in 1974, and by 1979 fibers had been made with close to the theoretical transparency. The first intercity connections began in 1983, a total development time of little more than a decade!

The fiber optics communications lines are made of exceedingly high purity silica, doped usually with germanium oxide, and drawn down to filaments the size of a human hair, about 100 micrometers, or 4–thousandths of an inch. Using tiny solid-state lasers, usually made from gallium arsenide or indium gallium arsenide phosphide, to generate the signal these fibers can carry many more voice circuits than a copper cable. They are not just speculative devices. Over the past four years, more than one billion voice circuit miles of these cables have been installed, which equals the total metal wire circuit mileage in use in 1984. A transoceanic cable, capable of carrying 40,000 simultaneous conversations is scheduled to begin operating in 1988; in contrast, the latest co-axial cable which was laid in the 1970s had a capacity of 10,000 conversations.

Optical transmission lines also require suitable solid-state lasers to send the necessary signal, and a variety of materials technologies have been developed for the fabrication of these devices. In general, these require a means for laying down a succession of thin films of group IIIa (e.g., gallium) and group Va (e.g., arsenic) elements, and as a consequence lasers can be designed to produce light of exactly the optimum wave length for the application.

Work is continuing most actively in these fields, and further accomplishments can be expected.

NOTES

1. Adapted from the *Metals Handbook* (Metals Park, Ohio: ASM International, 1984).

2. W. David Kingery and Pamela B. Vandiver, *Ceramic Masterpieces* (New York: Free Press, 1986).

3. *Chemical and Engineering News,* August 24, 1987.

4. *Chemical and Engineering News,* January 28, 1985.

5. W. Dale Compton and Norman A. Gjostein, ''Materials for Ground Transportation,'' *Scientific American,* 255 (Sept. 1986), p. 93.

6. Data from Keshav V. Datye and A. A. Valda, *Chemical Processing of Synthetic Fibers and Blends* (New York: Wiley-Interscience, 1983).

7. T. H. Geballe and J. K. Hulm, ''Superconductivity—The State That Came in from the Cold,'' *Science* 239 (1988), p. 367. This is an excellent current review of both science and technology.

8. J. G. Bednorz and K. A. Müller, *Z. Physik* B64 (1986), p. 189.

BIBLIOGRAPHY

There are many sources of information on materials, both classical and high-technology, but most of the publications are so limited that they are valuable only to specialists. Two issues of *Scientific American,* vol. 217 (Sept. 1967), pp. 68–254, and vol. 255 (Oct. 1986), pp. 50–292, are devoted to materials and present a particularly balanced and exciting but not overly optimistic view of materials science and technology. *Science,* vol. 226 (Nov. 9, 1984), pp. 615–63, contains many articles on materials research. The paper by M. E. Lines on fiber optics is particularly informative. *Science,* vol. 235 (Feb. 27, 1987), pp. 997–1029, is also devoted to materials science. A careful perusal of these four journal issues will give a very good feeling for the scope of materials research and technology, and many independent estimates of probable future accomplishments.

More specific data may be obtained from handbooks and encyclopedias. Two good ones are: *Metals Handbook* (Metals Park, Ohio: ASM International, 1984). A multivolume compendium revised from time to time; and the *Encyclopedia of Polymer Science and Engineering,* 2d ed. (New York: Wiley-Interscience, 1985).

3

Lasers: Now the Age of Light

Joseph W. Haus and John Schroeder

HISTORICAL INTRODUCTION AND TECHNICAL BACKGROUND

A new era is dawning, the era of photons or light. Across our planet, both on the surface and below, a myriad of new communication technologies based on the concepts of photonics, comprising lasers as light sources, ultrapure glass fibers as light guides, and new exotic materials, is challenging the supremacy of the existing electronic technology. With extreme speed the new technology of photonics promises to overtake the powerful but now conventional electronic technology. The existing electronic age in communications may soon change into the age of optics, where light from lasers is the starting point of many devices.[1]

It was just over a quarter-century ago that the first operational laser was reported by T. H. Maiman. Laser development proceeded rapidly after Maiman's experiment. It was from the beginning an international effort. It is possibly this openness in the community that has in large measure contributed to the rapid maturation of the field.

Electromagnetic radiation is used in many aspects of our daily lives. Ubiquitous radio and television communications use frequencies of electromagnetic radiation up to 100 megahertz (i.e., 10^8 cycles per second—100 MHz). The corresponding vacuum wavelength of the radiation is found by taking the speed of light divided by the frequency, so 100 MHz corresponds to a wavelength of 300 cm. The radiation originates in an electronic oscillator which accelerates electrons in an antenna. Whenever charged particles, such as electrons, are accelerated they emit electromagnetic radiation, which then propagates through free space. The signal sent by the transmitting antenna is received by an antenna attached to our radios and televisions; this reception is achieved by the inverse process of the transmission, electromagnetic waves accelerate the electrons in the antenna, and these accelerations are selectively amplified by tuned circuits. The radiation generated in this way is called *coherent,* since it is emitted over a narrow frequency band.

For shorter wavelength electromagnetic radiation, accelerating electrons in oscillators becomes difficult. In the microwave region, which extends to wavelengths between about 1 m and 1 mm, a new type of generator must be used to create the electromagnetic waves. Since these wavelengths are convenient lengths for constructing devices, a microwave generator always has a resonant cavity with physical dimensions around the desired wavelength that determines the resonant frequency. The simplest such generator is the klystron tube, which uses a stream of electrons interacting with electromagnetic radiation in a cavity tuned to a particular microwave frequency.[2] The electromagnetic wave is amplified by interacting with the electrons, thus transferring energy from the electrons to the field. Similarly, a second device, the traveling wave tube, uses a stream of electrons which amplify electromagnetic waves traveling along a helix-shaped conductor. This technology is important in radar, high-capacity communication, and navigation.

Coherent radiation at still shorter wavelengths was not practically achievable by the existing electronic devices developed before 1950. It was time for a revolutionary concept—the stimulated emission of electromagnetic radiation.

The concept of stimulated emission was first enunciated by Albert Einstein in 1916,[3] as an alternative proof of Planck's law for black-body radiation. Black-body radiation is the electromagnetic emission from matter and is in thermal equilibrium with it. This radiation depends on the temperature of the matter, but not on the specific geometric shape or material characteristics of the body. Black-body radiation is *incoherent*; it spans a continuous range of frequencies and the amplitude, phase, and polarization of the electromagnetic fields randomly vary. Planck laid the foundation stone for quantum mechanics by his explanation of the black-body radiation spectrum.[4] Further developments of the quantum theory explained the discrete lines (e.g., Balmer series) in atomic spectra by allowing only discrete energy levels E_n to be available to electrons bound with the nucleus. These levels are referred to as electronic states; and for neutral atoms there are an infinite number of these states (see Figure 3.1).

Under certain circumstances, only two electronic levels need be considered. The excited state, $|2>$, has an energy E_2, and the ground state, $|1>$, has an energy E_1. The energy difference is denoted as $\Delta E = E_2 - E_1$. The state $|1>$ is connected to state $|2>$ by absorption of light which excites an electron from the ground state to the excited state. Light has qualities that can be attributed to particles called photons, which have frequency $\nu = \Delta E/h$. The constant h is called Planck's constant.

The concepts of absorption and gain are illustrated in Figure 3.2. They can be explained by an analogy with chemical reactions. In this analogy, we use only two-level atoms. In order for the reaction to occur there must be electrons in state $|1>$; this population number is denoted as N_1. This is the absorption process, and the number of photons as well as electrons in state $|1>$ are reduced by one. The

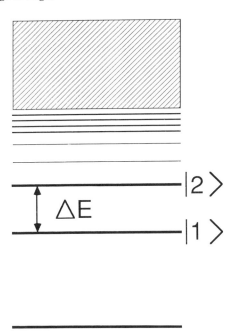

Figure 3.1 Schematic illustration of an atom with many bound states and a continuum. The two states of interest are labelled |1> and |2> in this figure; the state |1> is designated the ground state because it has the lower energy of the two.

product of this reaction is an electron in state |2>; its population has now been increased by one. The inverse process can occur in two ways: the population of the excited state, N_2, can spontaneously decay into a photon and an electron in the ground state, or the presence of photons can catalize the reaction and help to increase the number of photons already present. The latter process is called "stimulated emission" and is essential to the operation of a laser. The medium will absorb more photons than it emits if more atoms are in the ground state (i.e., $N_1 > N_2$) as depicted in Figure 3.2(a). A net gain in the number of photons requires a population inversion, $N_2 > N_1$, as shown in Figure 3.2(b). Unfortunately, for atoms in equilibrium with their environment, the population of the ground state is always larger than the excited state. Inversion of the population required for gain is only possible when the atoms are far from equilibrium.

Weber was the first to state that this inversion would lead to amplification.[5] C. H. Townes, and independently A. M. Prokhorov and N. G. Basov, worked out principles of microwave amplification by stimulated emission of radiation,

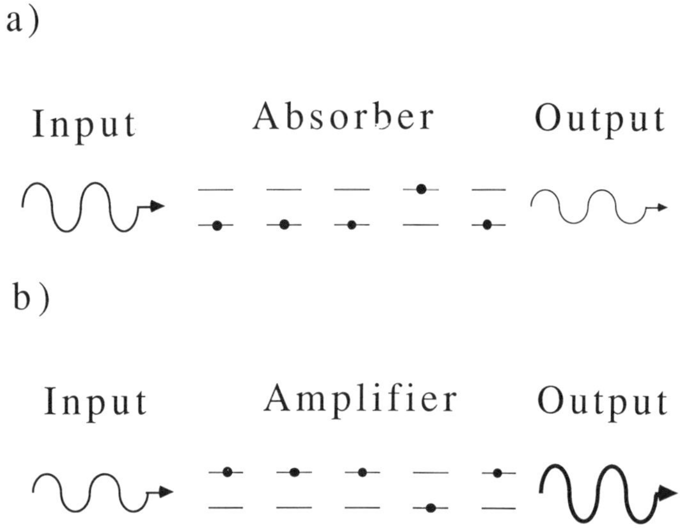

a)

Input   Absorber   Output

b)

Input   Amplifier   Output

Figure 3.2 A photon is traveling through two media illustrated by two-level atoms. If an atom is excited, a heavy dot is shown on the higher line; otherwise the dot is drawn on the lower line. In (a), there are more atoms in the ground state ($N_1 > N_2$) and the light is absorbed in the medium; in (b), more atoms are excited and the light is amplified by the medium. The absorption in (a) and gain in (b) is called saturable, because both processes will eventually be stopped when $N_1 \simeq N_2$.

which has the more common acronym of *maser*. To achieve the inversion, Townes' scheme separates excited-state ammonia molecules from the ground-state ones.[6] The excited molecules are inserted into a cavity tuned to the transition frequency and the microwave radiation is amplified. Basov and Prokhorov used three-level schemes; in each case the excitation is from level $|1>$ to level $|3>$.[7] In Figure 3.3(a) the population is inverted between levels $|3>$ and $|2>$, $N_3 > N_2$, and in Figure 3.3(b) the population of level $|1>$ is depleted so that $N_2 > N_1$. In both cases the atoms are far from thermal equilibrium and a net gain in the number of photons can be achieved.

Soon after masers were developed, work continued on extending these coherent electromagnetic generators to the optical regime. The result of these efforts was the *laser* (light amplification by the stimulated emission of radiation). It was Townes and A. L. Schawlow, G. Gould, and A. M. Prokhorov who independently determined the conditions for laser operation.[8]

a)

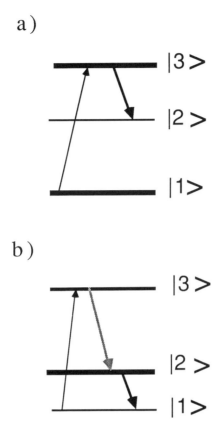

b)

Figure 3.3 (a) A three-state atom with excitation between states $|1>$ and $|3>$ and lasing between levels $|3>$ and $|2>$. (b) A three-level pump scheme with depopulation of state $|1>$ by excitation to state $|3>$. The state $|2>$ achieves a population inversion relative to the ground state $|1>$.

ESSENTIALS OF A LASER

A laser device is an optical oscillator that emits intense, highly collimated, highly polarized beams of coherent radiation. Three parts are crucial to its operation: an external energy source or pump, a working or amplifying medium, and an optical cavity or resonator.

The pump is a source of energy that brings about a population inversion in the laser medium. Amplification of a photon radiation field will occur only in a laser medium where population inversion exists between two energy levels. If this is not the case, then any light passing through the laser medium will be severely attenuated. Pumping in a laser medium can be optical, thermal, chemical, or electrical in nature; what is important is providing energy that can be coupled into the laser medium to excite the atoms and ions and bring about the required population inversion. For gas lasers such as the argon-ion or helium-neon the most common pumping process is an electrical discharge. For solid or liquid lasing media, the most practical method is optical pumping. Optical pumping is achieved using flash lamps.

The amplifying or laser medium may be a gas, liquid, or solid. The particular element, or combination of elements, used is predetermined by the desired wavelength of the laser radiation. Laser action has previously been observed in more than half the known elements and several thousand transitions have been identified in gases that could be usable as laser media. Four of the most widely used transitions in gases provide the wavelengths 488 nm (i.e., $1 \text{ nm} = 10^{-9} \text{ m}$) and 514.5 nm visible radiation from argon-ion gas, the 632.8 nm radiation from neon gas, and the 10.6 μm (i.e., $1 \mu\text{m} = 10^{-6} \text{ m}$) infrared radiation from the carbon dioxide (CO_2) molecule. In some laser media one has a host medium with impure atoms with a lasing transition (e.g., the ruby laser and the Nd-YAG laser). An amplifying medium must have the ability to support population inversion between two energy levels of the active atoms. This is brought about by exciting more atoms into a higher energy level than exist in a lower level. Without pumping (or excitation), the higher energy states will always be less populated than the lower energy states as demanded by the equilibrium distribution. Hence, pumping is necessary to produce the forced condition of population inversion.

A laser's third basic element is an optical resonator which confines and channels the photons through the amplifying medium (see Figure 3.4). The simplest Fabry-Perot resonators or optical cavities consist of a pair of precisely aligned flat or spherical mirrors (usually termed a Fabry-Perot cavity; in essence, a Fabry-Perot Interferometer etalon with large separation). One mirror allows about 100 percent reflectivity while the other is less than 100 percent, enabling the internal reflecting beam to escape and become the laser output.

The optical cavity separation and the mirror geometry determine the structure of the electromagnetic field in the laser cavity. Many transverse radiation patterns (called TEM modes) are present in the typical laser output beam, making it a multimode laser. By suppressing the gain of higher order modes a laser can be made that operates in a single fundamental mode. The reasons for using a single mode are to reduce the noise in the laser output and to control the spreading of the beam.

There are many other important resonator designs. One important class is unstable resonators, which allow energy to escape from the cavity by passing

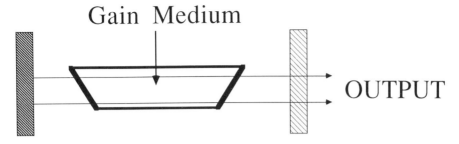

Figure 3.4 Schematic diagram of a laser with Fabry-Perot cavity. The mirrors are shown as planes here, but in practice they are usually concave. The mirror at the output is partially silvered to allow light to escape. The lasing medium is contained in the trapezoid-shaped structure between the plates. The angles of the trapezoid are chosen to minimize reflection of a particular polarization of light. These faces are called Brewster angle windows.

around the mirror edges or by being deflected from their path in the cavity (Figure 3.5). They are used for high gain media, when high power levels are present in the cavity, enabling the laser to operate efficiently with a large output coupling of the cavity. The mirrors can be totally reflecting, thus eliminating complicated coatings. The power output is efficient and the transverse structure is easily controlled.

A second important resonator is the ring cavity pictured in Figure 3.6. This can be operated in a running wave mode in which gain is suppressed for photons in one direction or counter-propagating waves can be sustained in the cavity. As will be discussed below, these lasers now play a prominent role in selected technical developments.

LASER LIGHT CHARACTERISTICS

Laser light is almost pure in color, i.e. it is of a single wavelength or frequency. The monochromaticity is measured by the width of its spectral lineshape or linewidth. To obtain a feel for the linewidth of a laser compared to an ordinary light source, let us consider some typical examples of a discharge lamp versus a helium-neon laser. The ordinary discharge lamp typically has a spectral linewidth of 90 Gigahertz (90×10^9 Hz), while the best helium-neon laser has a linewidth of about 7.5 Kilohertz (7.5×10^3 Hz).[8] Argon-ion lasers operating at single mode have a linewidth of about 10–12 Megahertz.

The optical property that makes the laser unique from other light sources is coherence. The laser is the first truly coherent light source. Coherence is the measure of the degree of phase and amplitude correlation that exists in the

a)

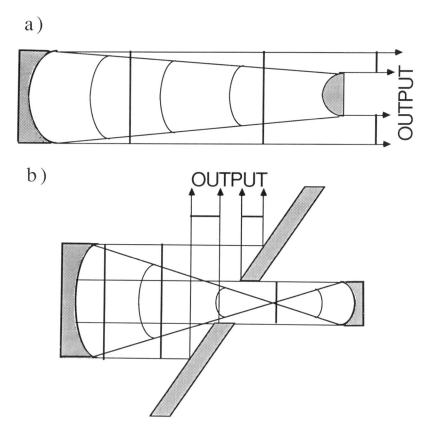

b)

Figure 3.5 Two designs for unstable resonators. The mirrors are totally reflecting. The lasing medium is often unconfined as in high-power chemical lasers. The light may simply bypass one of the mirrors as in (a), or a second mirror may be inserted in the cavity to ''scrape-off'' the light from the cavity.

radiation field of the light source as a function of time and spatial separation. Thus, two types of coherence exist: temporal and spatial. Temporal coherence is the measure of the degree of monochromaticity of the light and spatial coherence is the measure of the uniformity of the phase across the optical wavefront. Note that only a laser that oscillates in a single axial and transverse mode emits highly coherent light. A multimode laser, while emitting more light, may not be any more coherent than a suitably filtered thermal source.[9] But for typical single-mode lasers, both the spatial coherence and temporal coherence of laser light are far superior to that of thermal sources. The coherence time of a laser is the average time interval over which one may continue to predict the correct phase of

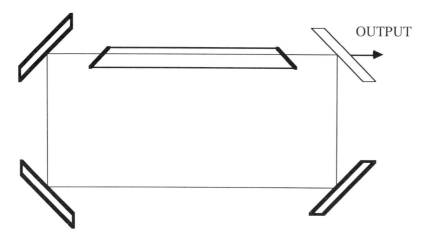

Figure 3.6 A ring cavity shown with four mirrors. The output mirror is partially silvered and the lasing medium is in the trapezoid.

the laser beam at any point in space. The coherence length is the average length of the light beam along which the phase of the wave remains constant. The coherence length (l_c) is related to the coherence time (τ_c) by $l_c = c\,\tau_c$, with c being the speed of light ($\sim 3 \times 10^8$ m/sec). The best helium-neon laser may have a coherence time on the order of milliseconds (10^{-3} sec), while a sodium discharge lamp has a coherence time of about 10^{-10} sec.[10] With such numbers the coherence length of the helium-neon laser is many hundreds of kilometers compared to the sodium lamp's coherence length of less than a centimeter.

Laser beams possess a high degree of beam directionality. A laser can generate a beam of precise definition and minimum angular spread. The reason for the high degree of directionality of a laser beam is the design of the optical cavity and the coherent and highly monochromatic nature of the light generated therein. The beam spread angle, θ, is given by $\theta = 1.27\lambda/D$, with λ and D being the wavelength and the diameter of the laser beam, respectively. The relationship for the beam spread angle is similar in concept to the diffraction angle that one considers if the angular spread in light generated by the diffraction of plane waves passing through a circular aperture is to be calculated. Here, the pattern consists of a central bright spot (called the Airy disk)[11] surrounded by a series of bright concentric rings. Diffraction effects play a precise role in the angular spread of a laser beam. The beam waist (diameter) is determined by the design of the laser cavity and depends on the cavity mirror spacing and the radii of curvature of the cavity mirrors. With proper design, a laser may be built to have a high degree of directionality and extremely low beam spread. As an example, let us take an argon-ion laser operating at 488 nm with a beam waist diameter of 1.8 mm. Here the angular spread will be $\sim 3.4 \times 10^{-3}$ radians, or an increase in the beam width of about 3.4 cm every 1000 cm. This number certainly provides a measure of the high degree of directionality that can be achieved with lasers.

Laser light is said (quite correctly) to be many times brighter than the sun. Typical laser intensities range from ~ 1 mW for an helium-neon gas laser to 10^{14} W peak power as found in neodymium glass lasers used in laser-induced fusion work. Using these two extremes of 1 mW and 10^{14} W, the photon output of lasers varies from about 10^{16} photons/sec to about 10^{33} photons/sec (here we assume an average energy of 10^{-19} J/photon). If a broadband black-body radiator (thermal source) is considered, with a radiating surface equal to the beam waist of the 1 mW helium-neon laser (i.e., 0.5 mm [area $\cong 2 \times 10^{-3}$ cm^2]), and wavelength of $\lambda = 632.8$ nm, linewidth about ($\Delta\lambda \approx 100$ nm) or $\sim 7 \times 10^{13}$ Hz and temperature of $\sim 1000°K$, the photon output rate of the black-body radiator is determined from Planck's theory to be about 10^9 photons/sec. However, if we take into account the directionality of both sources, the difference is even more dramatic. The helium-neon laser emits 10^{16} photons/sec into a solid angle of about 2×10^{-6} steradians, while the black-body source emits 10^9 photons/sec into a solid angle of 2π steradians. Therefore, if we determine how many photons are emitted from the black-body source in the solid angle equivalent to the laser solid angle, we find the number to be about 3×10^2 photons/sec. Hence, the differences on the order of 10^{14} to 10^{31} give a feeling for the brightness or irradiance of a laser compared to a black-body source.

The laser is the first true system that allows the focusing of light to a diffraction-limited point image. The combination of a nonpoint source and incoherent light as found for thermal sources leads to fairly large image sizes. The laser, however, radiates very intense, coherent light that appears to come from a point source, and it is these unique properties that allow us to surpass the limitations that prevented thermal sources from being focused to a very small point. It is possible to focus laser light to a diffraction-limited Gaussian spot of diameter $d \approx f\theta$, where θ is the beam divergence angle given by 1.27 λ/D; and f is the focal length of the lens employed in generating the spot size. Typically, with a lens of focal length 50 mm and an incident laser beam of divergence $\theta \approx 10^{-3}$ to 10^{-4} radians, spot sizes of 50 to 5 μm in diameter can easily be obtained. Laser light can be focused to spot sizes on the order of a wavelength of the light; this makes it possible to drill hole sizes on the order of the wavelength of the incident light into very hard material.

Laser oscillators normally operate at several optical frequencies simultaneously unless special single frequency techniques are used. A 1 m mirror separation is about two million wavelengths and a cavity will have resonances spaced every half-wavelength. The resonant frequencies corresponding to these wavelengths are spaced by a frequency difference $\Delta\nu = c/2L$, where c is the velocity of light and L the effective cavity length (see Figure 3.7). For instance,

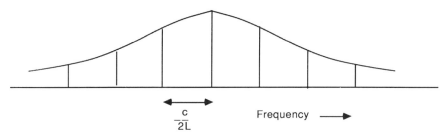

Figure 3.7 The mode spacing lines are distributed evenly across the gain profile of a laser. All lines inside the curve will be amplified.

in a typical argon-ion laser, $L = 1.05$ m, making $\Delta\nu = 143$ MHz. With a prism the Doppler-broadened argon gain profiles have bandwidths of more than 5000 MHz, so that a high-gain transition can provide oscillations at more than twenty frequencies.

SPECIFIC LASER TYPES

Lasers may be classified in many ways. The lasing medium may be used to group them (gas, liquid, or solid). The technique of pumping is another way to distinguish lasers, or they can be classified by the spectral region in which they emit (i.e., visible, infrared, or ultraviolet).

Ruby Laser

This laser consists of a single crystal ruby rod made of aluminum oxide (Al_2O_3) with a small amount of chromium oxide (Cr_2O_3); a xenon flashtube in a helical configuration surrounds the ruby rod. This laser is optically pumped by the xenon flashtubes while Cr^{+3} ions are responsible for the emission of the light by the crystal. The ends of the ruby rod are either at Brewster's angle, for which one polarization has zero reflectance, or there are antireflection coatings on the ends. Dielectric reflectors are located beyond the ends of the ruby rod to provide the proper optical cavity. The energy of the ruby transition is about 1.8 eV, which corresponds to a wavelength of 694 nm.

The output of a ruby laser is an irregular series of pulses primarily due to its multimode oscillations. The laser may emit 2 Joules or more for every pump pulse and if the pulse width is about 10^{-3} sec, the output pulse will have the average power of a few kilowatts. The ruby laser may be Q-switched to attain high peak power. Q-switching is a technique that artificially impairs the optical path in a laser so that the onset of laser oscillations is delayed and the energy in the cavity can be more efficiently used.

Neodymium Laser

This is another optically pumped laser and a good example of a four-level laser. The active Nd^{+3} ion is incorporated into many hosts, especially certain crystals and glasses. Hence, Nd:YAG (YAG—for yittrium aluminum garnet) and Nd:glass oscillate at about the same frequency with the output in the near infrared, at 1.06 μm.[12] The Nd:YAG laser is most often used in semicontinuous fashion, with a very high pulse repetition rate and a pulse power output in the kilowatt range. Nd:glass are usually operated in single pulses. The advantage of a glass rod versus a single crystal rod is that high-quality glass laser rods can be produced in almost any diameter to give high power with relatively low power density. Again Nd:glass lasers are Q-switched to produce very high power pulses. Pulses with peak power in excess of 10^6 MW have been generated for use in laser research.

Gas Lasers

There are four representative classes of lasers that use a gaseous medium. In order of discussion they are neutral gas lasers, ion lasers, carbon dioxide lasers, and excimer lasers.

Representative of neutral gas lasers is the common helium-neon laser invented by Javan and Bennett in 1960.[13] Population inversion was achieved by exciting helium atoms through electron impact. The energy is transferred to the neon atoms through collisions. This laser operates continuously with emission in the infrared ($\lambda \sim 2.8 - 4.0$ cm and $1.1 - 1.5$ μm) and the visible ($\lambda = 0.59 - 0.73$ μm). The most commonly observed emission is at $\lambda = 632.8$ nm, which is the characteristic red light of these lasers. Helium-neon lasers operate at low power levels in the visible and are used as pointers during lectures, for optical system alignment, holography, and a host of other applications.

The argon- and krypton-ion lasers are representative of a class of gas lasers that operate continuously (CW) and have high plasma temperatures. Argon properties are better understood, and for this reason the discussion will deal with a brief explanation of argon gas media. The argon-ion laser can be made to emit at various wavelengths in the blue-green end of the visible spectrum, with the most important being the 488 nm and 514.5 nm lines. With special optics, argon-ion lasers oscillate at twelve different wavelengths from the infrared to the ultraviolet. The krypton-ion laser emits predominantly in the red wavelengths and can exhibit fifteen different wavelengths in its output spectrum.

The energy level diagram of singly ionized argon is given in figure 3.8. It is valid to assume that the two ground-state sublevels of the $4s^2P$ states that make up the two lower states for argon-ion laser transitions have short lifetimes and extremely high probabilities of emitting energy and dropping to the argon ion ground state. Whereas in a neutral atom laser the greater part of the entire

A⁺ ENERGY LEVELS

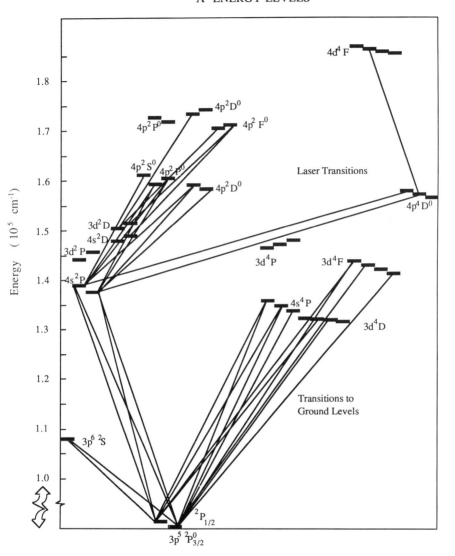

Figure 3.8 The energy level diagram of an atomic gas can be very complicated, as this diagram for simply ionized argon shows.

population is in the ground state, the population at any given time in an ionic ground state is not very large due to recombination processes that return the ions to levels in the neutral atom energy level scheme. Hence, absorption does not develop a "bottleneck" that would build up to a population in the lower levels by collisions.

Since the excitation process that generates the population inversion in argon-ion lasers requires more than one collision to reach the final upper state of the laser transition, the gain and power outputs vary approximately as the square of the current density. The close relation between current density and input power density dictates that high input power densities are desirable for maximum output power.

The argon-ion lasers or krypton-ion lasers are primarily research tools, excitation sources for spectroscopist or optical pumps for dye lasers. They are also employed in the medical field for surgery.

If infrared frequencies are desired, the molecular CO_2 laser may be used at 10.6 μm. In this laser the important transition occurs between the vibrational levels of the CO_2 molecule. CO_2 lasers may either be in a CW or pulse mode (Q-switched); in either case, relatively high power outputs are achieved.

The excitation in this type of gas laser is a glow discharge, an arc discharge, or radio frequency discharge. Another class of lasers, of which CO_2 is an appropriate medium is the TEA laser (transversely excited atmospheric pressure laser). The TEA laser is always in the pulse mode and is excited by an arc discharge at about atmospheric pressure. The CO_2 TEA lasers operating at atmospheric pressure require simple gas handling and gas exchange systems; consequently, they are of relatively low cost.

The primary use of the high power density CO_2 laser at 10.6 μm is for cutting metals and cloth and for welding. CO_2 lasers may also be used as drills for hard and somewhat brittle materials, such as diamonds, tungsten carbide, and boron-nitride, or to fabricate precision drawing dies or other thin metal-forming dies of extremely small dimensions.

For ultraviolet radiation excimer molecules have been used as a laser medium; this was first discussed in 1960 by F. G. Houtermans.[14] Excimer molecules are atoms which can be bound in an excited state, but dissociate into atoms in the ground state. An example of such metastable molecules is a dimer made of rare gas atoms (e.g., He_2, Ne_2, Ar_2, or $KrAr$, etc.). Since the atoms have closed electronic shells there is no tendency for them to form a bound state, unless they are excited. They are the ideal laser medium in the sense that the ground state population $N_1 = \emptyset$. Once the molecule dissociates, there is no absorption of a photon by a ground to excited state transition. Of course, many other excimer combinations exist and are commercially available, such as the rare-gas halogen laser media (ArF, $KrCl$, XeF, etc.). These lasers operate in the ultraviolet and have a wide range of applications because their energetic photons easily break chemical bonds.[15]

Dye Lasers

The organic dye laser is an example of an important class of optically pumped lasers. The active lasing medium in such a device is an organic dye contained in a liquid solvent. The dye molecules are essentially three-level systems; the appropriate energy level scheme is found in figure 3.9. The levels usually have a lifetime that is on the order of microseconds; consequently, great pumping power is required to sustain a population inversion.

The organic dyes also have a fourth level or triplet level which does not contribute to the lasing process. The organic molecules in level 2 decay to the triplet level in about a microsecond, but the triplet level is very long-lived so the molecules do not quickly return to the ground state. Lasing action ceases when a large portion of the dye molecules are in the triplet level.[16]

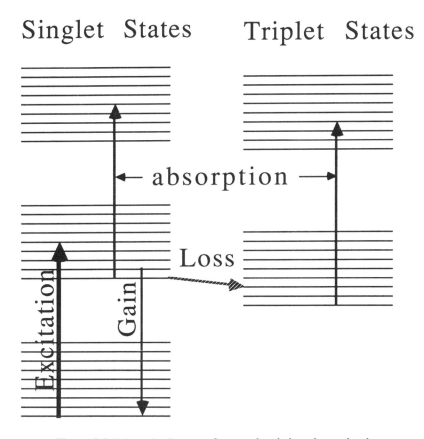

Figure 3.9 Schematic diagram of energy bonds in a dye molecule.

The use of very high speed discharge lamps as optical pumps (microsecond duration) forces the dye to lase efficiently before many molecules are lost to the triplet level. This process tends to minimize the detrimental effect of the triplet state on the lasing efficiency. For dye lasers that are pumped continuously with gas lasers (i.e., argon-ion lasers), the triplet-level problem is partially overcome by passing the dye solution rapidly through the cavity. With small pumping volumes and high flow rates, the molecules are physically removed from the cavity before many of them are lost to the triplet level.

Dye lasers with all their delicate problems are nevertheless of considerable importance because of their tuneability over broad wavelength regions. Several dyes are available and each has a broad fluorescence spectrum; the dye laser with different dyes can produce coherent radiation at any wavelength in the visible spectrum.

Ultrashort Pulsed Lasers

There has been steady progress toward generating even shorter pulses of coherent light. Lasers are now able to produce pulses as short as six femtoseconds (i.e., 6×10^{-15} sec). This time is so short that only a few oscillations of the light wave are contained within the envelope of the pulse.

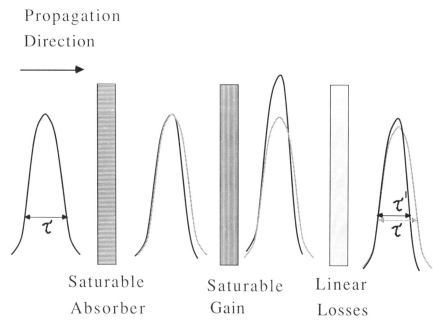

Propagation
Direction

Saturable
Absorber

Saturable
Gain

Linear
Losses

Figure 3.10 Illustration of pulse shortening using a saturable absorber and saturable gain dye. The pulse width is shortened when compared to the original pulse.

Femtosecond pulses are generated using ring laser cavity design with dye media. The dye molecules are chosen because of their broad frequency response. One mechanism for shortening the pulses is the use of dyes with saturable absorption and saturable gain (see Figure 3.2). In a single pass, illustrated in figure 3.10, the pulse is preferentially absorbed on its leading edge and the gain in the second medium is also on the leading edge of the pulse. The net effect of these two processes is to shorten the pulse width. In a ring cavity, the pulse is repetitively shortened in each round trip through the saturable media.

Pulses of light on the order of femtoseconds are widely used in biology, chemistry, and physics. Their temporal resolution is important for measuring relaxation processes and transport properties in gas, liquids, and solid materials. One pulse of light is used to pump the material and a second pulse is continuously time delayed to probe the optical absorption, dispersion, or nonlinear response of the material.

Semiconductor Lasers

Semiconductor lasers emit light when carriers recombine in the active semiconductor material. These lasers are constructed from several layers of material with different doping and composition (figure 3.11). These variables are used to control the band gap and the index of refraction. Materials with an excess of

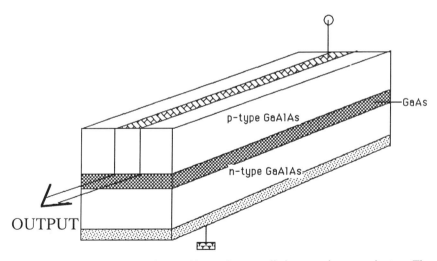

Figure 3.11 A semiconductor laser with a voltage applied on a strip across its top. The base of the laser is grounded. Holes from the p-doped layer on the top and electrons from the n-doped layer on the bottom are injected into the active GaAs layer. The electrons and holes recombine and emit a photon. The ends of the material form a natural Fabry-Perot cavity.

electrons are called "n-doped" and materials with a paucity of electrons are called "p-doped." The latter material behaves as though there were an excess of particles with a positive charge (holes). In semiconductor lasers these particles are injected into a region by applying a voltage; they recombine and emit photons that are subsequently amplified by stimulated emission. The wavelength of the light is determined by the bandgap of the active material. The light is confined to the active layer by the waveguide effect of total internal reflection at the lateral boundaries.[17] The light is trapped in a Fabry-Perot resonator by reflection at the end faces. The laser action is achieved above a threshold current for the injected carriers when gain overcomes absorption in the medium. Semiconductor lasers operate at infrared frequencies, though some are available in the visible regime. The GaAs laser operates in the infrared; lead-salt lasers access IR wavelengths between 2.7 and 30 μm.

Semiconductor laser diodes are taking a large share of the laser market. These lasers have been operating from infrared to visible wavelengths; the vast majority have been put into compact disk players and low-cost laser printers.

The development of lasers is a multidiscipline activity with expertise in electrical engineering, physics, chemistry, and materials science required. From the beginning it has been an international cooperation[18] and competition that has resulted in a large and varied array of lasers.

MEDICAL APPLICATIONS

The medical applications of lasers are not restricted to a single laser type.[19,20] Argon-ion, CO_2, Nd:YAG, dye, krypton, and He-Ne lasers are all useful. The applications require about 10^9 Joules of laser light. The medical procedure of interest here is the absorption of light to heat biological material. This is an old principle in medicine that has been considerably refined from the days when hot irons were used to stop hemorrhaging. Laser light, because of its monochromaticity, can be selectively absorbed by tissue. For instance, the ability of some lasers to seal blood vessels by cauterizing them makes this technique useful for some surgery, such as heart and intrauterine operations where blood-rich tissue is a problem. Internal bleeding can be stopped by using the green light of an argon-ion laser, since it coagulates blood without burning it.

Laser angioplasty offers the possibility of treating several diseases, including coronary artery disease, by using an optical fiber to bring the laser light to the diseased tissue. Blockage is removed by photoablation using pulsed excimer lasers. Trials indicate that this procedure clears arteries better and more completely than balloon angioplasty, which removes the deposits on artery walls by pushing them out of the way. This technique could replace many coronary bypass operations. Nd:YAG lasers have been used to remove oral cancer; this procedure of selectively absorbing light in cells can be used for several diseases (e.g., removal of scar tissue from the heart) where previously open heart surgery was required. In ophthalmology the most popular lasers are argon-ion and Nd:YAG. The Nd:YAG laser is well suited for the removal of the lens. In cataract removal, an estimated 40 percent of the cases develop clouding of the posterior capsule. The laser procedure vaporizes this tissue and restores vision without cutting. Eye tissue (such as the cornea) can also be ablated by lasers, and retinal photocoagulation is used to correct glaucoma. Radial keratotomy is a procedure whereby the surgeon reshapes the lens of the eye by cutting fine lines in the cornea with excimer lasers; it can correct certain distortions that otherwise require glasses or contact lenses. Another experimental surgical technique to correct vision is laser refractive keratoplasty. This procedure uses an excimer laser to sculpt the cornea and shape it to correct far-vision problems. These techniques are highly experimental and long-term effects will need to be addressed before they can be widely marketed.

Endoscopy is the technique of inserting an optical instrument, called an endoscope, into the patient's body cavities through incisions in the skin. The doctor can view the diseased area and then insert an optical fiber into the endoscope and deliver laser energy where it is needed and in controlled amounts.

Lung tumors have been ablated by Nd:YAG lasers that restore air passage through the channels of the endobronchial tree. Early stages of lung cancer have been treated by this technique and it shows some promise in controlling the spread of cancer. The laser has been also applied to stop hemorrhages, a postoperative complication that can occur when operated tissue falls away and opens a major blood vessel.

Fuji Optical has made synthetic holograms from tomographic images, which when viewed with laser beams, show three-dimensional images. The visual rendering of the information could play an important role in deciding options available to surgeons.

Lasers are used in medical research to study the dynamics of proteins, nucleic acids, and other molecules.[21] All time scales become significant for understanding the molecule's role in biological environments. Vibrational dynamics is studied by Raman and coherent anti-Stokes Raman spectroscopy, chain dynamics is investigated through picosecond fluorescence, and femtosecond spectroscopy can give information about the transfer of energy in these complex chemicals.

BUSINESS/INDUSTRY APPLICATIONS

Lasers are already making their way into offices, businesses, and industries. It is to be expected that networks with laser links through fiber optic cables will be an integral part of the future office. Laser printers are used with word processors for high quality, inexpensive copies of documents.[22] An image is written onto a drum using the laser and by a xerographic process the image is deposited onto paper. Letters of various fonts and pictures can be put onto paper; the process is fast with 10 pages per minute for inexpensive laser printers now on the market. Laser readers are used to transmit high-quality facsimiles and the documents are printed by laser printers. Bar code laser readers in supermarkets eliminate mistakes in pricing and provide continued monitoring of inventory. Hand-held versions of bar code readers with semiconductor lasers remove inventory drudgery, allowing time to be spent on more productive work.

Nd:YAG lasers have been used to expose printing plates. The process has speeded up the production of newsprint by allowing the printer to go from a computer directly to page makeup. The common application of this technology is in business-form printers which use a single argon-ion laser. Lasers are used to separate colors in a color photograph into a subset of four primary colors. The prints are then reproduced on four negatives which are used to produce full-color pictures in a magazine or book.

All holograms are made using a laser, but techniques have been developed to observe the holograms in white light by transmission or reflection of the light. These holograms have found an important application in credit card security, since these images are made from a technology not ordinarily available to forgers.

The laser is revolutionizing the printing industry with laser typesetting techniques; a cousin industry, graphic arts, uses lasers for printing and image-processing optical disks are used for mass storage of information; disks now on the market can write over ten gigabytes of information.[23] This is a write-only medium now, but with magnetic materials assisting the next generation of videodisks, high-storage density with erase and rewrite options is also available.[24]

Integrated optical devices are used to manipulate light signals.[25] These devices include switches, switching networks, high-speed modulators, filters, and wavelength multiplexing circuits. Several materials can be used to form waveguide structures; some may be doped such as the titanium-doped lithium niobate crystals. Other materials are alloys, like the GaAs/GaAlAs structures used in semiconductor lasers. In figure 3.12(a) an optical switch is shown. This is a four-port device which can, by application of a small voltage, switch a signal from an input port to an output port. The voltage changes the index of refraction and thus the coupling of the two waveguide structures. The switches can be put together to form a switching network as shown in Figure 3.12(b) for eight bits.

Other integrated optical devices include the Mach-Zehnder modulator, which splits an input signal, changes the phase of one, and recombines them at the output, thus providing a modulated signal; a schematic of this device is shown in figure 3.13. Acousto-optic Bragg cells are used to deflect light in the structure and three-port junctions split the signal into two channels. Filters are used as building blocks of optical wavelength multiplexers. The corrugated surface of a

a)

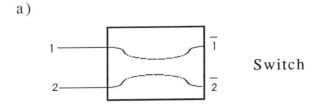

Switch

b)

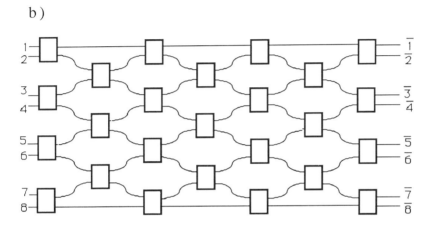

Switch   Array

Figure 3.12 (a) An electro-optical switching device, which couples two paths. The input may be from port 1 or 2 and output depending on the voltage applied can be at either of two ports. (b) An array of electro-optical switches which can be used to switch eight bits of information at the input to any of the eight output ports.

waveguide is matched to a particular wavelength; it acts as a wavelength selector to couple light into the waveguide. Several wavelength selectors together on a chip can be used to multiplex signals onto an optical fiber; at the other end, a similar set of wavelength selectors can be used to redirect the signals into the appropriate channels, thus performing the demultiplexing operation.

Lasers are finding their way into microelectronic applications.[26,27] Excimer lasers are being used in (integrated circuit) IC research and fabrication for help in etching, deposition, and doping of thin films. They are also used to ablate photoresist by photodecomposition. Lasers are needed to identify small particles (under one micrometer) in IC processing—especially as the dimensions of gates

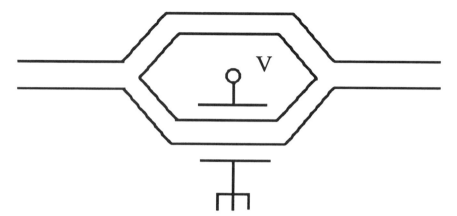

Figure 3.13 A Mach-Zehnder interferometer. A signal at the input is divided into two arms of the interferometer; an applied voltage delays a signal in one arm relative to the second arm.

on surfaces are reduced below one micrometer. Here again, light-scattering methods are sensitive enough to detect particle sizes to within a few Å, and nonlinear optical methods can be used to ablate or push, by radiation pressure, particles from the surface.[28] Another use of the laser is to cut connections to faulty gates on integrated circuits and to solder in their place a redundant replacement gate. Femtosecond laser spectroscopy has been used to directly test transistor switching speeds, where no other method was available.[29,30] With the use of gallium arsenide technology, a new type of ultrafast transistors called modulation-doped field-effect transistors has been invented and their switching times of about ten picoseconds have been measured by the new spectoscopic technique. The time resolution is on the order of two picoseconds, and there is no reason why this cannot be improved as instruments with subpicosecond resolution become available in the future.

Semiconductor lasers will undoubtedly also find use in chips as GaAs is a material with fast electronic switching and excellent optical waveguiding properties. One thrust of DARPA's (Defense Advanced Research Project Agency) funded research is to integrate optical and electronic components.[31] The optical components would alleviate clock skew caused by RC time constants in electronic conduction, and they do not require coaxial shielding of different light signal inputs; the cross-talk is thereby eliminated. The partnership between optical components and electronic components is a new one, but it will undoubtedly be a fruitful synergism.

Another important area of laser development is in the automation of various industries.[32] The factories of the future will be filled not with people but robots.

Some robots will have lasers to cut, weld, and drill. CO_2 lasers with 500W of CW power are used to melt or vaporize the material; similarly, surface hardening by heat treatment of the materials with lasers is cost effective. CO_2 or Nd:YAG (high repetition rate) lasers are used for plastics, wood, ceramics, and steel to cut through the object and create complex shapes.

Lasers have already found uses in industry to measure rotation; for instance, the ring laser design of a gyroscope has increased the sensitivity of rotational measurements. These laser gyroscopes are now being installed in the new generation of Boeing 767 jets and the European Airbus. They are cost effective and do not require expensive maintenance.

Measurement of length with lasers has been done in a variety of ways. For instance, interferometers like the Michelson interferometer can measure lengths to an error of about $\Delta L \approx 10^{-6}$ cm; the theoretical limit would be many orders of magnitude smaller if thermal and microphonic effects were eliminated. To measure long distances, a beam is modulated and the change of phase at several frequencies can be used to determine accurately the distance (up to about 80 km). For much longer distances, pulse echo methods have found application by monitoring the time of flight until the laser pulse returns. This method can be used for timing in navigation, turbulence measurements, air travel, and air pollution emission monitoring. Velocity measurements can be made by Doppler effect mixing the laser light with the scattered light and measuring the beat frequency.[33]

Lasers will provide multidimensional metrology of two- or three-dimensional objects for multiaxis measuring machines and industrial robots. Holographic interferometry is used to record the amplitude of vibration of machines and to give information about excessive motion that can lead to breakdown of machines;[34] other methods rely on the placement of accelerometers which need to be mounted and may change the vibration characteristics.

Interferometers, such as the Twyman-Green or Fizeau interferometer,[34] are used for testing curved and flat surfaces. This array of instruments can be used for displacement, velocity, flatness, pitch, jaw, and many other essential properties of a piece being manufactured.

LASERS IN COMMUNICATIONS

During the last decade the number of fiber optic waveguide-based communication systems has increased manyfold, primarily because of significant reductions in the loss characteristics of the optical fibers and major breakthroughs in achieving stable and long-working lifetime semiconductor lasers. Most of this spectacular growth has been in high capacity systems in long-distance, single-mode fiber communication networks.[35] At present, the predominant operating wavelength is at 1300 nm generated by InGaAsP/InP-based semiconductor lasers. As far as loss characteristics go, it is most beneficial to operate a fiber optic waveguide system at the longest wavelength possible, since the intrinsic Rayleigh scattering in a fiber optic material falls off inversely with the fourth power of the wavelength. Such high-purity glass for fiber optic application has been produced with the consequential extremely low absorption characteristics, that the intrinsic Rayleigh scattering now is the limiting criterion for long range transmission of light signals.[36] An additional intrinsic light attenuation process present in all optical materials is the absorption due to molecular vibrations at wavelengths in the near infrared regime (multiphonon absorption). The lowest possible attenuation in an optical fiber is determined by a delicate interplay between the Rayleigh scattering and multiphonon absorption. These effects place silica fibers at a theoretical limit of about 1550 nm and in practice minimum losses of about 0.1 dB/km have been realized in silica fibers.[37] Halide glasses have their practical minimum loss wavelength at about 2550 nm and a lower intrinsic attenuation is possible. Achieving 10^{-2} to 10^{-3} dB/km at 2550 nm may not be ruled out,[38,39] and it may become possible to have a transatlantic communication channel without repeaters (light amplifiers).

Various laser types or structures are employed in communication systems. The most successful seem to be the general class of buried heterostructures produced by liquid-phase epitaxy techniques (LPE).[35] The power output of such lasers is typically from 10mW to 30mW, with a modulation bandwidth on the order of 500 MHz. Reliability of the communication laser requires a lifetime in excess of 10^5 hours for use in inaccessible terrain such as the ocean floor, whereas shorter lifetimes may be equally useful for terrestrial communication systems. Most of the semiconductor lasers available today operate at least at 1300 nm and 1550 nm, at the wavelength of minimum loss for silica-based fibers. Current research efforts are trying to extend the frequency spectrum such that semiconductor lasers may operate reliably beyond 1550 nm.

Most lasers in fiber optic communication systems are produced by liquid-phase epitaxy,[35] which has been successfully augmented for multiple unit production facilities. Some problems do exist in the uniformity of the epitaxial layers grown by this technique. Newer techniques such as molecular beam epitaxy (MBE) and metal-organic chemical vapor deposition (MOCVD) have greatly advanced the growth of uniform epitaxial layers and it is possible that both MBE and MOCVD offer great adaptability for achieving higher manufacturing yields and thereby further reducing laser costs.[35] Gas-source MBE has been found to produce atomically sharp interfaces between different material layers, thus allowing engineering of materials with novel electronic and optical properties. For example, AlGaAs lasers, MBE grown, with tailored bandgaps and multiple quantum wells exhibit superior performance,[40] and these techniques may well work when applied to InGaAsP lasers to produce a superior product.

Today the state of the art in low-cost, high-reliability room temperature semi-conductor lasers seems to be limited to less than 2000 nm in wavelength if InP-based materials are used. If halide-based fibers are to become viable, then lasers operating from 2000 nm to 5000 nm must be produced. GaSb or InAs are materials that may work in that wavelength region.[35]

LASERS IN CHEMISTRY

The laser's superior monochromaticity and high intensity can be used selectively to enrich the products of chemical reactions. Before the laser, heat or flames were the available sources of photons for breaking chemical bonds. These are broadband sources; hence, there was little control over the molecules that were transformed under this process. The most controversial application of laser photochemistry was isotope separation;[41] by precisely tuning the laser to an electronic excitation of a particular isotope, the molecule with the desired isotope could be ionized and then separated. When the nuclei are heavy, isotopic mass differences are small and the molecules are difficult to separate. At Lawrence Livermore a two-story system of copper vapor and dye lasers has been built to enrich uranium. This technology is expected to be a commercially viable alternative to gaseous-diffusion enrichment techniques in the near future.

Light detection and ranging (LIDAR) can be used for remote sensing of environmental conditions.[42] The lidar principle is based on the scattering of a light pulse from molecules, clouds, or dust in the atmosphere. During the interaction of light with these constituents, the scattered light has characteristic shifts of wavelength that give information about the composition and physical state of the atmosphere. The delay times of the return pulse provide the ranging information.

Lidar technology has been used to monitor the ash from the volcanic eruptions of Mount St. Helens and El Chicon thus serving as a tracer for global wind and circulation patterns. It provides useful information about atmospheric temperature and pressure conditions as a function of altitude, and can provide detailed meteorological data.

The sensitivity of lidar has been extended to detecting chemical species from the parts per billion level and the range is up to tens of kilometers. The future of lidar includes ozone layer studies, space exploration, and weather forecasting.

Tomography has been most commonly found in medical applications using X-ray or nuclear magnetic resonance imaging techniques. Optical tomography can provide three-dimensional reconstruction of systems such as the atmosphere, flames, plasmas, and fluid flows. Good reconstructions of images have been obtained; for instance, in flames a range of temperatures differing by over two orders of magnitude can be distinguished and spatial resolutions to 100 μm have been performed. The method works only in transparent media, and phase measurements can be used that do not rely on optical resonance.

LASERS IN ENTERTAINMENT

Laser shows were once quite the rage at rock events or science exhibits. Holographic pictures have found their niche in the art world; there is the Museum of Holography in New York, a permanent exhibit at the Royal College of Arts in London, and in Paris, a two-minute holographically recorded movie can be seen. It would be interesting to speculate that perhaps this technology will also revolutionize the entertainment industry as films once did. Holographic pictures in magazines, such as already appeared on the covers of *National Geographic,* could be commonplace.[43] Even advertisements with this technology may become popular. Holographic video games have become a minor industry.

Rainbow holograms are the result of making a hologram of a portion of a hologram.[44] This was first performed by Stephen A. Benton, who masked part of a hologram to create a new hologram. Since all information is stored everywhere on the hologram, the original picture was still present, but with a limited viewing perspective. The hologram image created by white light can be seen in different colors as the head is moved from side to side. This has been used to create interesting artistic effects in holographic art.

An image from a hologram can also be projected onto a screen, when light from the counter-propagating direction illuminates the film. The counter-propagating direction is reversed by 180° from the original reference beam used to illuminate the hologram.

The audio compact disk (CD) player, unlike the video disk, is rapidly grabbing a large share of the market. The heart of this new technology is a semiconductor laser which directs light to the optical disk. The reflected light is modulated by the disk's surface and the detector senses the charge of light intensity. This technology is able to reproduce high-fidelity sound and the surface does not wear from mechanical contact.

LASER FUSION

Lasers may provide the solution to creating controlled thermonuclear reaction.[45] The temperatures required for this reaction are about 10^8K. Scientists believe the goal of releasing more energy (in the form of neutron yield) than was used in the process can be attained by powerful lasers that are focused onto a fuel pellet containing deuterium and tritium. The laser pulses ionize the outer atomic layers and cause a compression of the material inside that can increase the density by a factor of fifty. The high temperature and density created by the sudden compactification can cause the atomic nuclei to fuse and release prodigious amounts of neutrons.

The amounts of available fuel for creating fusion power are essentially unlimited, since it is extracted from water, albeit in small amounts. However, the efficiency of the process is impressive and only relatively small amounts are required. Work on laser fusion is in progress in the United States—at Lawrence Livermore National Laboratory,[46] where the NOVA laser facility is located, and at the University of Rochester and Los Alamos National Laboratory. Considerable research efforts are also being made in the Soviet Union, England, France, and Japan.

MILITARY APPLICATIONS

It is no surprise that lasers would find their way to defense applications. The smart bombs employed in Viet Nam were fitted with laser-seeking heads to reach targets such as bridges, power plants, or industrial plants. Laser-guided weapons and tracking have been a part of the battlefield scenario and will be integrated into space technology if the Strategic Defense Initiative (SDI) is developed.

Many more laser applications will undoubtedly be developed for battlefield use. Fiber optic guided missiles (FOGM) are already being tested with 40 km of spooled cable; these systems transmit light through the fiber optic cables to guide the missile to its target.[47] One application of fiber optics and lasers is the ADOCS army program to send signals from pilot control to mechanical control devices (so called "fly by light").[48] The test bed is the Sikorsky UH-60 Black Hawk helicopter. The navy is developing a fiber optic link to sensors for antisubmarine warfare with the ARIADNE program; optics to replace mechanical or electrical connections is being used in surface ships in the AEGIS program (e.g., USS Mobile Bay) and may be incorporated in submarines. Laser correlators will be used for target recognition and missile guidance.[49] These devices, using a principle of pattern recognition conceived by van der Lugt, have a hologram with stored information and a laser to correlate the input scene with objects stored on the hologram.

Laser communications through optical fibers will replace cables now used on battlefields, since such fibers are radiation resistant, immune to electromagnetic pulse, electromagnetic interference, and radio frequency interference, and cannot easily be tapped. Laser gyroscopes are used for navigation in military jets and in ships as well.[50] They are robust, relatively inexpensive, and do not require expensive maintenance.

The development of laser remote sensing from space using LADAR[51] (laser detection and ranging) will be accompanied by high throughput computational needs, another problem that could be addressed by optical computers.[52] The ability of CO_2-based ladars to detect small metallic cross-sections, such as anten-

na towers, wires, and poles, makes it the ideal system to be employed in helicop-
ters as the heart of the obstacle and terrain avoidance system.[53] A high power
laser's ability to destroy missiles has been the source of a great deal of controver-
sy. The proposal for Strategic Defense Initiative includes land-based free electron lasers or chemical lasers as well as space platform systems fitted with
chemical, X-ray, or other high power lasers.

A free electron laser (FEL) uses a relativistic beam of electrons and passes
between a row of alternate-poled magnets as shown in figure 3.14.[54] The
magnetostatic device is called a wiggler or undulator. The electrons are peri-
odically accelerated by the wiggler magnets, much like the traveling-wave devices used in microwave electronics, thus emitting electromagnetic radiation.
The FEL is tuneable over a wide range of wavelengths, from millimeters to the
X-ray regime. Since it requires an accelerator to give the electrons relativistic
speeds, this laser is ground-based. Strategic defense scientists, therefore, envision that the laser light would be sent through the atmosphere to mirrors that
would target and focus the radiation. High powers have already been demonstrated: 1 GW average power at 1 mm wavelength and 1 MW at the 1 μm (i.e.,
1000 nm) wavelength.[55]

Another potential laser weapon is the chemical laser. The active medium is a
gas of molecules created by mixing reactive chemicals. The energy stored in the
excited molecule is lost by emission of a photon. The molecules are swept out of

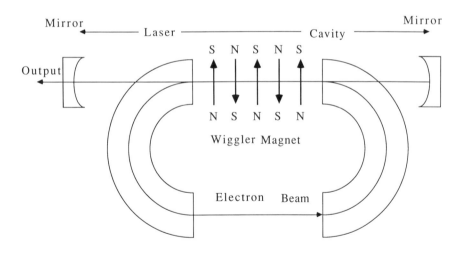

Figure 3.14 A schematic of the wiggler magnets and electron path in a free electron laser
(FEL).

the ground state by a vacuum. These lasers can achieve very high gain; therefore, an unstable resonator design is appropriate. The HF laser would be deployed on space platforms since the lasing wavelength ($\lambda = 2.8$ μm) is strongly absorbed in the atmosphere. The DF laser, which replaces hydrogen with the isotope deuterium, could be a ground-based laser since its operating wavelength ($\lambda = 3.8$ μm) is not strongly absorbed by the atmosphere.

Recently a high-efficiency chemically pumped iodine laser has been developed. Research is underway to develop its potential for high power applications in the military.

There has been relatively little discussion about X-ray and gamma-ray laser technology. Reportedly, X-ray lasers, pumped by radiation from a nuclear explosion, would be operated without a cavity and presumably enhance the brightness of X-rays incident on the targets, over that which would normally occur from a nuclear explosion, by six to twelve orders of magnitude. Gamma-ray lasers would be made of a material with energy stored in a long-lived isomeric nuclear state. A transition to the lasing level is triggered by a pump in the optical regime.

FUNDAMENTAL RESEARCH

Lasers have had a substantial impact on basic science. They can be tuned to particular optical transitions of atoms or ions. By properly detuning a laser from an atomic transition, the atom can be made to selectively impart some of the photon's momentum to the atom. This technique has been used to slow down ions and atoms, cooling the atoms by removing kinetic energy.[56] Trapping ions is a relatively straightforward procedure with a Penning trap. For neutral atoms, researchers rely on an electric dipole force exerted on the atom by a gradient of the laser intensity. Researchers at AT&T Bell Laboratories have demonstrated a trap of this type using six unfocused laser beams to cool the atoms; the light field creates an environment for the atoms that is difficult to escape. It has been coined "optical molasses" because of this property. As a spinoff of this technology, scientists hope to study collective quantum effects, since the temperature is 240μK. The trapped atoms are separated by about thirty nm, so it may be possible to achieve a phase transition called condensation with neutral atom traps.

Strong-field tests of quantum electrodynamics have been made possible by lasers.[57] When a laser is tuned close to the transition frequency of an atom, the scattered radiation is called resonance fluorescence. In strong fields, the spectrum of scattered light becomes complicated. Remember, the spectrum is the separation of the light into its different frequency components; for a single-mode laser there is only one sharp maximum in the spectrum at the laser frequency. However, in scattered light from strong laser fields, instead of a single peak at the laser frequency, two symmetric side peaks develop and their frequency shift is proportional to the electric field amplitude of the laser. The relative widths and heights of the three resonances was predicted by Mollow[58] and later observed by Wu et al.[59] in agreement with the theory.

Other tests of the quantum electrodynamical basis of the laser itself have been devised.[60] In the transient regime, when the laser is turned on, its coherent field is created by amplified spontaneous emission. The random release of spontaneous photons has statistical properties which can be theoretically calculated in this transient regime. The quantum noise is amplified to macroscopic levels and is an easily observable effect. When the mirrors of the cavity are removed, the quantum noise can, under suitable conditions, be amplified to give an intense and very short pulse of electromagnetic radiation called superfluorescence.[61]

The features of superfluorescence can be theoretically quantified, and many have been verified by experiment. It is of interest not only for its application to strong-field quantum electrodynamics, but also as a configuration for ultraviolet sources and possibly coherent X-ray sources. Another coherent transient source with a close analogy to superfluorescence is called stimulated Raman scattering. Raman scattering is the observation of light at a frequency ν_s (so-called Stokes' frequency), though an exciting laser pulse of frequency ν_L is not in resonance with an allowed transition in the medium. The effect is caused by the scattering of light waves from molecular or electronic vibrations or longitudinal-optical phonons in solids. The frequency shift, depending on the medium, can be from 10^{12} to 10^{14} Hz. The initiation of Stokes' radiation is due to spontaneous emission. There are important new features to this process, such as the formation of solitons at the Stokes' frequency at the expense of depleting the laser pulse.

Other strong-field effects could be studied. In ionizing transitions, an asymmetric resonance has been observed in the spectrum of emitted photons (called the Fano spectrum in atomic physics).[62] Tuning a laser to this transition is expected to give effects similar to the resonance fluorescence spectrum, but is further complicated by the interference between electrons in the atoms which gives rise to the Fano profile.[63] Although as yet unobserved, experiments verifying these theories would provide a new test of strong-field quantum electrodynamics. Intense lasers also make possible the study of multiphoton ionization of atoms. The comparison between theory and experiment has proven successful. For instance, in 22-photon ionization of helium, the cross-section has an intensity dependence proportional to $I^{22\pm0.2}$ in agreement with theoretical calculations of photon cross-sections.[64] Other quantitative comparisons between theory and experiment have been made possible by these high-power lasers, but new puzzles have been found as well.[65] It remains a vigorous and important field of research.

Molecular spectroscopy should benefit from multiphoton ionization, since new states can be reached and identified by ionization spectroscopy. Competition between resonant multiphoton ionization and spontaneous emission back to the ground state in the ultraviolet can be exploited to make a new class of coherent vacuum ultraviolet sources.[66]

Recent research by Brillet and Hall[67] increased the sensitivity of the Michelson and Morley experiment by several orders of magnitude; they were able to establish the correctness of Einstein's theory of special relativity and rule out ether drag effects.

Testing Einstein's general theory of relativity has been an extremely difficult endeavor.[68] Laser ranging using retroreflectors placed on the moon provided a test of Einstein's equivalence principle for the general theory of relativity.[69] In this experiment the body being tested was the moon. This experiment is also significant in that it used retroreflectors carried to the moon by two Apollo missions and two retroreflectors brought by the Russian Lunaklod mission. The accurate positioning of the moon required retroreflectors at several locations to determine the librations of the moon. The U.S. McDonald Observatory with its 2.72 m telescope was used to transmit and receive low pulses and track the moon to within a few centimeters. The experiments proved inertial and gravitational masses are the same to within five parts in 10^{12}.

Lasers may also provide the key to the detection of elusive gravitational waves, for which there is only indirect astrophysical evidence so far.[70] The new generation of gravitational wave detectors will use a Michelson interferometer arrangement with mirrors affixed to masses set in motion by a passing gravitational wave.[71] Prototype systems have been developed in Glasgow, Scotland, Munich, Germany, and Pasadena, California. Larger systems are now under construction.

Gravitation wave research has also spurred a search for quiet light known as squeezed states.[71] Already reductions in noise of 50 percent or more below the vacuum fluctuation level have been achieved. According to quantum mechanics, any measurement of the amplitude or phase of light is accompanied by some uncertainty; even the ''vacuum state'', a state with no photons, has quantum-mechanical fluctuations. This should have important applications to optical communications as well as measurement science in general, and gravitational wave detection in particular. A new type of laser made with this light would have noise in one quadrature of the signal.

Ring-laser gyroscopes rely on the phase shift of light traveling in opposite directions within the ring. The phase shift is sensitive to the angular rotation of the ring laser with respect to a local inertial reference frame. The light that has traveled in opposite directions is recombined and the interference fringes determine the phase shift; this is called the Sagnac effect and although, as mentioned earlier, it is the basis of navigational gyroscopes, it can also be the basis of designing extremely sensitive tests of general relativity.[72] For example, Einstein's general theory of relativity has no preferred reference frame, while other theories involve a preferred frame; another example is the measurement of a rotation because the earth drags the local inertial frame (the Lenz-Thirring effect). Recently, Scully and coworkers[73] proposed a correlated emission ring laser design that would improve the sensitivity of ring-laser gyroscopes. This work could impact future tests of general relativity.

A direct test of Wegener's theory of plate tectonics was made possible by the laser geodynamic satellites (LAGEOS).[74] These satellites are equipped with retroreflectors in order to reflect short pulses of light back to earth. Lasers are placed at several locations on earth and are used to monitor the relative distance between these locations with an accuracy of within a few centimeters. Over a period of months or years, the motion of the continents has been registered.

The foundations of quantum mechanics have been controversial since the theory was first developed.[70] There are alternative hidden variable theories; as espoused by Bohm, the various parameters for a particle's complete dynamics are determinate in this viewpoint; however, these parameters are hidden from us. Bell formulated a theorem based on classical logic which allows a class of the hidden variable theories to be experimentally tested.[75] Such a test was performed by Fry and Thompson, who used a tuneable dye laser and examined correlations between photons emitted in a cascade of transitions ($7^3S_1 \rightarrow 6^3P_1 \rightarrow 6^1S_0$) in mercury vapor.[76] The results agree with the predictions of quantum mechanics; the predictions of hidden variable theories are violated.

Lasers have also opened up the field of nonlinear optics. Nonlinear response of atoms and molecules is observed in all forms of matter: gas, liquid, solid, and even plasmas. The polarization of the medium is not simply proportional to the applied electromagnetic field. When the laser light is strong enough, there will be a nonlinear response of the medium. The nonlinear response can be exploited to observe a rich variety of phenomena. In 1961, soon after the invention of the laser, Franken and coworkers[77] performed the first experiment in nonlinear optics by generating the second harmonic wavelength $\lambda = 347$ nm in a quartz crystal from ruby laser light $\lambda = 694$ nm. The generated second harmonic radiation has been used as a coherent source at frequencies where no laser is available and has been a tool for pulse duration measurements by determining the length of crystal over which second harmonic radiation is produced. It has been an important contributor to laser fusion, where the efficiency of laser energy transfer can be increased by shortening the wavelength. Using two lasers tuned to different frequencies, coherent light at a new wavelength can be created in nonlinear materials (parametric conversion).

Third harmonic frequencies can also be generated, but this is difficult because of the absorption and dispersion in the medium. The index of refraction of the medium is changed by the nonlinear response and the beam can become focused to the center, just as a lens concentrates a beam of light. The phenomenon is called self-focusing of light.[78]

Other interesting and useful phenomena are stimulated Brillouin scattering, stimulated Raman scattering, and Kerr effects.[79] Stimulated Brillouin scattering is possible in a material that has pressure dependence of the polarizability. Light excites sound waves in the medium by electrostriction forces, the grating formed by the sound waves sets up an index grating that in turn scatters light backward. The scattered light, because of the phonon scattering, is shifted in frequency by about 10^9 Hz. Kerr effects can arise in molecular fluids which have an anisotropic polarizability. The electric field produces a torque on the molecules, causing them to reorient and thus changing the index of refraction. As one might expect, this is a slow nonlinearity since the molecules must be reoriented.

The complete theoretical treatment of the material may demand a solution of differential equations for material properties. This effort has been necessary to explain, for instance, the unusual transparency of materials to strong light pulses, so-called self-induced transparency found when a pulse propagates in a nonlinear medium.[80]

OPTICAL PHASE CONJUGATION

This phenomenon refers to the phase reversal ability of a nonlinear optical material.[81] If a plane wave is observed during its passage through a turbulent atmosphere, then this effect will reflect the light in such a way that it retraces the same path and returns as a plane wave. Optical phase conjugation has applications where there is a need to compensate for aberrations introduced in a wavefront. This field is the domain of adaptive optics, and reflectors of the type described above are referred to as phase conjugate mirrors.

The phenomenon was observed using stimulated Brillouin scattering by Zeldovich in the Soviet Union.[82] Hellwarth[83] in the United States predicted it would occur in other nonlinear media by mixing a signal wave together with two pump waves having the same frequency, to create a fourth wave conjugate to the signal. The process is called degenerate four-wave mixing. There have since been many different schemes developed to create optical phase conjugation. The phenomenon has been observed in gases, liquids, crystals, glasses, aerosols, and plasmas. Many materials have been used: semiconductors, inorganic dyes, and polymers can all be used as nonlinear media in which to mix the laser beams.

The four-wave mixing geometry is analogous to the phenomenon of holography discussed earlier, only here the wavefront is reconstructed from a material that can be erased. There is no film and no developing procedure. In four-wave mixing as illustrated in figure 3.15, the signal mixes with a pump wave to create an interference grating in the medium; the information from the object is thus said to be written into the medium. The second pump wave must come from the opposite direction of the first pump; this wave scatters off the interference pattern created by the signal and first pump wave to create the conjugate wave. Applications include photolithography, optical communication, high power laser development, signal processing, interferometry, and image processing.[84] This phenomenon has captured the imagination of many researchers around the world.

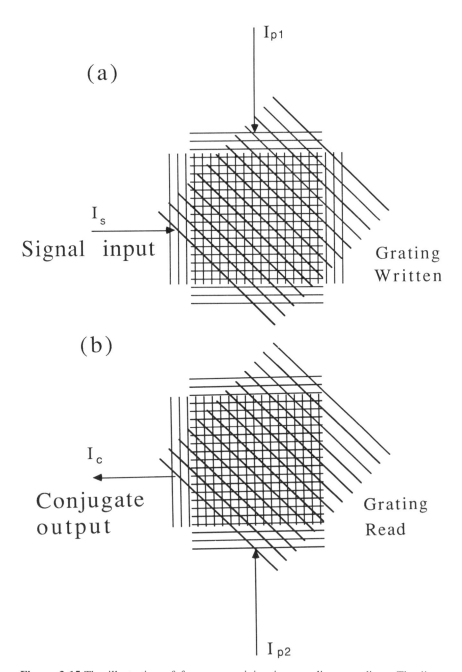

Figure 3.15 The illustration of four-wave mixing in a nonlinear medium. The lines illustrate the maximum amplitudes of the waves. (a) The signal wave, I_s, and the first pump wave, I_{p1}, interfere with one another and imprint their interference pattern in the medium. (b) The second pump wave, I_{p2}, is scattered off the interference pattern, but only in a direction that constructively interferes to form the conjugate wave I_c.

OPTICAL COMPUTING

Optical computing has developed into two different directions. One area is the performance of digital operations by developing new devices and architectures; the second is the traditional field of optical computing generally associated with problems such as signal processing. Imagine doing digital optical computing with photons rather than electrons.[85] Since photons are uncharged particles, they do not interact significantly with one another in free space. They can be confined in rays and propagate along a straight line. Electrons must be confined to wires and careful shielding must be used to prevent cross-talk between the various components.

One of the basic elements of electronic computing is a gate that has two different output voltages for the same input voltage. Such a gate is called bistable. Optical analogues of this device have been under investigation since the mid-1970s and materials with especially large optical nonlinearities have been found. The output of the device can be one of two different intensities for the same input intensity. This field of nonlinear devices that are driven by photons is termed photonics and, as the name implies, the goal is to design devices that perform with photons what their counterparts in electronics perform with electrons.

The field is literally in its infancy and if a multitude of problems are overcome, researchers may find the fruits of their labors culminating in a supercomputer that would surpass any electronic machine in performance. One reason for this optimism lies in the inherent massive parallelism of optical devices; the photons are not restricted to propagate in the plane of the chip as are electrons; they can pass through the plane and many operations can be performed in parallel. By present-day materials technology, a chip 1 cm^2 could pack one million optically bistable gates. Since they switch in one nanosecond, the processing speed of the device in one clock cycle would be 10^{13} logic operations per second. This figure is larger than the rate of information processing by present-day electronic supercomputers, and does not reflect the limits of materials properties. Higher rates would be possible as the materials problems related to nonlinear optical devices are solved. Nevertheless, it would be wildly optimistic to believe that this new form of computing is just around the corner. More realistic is the gradual introduction of optical components in electronic computers to relieve bottlenecks and to improve computational efficiency.

The analog uses of optical computing are driving the technology into commercial use. The research areas are signal processing, pattern recognition, array processing, and artificial intelligence.[86]

The optical correlator developed for military target recognition is an example of the analog approach to optical computing. Like all optical pattern recognition, it is based on the Fourier transform, which is simply performed by a lens in optics. The van der Lugt architecture[87] for optical correlators is shown in figure 3.16. The Fourier transform takes a scene or a signal and decomposes it into a characteristic spectrum. If a hologram called a matched filter is placed in the focal plane of the lens, it will then be correlated with the incoming signal and the output contains only the information from the input scene that *matches* the image stored in the hologram. The output is a spot that corresponds to the position of the correlated image in the input scene. In order to do this processing, the light must be coherent over a wide aperture; the source is a diode laser in the optical correlator used by the military, but clearly there are many applications for this technology.

The factories of the future may be assisted by another novel optical architecture for pattern recognition and image understanding. This new computer tries to mimic the brain's functions by using a large number of highly interconnected processors. Such machines are called neural computers. One such model proposed by Hopfield[88] processes information in parallel. A set of devices called neurons communicate with each other by interconnections that store information which can be recalled. Each neuron processes the signals fed into it by its neighbors using a threshold operation, i.e., its output is either low or high depending on the sum of the input signals. Using the model, a partial picture of an object can be compared with stored objects and the one most closely resembling the partial picture is chosen. An optical architecture to implement this model has been proposed based on a holographic memory and nonlinear optical components for thresholding operations. Optical techniques have much greater potential in effectively expanding this model to complex objects because of the

MATCHED

INPUT   FILTER   OUTPUT

L1   L2

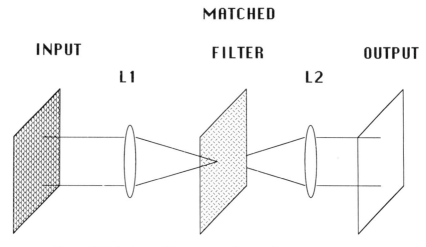

Figure 3.16 A simple illustration of the van der Lugt architecture.

massive parallelism inherent in optics and the ability to make global interconnections among different devices.

Optical neural computers have been able to take partial information and process it to retrieve complete information about an object.[89] This ability is called associative memory and is a significant aspect of the brain's computational power. The brain accomplishes this task by exciting neurons, which are also communicating with their neighbors. The result of the brain's computation does not depend on a single neuron, but on the collective behavior of many neurons.

The neurons of an optical neural computer could eventually use optical switching elements made from nonlinear materials. The memory can consist of a hologram or a nonlinear material that has the capability of learning new information. The connectivity and feedback is achieved by employing optical cavity designs; these include ring resonators and phase conjugate resonators.

Quo Vadis

The future development of both analog and digital optical computing will have a substantial impact on technology. These computers could perform the vast amount of computation necessary for a strategic defense shield, the rapid analysis of a critically ill patient and subsequent identification of medication from a large data bank, and the decision process for a robot operating on another planet. It will be a challenge to solve the myriad of problems in implementing this new technology, but it does not seem out of reach.

The U.S. government is planning for a controversial strategic defense shield that will eliminate the danger of a nuclear holocaust. The centerpiece of this system are lasers with the ability to direct their energy at projectiles and disable them. These lasers may be X-ray, gamma-ray, free-electron, or chemical lasers. Of course, these same lasers could be used to destroy all communication and surveillance satellites in a matter of seconds. There would be no warning of such a sneak attack and the opponent would be vulnerable to attack without any early warning system. Lasers in space remove the possibility of any reaction time. This future is already developing with the recent reports of ground-based Soviet and U.S. lasers, already operational, that are used to blind satellites or destroy their surveillance sensors.

We envision vast changes in medicine in the future. Many forms of surgery will be obsolete. Lasers guided by optical fibers will replace a large number of surgical procedures. An operating room may be equipped with a bank of lasers that each perform specific tasks. Physicians will also be aided by optical computers that are programmed to recognize and prognosticate diseases and illnesses based on incomplete observations. Holographic displays will provide the doctor with a three-dimensional image of the body. Lasers will also analyze tissue and fluids from the patient's body, *in vivo*, to accurately determine the patient's health status.

The factory floor may have robots which can analyze and test an object. This process will be achieved by complicated optical pattern recognition computers. The robots will also be equipped with an array of lasers that cut, weld, drill, measure dimensions, and perform a variety of other tasks.

Rockets of the future will be propelled by laser beams, generated from lasers both ground-based and in orbit. The rockets will receive the energy and convert it into propulsion. The major advantage of this propulsion scheme is that the rocket will not have to carry fuel on board, permitting a large weight reduction of the vehicle. In space, solar energy will be used to pump a lasing medium, and the output power will be directed to rockets, space stations, and power stations on earth.

Throughout the history of mankind many political and economic revolutions have taken place. Usually these revolutions are labor intensive, with intellect and creativity being relegated to a secondary place. This new era, or this new revolution, involving light is information intensive. The First Industrial Revolution came about primarily due to the engineering achievements of man in developing machines which eventually relegated horses to pasture. This First Industrial Revolution fueled by great engineering achievements then spawned many new sciences (i.e., thermodynamics, mechanics, and elasticity). The Second Industrial Revolution had its advent with electricity and electronics; first came the science, then the engineering, followed by gadgetry and devices. Great scientists like Faraday, Maxwell, and Hertz set down the basic laws of electricity that later allowed engineers to produce useful items such as the light bulb and the electrical machines and components that make it functional. Their results were the foundation of communication systems. The Third Industrial Revolution, which involves light, has come about primarily due to the exercising of the greatest nicety of thought; and hence, intellect or mental creativity and information are its main ingredients.

Quantum mechanics showed scientists how to manipulate electrons in semiconducting materials; the result was the transistor, and eventually the multiple transistor or integrated circuit. Now it is the task of this same logical train of thought to guide the scientist in manipulating photons in any optical material (photonics[90]). At the core of this new revolution, which is more information intensive than any before, is the ultimate source of all photons, the laser.

The evolution of the laser has certainly played a crucial role in the development of lightwave communications, optical logic devices, and all optical circuit elements. The latter two in coupling with the lightwave communication technology offer the exciting possibility of replacing electrical currents by optical beams in new classes of information-processing devices. In lightwave communications the laser has realized its full potential and is bringing to its innovators indications that point toward increased productivity and commercial profit. Information processing or optical computation has not yet realized its full potential since many of its necessary ingredients are just now in a conceptual stage. This field is perhaps hindered by the belief that a gradual evolution of ideas and concepts from the all-electron computer to the all-photon computer must be achieved by a hybrid evolution incorporating photonic devices in an electronic computer.

A hermaphrodite of existing electronic computers and new photonic concepts will not yield an optical computer that can compete in speed and capacity with the best existing electronic computers. New radical thought processes involving only photonic techniques will be necessary for optical computing to realize its great potential.

Indeed, the impact of lasers on our future is just beginning to be fathomed. As in any other technology, adverse as well as beneficial applications will co-exist. The inevitable result of this fantastic new technology is that its impact will be judged by all the people of the world, not merely the scientists and engineers.

NOTES

1. *Time*, October 6, 1986, p. 5.

2. D. L. Webster, *J. Appl. Phys.* 10, 311 (1939); R. H. Varian and S. H. Varian, *J. Appl. Phys.* 10, 321 (1939); M. Choclorow and C. Susskind, *Fundamentals of Microelectronics* (New York: McGraw-Hill, 1964).

3. A. Einstein, *Physikalische Zeitschrift* 18, 121 (1917).

4. M. Planck, *Verhandlung der Deutschen Physikalischen Gesellschaft* 2, 202 (1900).

5. J. Weber, Trans. IRE Professional Group on Electron Devices PGE D-3, 1 (1953); I. D. Abdella and C. H. Townes, *Nature* 192, 957 (1961).

6. J. P. Gordon, H. J. Zeiger, and C. H. Townes, *Physical Review* 99, 1264 (1955).

7. N. G. Basov and A. M. Prokhorov, *Doklady Akademiia Nauk* 101, 47 (1955).

8. B. A. Lengyel, *Introduction to Laser Physics* (New York: John Wiley & Sons, 1966).

9. M. Young, *Optics and Lasers*, vol. 5 (Berlin-Heidelberg: Springer-Verlag, 1977), chap. 7.

10. J. Strong, *Concepts of Classical Optics*, (San Francisco: W. H. Freeman & Co., 1958), p. 159.

11. M. Born and E. Wolf, *Principles of Optics* (Oxford: Pergamon Press, 1964).

12. E. Snitzer, *Neodymium Glass Laser* (New York: Columbia University Press, 1964), pp. 999–1019.

13. A. Javan, W. R. Bennett, Jr., and D. R. Herriott, *Physical Review Letters* 6, 106 (1961).

14. F. G. Houtermans, *Helv. Phys. Acta* 33, 933 (1960).

15. C. K. Rhodes, ed., *Excimer Lasers* (Berlin: Springer, 1984).

16. F. P. Schafer, ed., *Dye Lasers*, vol. 1 (Berlin: Springer, 1973).

17. G. P. Agrawal and N. K. Dutta, *Long-wavelength Semiconductor Lasers* (New York: Van Nostrand Reinhold, 1986).

18. M. Bertolotti, *Masers and Lasers: An Historical Approach.* (Bristol: Adam Hilger, 1983).

19. R. A. Kirschner, *Photonics Spectra* (Sept. 1987), 48.

20. D. Muller, *Lasers and Applications* (May 1986), 85.

21. V. S. Letokhov, *Nonlinear Laser Chemistry: Multiple-Photon Excitation* (Berlin: Springer, 1983).

22. *Lasers and Applications* (Oct. 1986).

23. Digest of papers for Topical Meeting on Optical Data Storage, Optical Society of America, 1984.

24. *Lasers and Optronics* (Sept. 1987), 77.

25. C. H. Lee, ed. *Piosecond Optoelectronic Devices* (New York: Academic Press, 1984).

26. T. A. Znotins, *Lasers and Applications* (May 1986), 71.

27. R. Dwight, *Laser Focus* (May 1986), 28.

28. A. Ashkin, *Physical Review Letters* 40, 729 1978).

29. J. A. Valdmanis and G. Mourou, *Laser Focus* (Feb. 1986), 84.

30. Idem., *Laser Focus* (Mar. 1986), 96.

31. J. A. Neff, "Electro-optic Techniques for VLSI Interconnect," in *Proceedings of AGARD Conference,* No. 362, 1985.

32. J. T. Luxon and D. E. Parker, *Industrial Lasers and Their Applications* (Englewood Cliffs, N.J.: Prentice-Hall, 1985).

33. S. L. Kaufman, *Lasers and Applications* (July 1986), 71.

34. C. M. Vest, *Holographic Interferometry* (New York: John Wiley & Sons, 1979).

35. C. Kumar and N. Patel, "Lasers in Communication and Information Processing," in *Lasers-Invention to Application,* eds. John R. Whinnery, Jesse H. Ausubel, and H. Dale Langford (Washington, D.C.: National Academy Press, 1987).

36. J. Schroeder et al., *Optical Engineering* 24, 697 (1985).

37. M. E. Lines, *Journal of Applied Physics* 55, 4058 (1984).

38. J. Schroeder et al. *Electronic Letters* 20, 860 (1984).

39. D. C. Tran, K. Levin, M. Burk, C. Fister, and W. Broer, *Proceedings of the Society of Photographers and Industrial Engineers Symp.* 618, 48 (1986).

40. W. T. Tsang, *Applied Physics Letters* 39, 786 (1981).

41. J. J. Snyder and R. A. Keller, eds. "Ultrasensitive Laser Spectroscopy," *Journal of the Optical Society of America* B2, (1985).

42. D. K. Killinger and N. Menyuk, *Science* 235, 37 (1987).

43. *National Geographic,* 165 (3), 1984.

44. J. Caulfield, ed., *Handbook of Holography* (N.Y.: Academic Press, 1979).

45. K. A. Brueckner and S. Jorna, *Reviews of Modern Physics* 46, 325 (1974).

46. R. S. Craxton, R. L. McCrory and J. M. Soures, *Scientific American* (Aug. 1986), 68.

47. *Lasers and Optronics* (June 1987), 24.

48. *Laser Focus* (Aug. 1986).

49. D. Casasent, *IEEE Spectrum* 18, 28 (1981).

50. J. F. Kreidl, *Lasers and Applications* (Feb. 1987), 18.

51. D. C. Morrison, *Lasers and Applications* (Sept. 1986), 20.

52. P. Speser, *Laser Focus* (Sept. 1986), 18.

53. A. J. DeMaria, "Lasers in Modern Industries," in *Lasers—Invention to Application,* eds. J. R. Whinnery, J. H. Ausubel, and H. D. Langford (Washington, D.C.: National Academy Press, 1987).

54. T. C. Marshall, *Free Election Lasers* (New York: Macmillan, 1985).

55. "The Science and Technology of Directal Energy Weapons", *Reviews of Modern Physics* 59 (3), pt. 2 (1987).

56. S. Chu, J. E. Bjorkholm, A. Ashkin, and A. Cable, *Physical Review Letters* 57, 314 (1986).

57. H. Walther and K. W. Rothe, eds., *Laser Spectroscopy IV* (Berlin: Springer, 1979).

58. B. R. Mollow, *Physical Review* 188 (1969).

59. F. Y. Wu, R. E. Grove, and S. Ezekiel, *Physical Review Letters* 35, 1426 (1975).

60. D. F. Walls, *Nature* 280, 451 (1979).

61. M. Gross and S. Haroche, *Phys. Reports* 93, 301 (1982); F. Haake, J. W. Haus, H. King, G. Schroeder, and R. Glauber, *Phys. Rev.* A23, 1322 (1981).

62. U. Fano, *Phys. Rev.* 124, 1866 (1961).

63. K. Rzazewski and J. H. Eberly, *Phys. Rev.* A27, 2026 (1983); J. W. Haus, M. Lewenstein, and K. Rzazewski, *J. Opt. Soc. Amer.* B1, 641 (1984).

64. L. A. Lompre, G. Mainfray, and J. Thebauld, *Revue Physique Appliquee* 17, 21 (1982).

65. P. Kruit, J. Kimman, H. G. Muller, and M. J. van der Wiel, *Phys. Rev.* A 28, 248 (1983).

66. J. Bokor, R. R. Freeman, and W. E. Cooke, *Phys. Rev. Lett.* 48, 1242 (1982).

67. A. Brillet and J. Hall, *Phys. Rev. Lett* 42, 549 (1979).

68. R.F.C. Vessot, *Contemp. Phys.* 25, 355 (1984).

69. C. O. Alley, *Quantum Optics, Experimental Gravitation and Measurement Theory* (New York: Plenum, 1983).

70. J. H. Taylor and J. M. Weisberg, *Astrophys. J.* 253, 908 (1982).

71. See note 69, esp. articles by the experimental groups.

72. A. Barut, P. Meystre, and M. Scully, *Laser Focus* (Oct. 1982), 49.

73. M. O. Scully, *Phys. Rev. Lett.* 55, 2802 (1985).

74. For further articles see *J. Geophysical Research* 90 (1985), pp. 9217–9438.

75. J. S. Bell, *Physics* 1, 195 (1965); *Rev. Mod. Phys.* 38, 447 (1966).

76. E. Fry and R. Thompson, *Phys. Rev. Lett.* 37, 465 (1976).

77. P. A. Franken, A. E. Hill, C. W. Peters, and G. Weinreich, *Phys. Rev. Lett.* 7, 118 (1961).

78. J. H. Marburger, *Progress in Quantum Electronics* 4, 1 (1975).

79. V. S. Letokhov and V. P. Chebotayev, *Nonlinear Laser Spectroscopy* (Berlin: Springer, 1977).

80. L. Allen and J. H. Eberly, *Optical Resonance and Two-Level Atoms,* (New York: Wiley, 1975).

81. A. Yariv, *IEEE J. Quant. Elec.* QE-14, 650 (1978).

82. B. Ya Zel'dovich, V. I. Popovichev, V. V. Ragul'skii, and F. S. Faizullov, *Sov. Phys. JETP Lett.* 15, 109 (1972).

83. R. W. Hellwarth, *J. Opt. Soc. Am.* 67, 1 (1977).

84. R. A. Fisher, ed. *Optical Phase Conjugation* (New York: Academic Press, 1983); B. Yu Zel'dovich, N. F. Pilipetsky, and V. V. Shkunov, *Principles of Phase Conjugation* (Berlin: Springer, 1985).

85. S. D. Smith, *Appl. Optics* 25, 1550 (1986).

86. "Optical Computing: A Field in Flux," *IEEE Spectrum* (Aug. 1986), 34.

87. T. Kohonen, *Self-Organization and Associative Memory* (Berlin: Springer, 1984).

88. J. J. Hopfield, *Proc. of the National Academy of Sciences* 79, 2554 (1982); idem, *Proc. of the National Academy of Sciences* 81, 3088 (1984).

89. Y. S. Abu-Mostafa and D. Psaltis, *Scientific American* (Mar. 1987), p. 88.

90. J. M. Rowe, *Scientific American* (Oct. 1986), p. 147.

4

Biotechnology

Arnold E. S. Gussin

Pick up any newspaper or magazine, any day, any place in the United States, and you are sure to find an article on the biotechnological revolution—usually not written for a scientifically trained audience, but for educated laypersons and people in business. These people are being inundated with articles that in past years would have caused them to turn to less formidable reading:

- Tobacco Plant with Firefly Gene Implant Glows
- Gene Responsible for MD Is Found
- Scientists Isolate Gene That Blocks Cancer Type
- Scientific Advances Lead to Era of Food Surplus Around the World
- Engineering Another Green Revolution
- Relaxation Urged in Gene-Splicing Rules
- FDA Approves First Genetically Made Vaccine
- Crash Program to Map Human Genetic Code Gets Growing Support
- Human Gene in Mice Producing Blood Substance
- In the Gene Lab, Scientists Manipulate Codes of Life
- Using Genetic Engineering to Make Tomatoes Taste Like Tomatoes Again
- Gene-Engineered Protein Aids in Faster Healing of Wounds
- Genetically Engineered Seeds, Plant Patent Protected
- Gene-altered Mice Make Human Protein in Their Milk

The list is long, and anyone could create his or her own. Mine comes primarily from the *New York Times,* the *Wall Street Journal,* and my hometown paper, the *Schenectady Gazette.*

If you restrict your reading solely to the business pages, you will come across these headlines:

- Biotechnology Units to Merge
- Fast Start for Bioengineered Drug
- Technology: Putting a Tag on Microbes
- Partnership Buyout by Genentech
- Bubbling Biotechnology
- Cloning a Cocoa Plant
- Technology: Gene Mapping Is Improved

On November 12, 1986, the *New York Times* published a page on business technology. Specifically, in a interview for an article entitled "A New Agenda for Tomorrow's Industry," Dr. Gerald O'Neill, professor emeritus of physics at Princeton University and an expert in the commercial applications of technology, noted that "American business . . . [if it is] to regain its economic fortunes in competition with Japan and Western Europe . . . will have to exploit market opportunities in six new global industries": magnetic flight, light aircraft, microengineering, genetic engineering, robotics, and space.

A 1985 seminar presented by Arthur D. Little Decision Resources promised "corporate planners, R&D managers, . . . senior executives, . . . management from the biotechnology, health care, food processing, pharmaceutical, agricultural, and chemical industries . . . investment analysts and venture capitalist" to assist them in working "this evolving technology into an overall corporate strategy in order to take full advantage of the opportunity it presents, while avoiding costly strategic errors."

Surely, the revolution wrought by biotechnology is upon us. Although we are on the threshold of great discoveries, "the public's anxiety about the technology, a relentless attack by critics, and violations of Government rules for biotechnology experiments by scientists have resulted in costly delays. Furthermore, the stock market collapse in October has dried up sources of investment income and reduced the chances that new projects will be started soon" (*New York Times,* January 17, 1988).

In June 1986, after two years of work by eighteen federal agencies and executive offices a "Coordinated Framework for the Regulation of Biotechnology" appeared in the *Federal Register* (FP 51, No. 123, pp. 23302–23393). The framework presents policy guidelines, based on scientific principles, for defining and regulating the environmental introduction of biotechnology products. The framework is conservative and overregulatory.

Public anxiety and federal overregulation may have an adverse effect on companies doing business in environmentally regulated fields. These two factors could lead to serious problems for companies. Any decrease in public support caused by public anxiety and/or government regulation could be reflected in decreased equity values and shortages of capital. For decades to come large continuous inflows of capital will be needed to satisfy the rigorous testing standards required for safety.[1] Thus there will be some lag time before genetic engineering exerts its full and expected impact on the world's economy. The public has forgotten that the genetic manipulation of nature for its benefit is not a new phenomenon. When people focus on the properties of the engineered organisms, and not on how they were produced, the revolution will be upon us in earnest.

Even busy executives had better begin to rectify their biotechnological illiteracy. They had better learn about DNA and how it may be manipulated to produce a desired result. For the purposes of this chapter, biotechnology is defined as gene splicing (recombinant DNA); this is the most predictable and precise method for manipulating genetic material in useful ways. After the basics of biotechnology (interchangeable with genetic engineering) are explored, the discussion will return to the marketplace.

DNA: THE MASTER MATERIAL

DNA is the genetic material. It contains (encodes) the information that parents pass on to their children and imparts to all of us our characteristics. DNA is part of our chromosomes. Each organism has a particular number of chromosomes. All human cells (except for sex cells) contain forty-six chromosomes (twenty-three pairs). When an egg which has twenty-three single chromosomes, is fertilized by a sperm with twenty-three single chromosomes, the resulting zygote (fertilized egg) has twenty-three pairs of chromosomes, for a total of forty-six. So we inherit long strands of a chemical, DNA, and it is the information in these strands that determines what we are to become.

DNA (deoxyribose nucleic acid) is a long chain of nucleotides joined together. A nucleotide is comprised of a sugar with five carbon atoms (formula 1), a

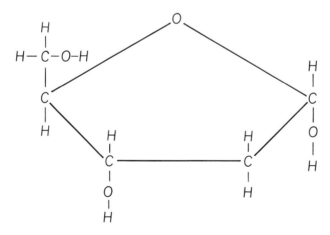

Formula 1 Deoxyribose

phosphate group (formula 2), and one of four nitrogen bases (formulae 3,4,5, and 6). Since there are only four nitrogen bases, there can be only four different nucleotides. In all DNA nucleotides, the sugar and the phosphate groups are identical; in fact, S (sugar) and P (phosphate group) are constant throughout the living world. The four bases are guanine (G), cytosine (C), thymine (T), and adenine (A). Figure 4.1 represents a nucleotide consisting of a P, S, and C. It is startling to note that the entire code of life resides in the arrangement of the four bases. That is, a gene is simply a long sequence of these bases (hundreds to several thousand) linked together. Figure 4.2 is hypothetical gene 1 and figure 4.3 is hypothetical gene 2. In creating gene 1, I chose any sequence of bases that came to mind; I used the same bases in creating gene 2, but presented them in a different order. In real genes, repetitions of any of these bases any number of times is permissible. But in a given gene the sequence of the bases is excruciatingly precise. One base exchanged for another, or one insertion or deletion of a base, changes the behavior of the gene.

Formula 2 Phosphate Group

Formula 3 Adenine   **Formula 4** Guanine

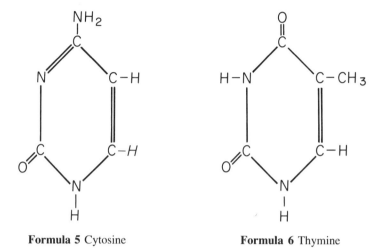

Formula 5 Cytosine   **Formula 6** Thymine

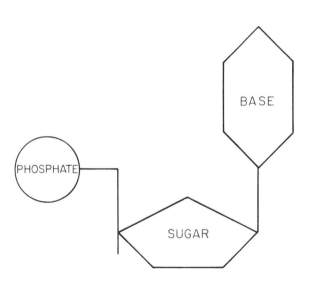

Figure 4.1 A Nucleotide

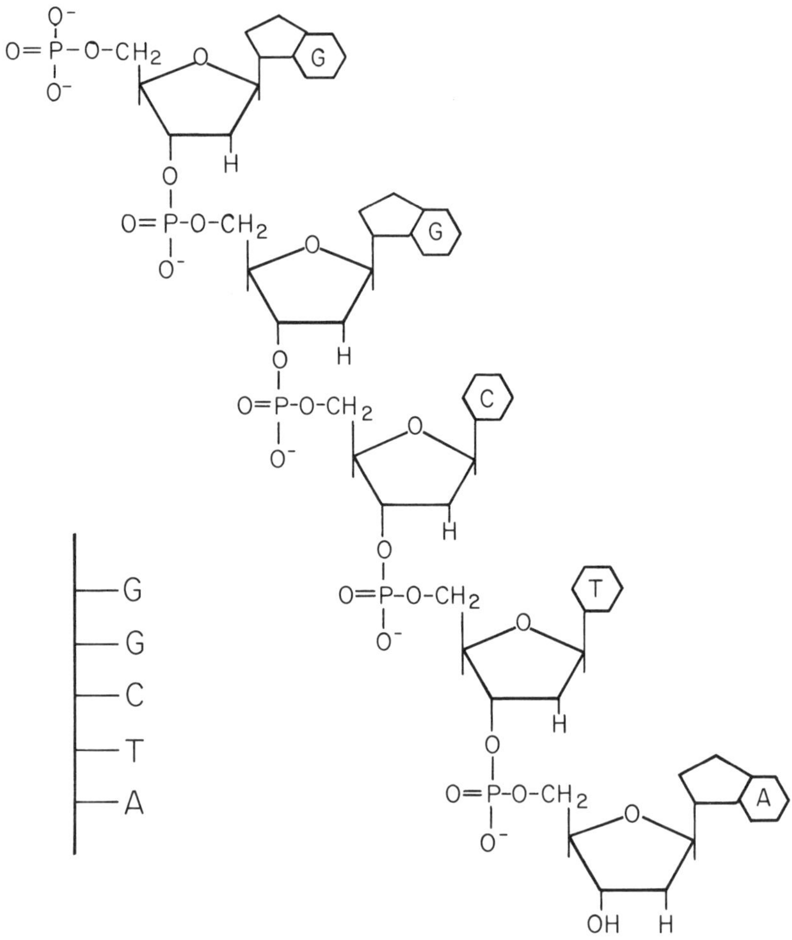

Figure 4.2 Hypothetical Gene 1

Usually, for expository purposes, nucleic acids (i.e., long chains of nucleotides which may include in their sequences one or more genes) are depicted as one-half of a ladder with rungs projecting out from an upright pole (figures 4.2, 4.3, and 4.4). Every organism has the same upright pole (the same repetitive sugar and phosphate groups). The bases, which are bonded to the deoxyribose sugar, are the projecting rungs, the informational component of the DNA molecule. The information encoded in these bases is eventually translated into the characteristics of an organism. DNA, however, does not exist as a single upright ladder, but as an entire ladder with two uprights and projecting bases which act

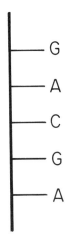

Figure 4.3 Hypothetical Gene 2

Figure 4.4 Nucleic Acid

as the rungs (figure 4.6). There are two complications. The first is that the ladder is helical (figure 4.5, the famous double helix discovered by James Watson and Francis Crick), and the second is that the four bases pair precisely, that is, the double-ringed adenine (A) always pairs with the single-ringed thymine (T), and the double-ringed guanine (G) always pairs with the single-ringed cytosine (C). This pairing is the result of the chemical sites available on each base for pairing with its correct neighbor; it ensures a precise geometry for the DNA molecule. With the information just presented it should be a simple exercise for the reader to write the sequence of bases for the nucleic acid complementary to the one depicted in figure 4.4.

The chromosomes, with their genes, are located in the nucleus of cells. The cell theory, proposed by the zoologist Jacob Schleiden in 1838 and the phys-

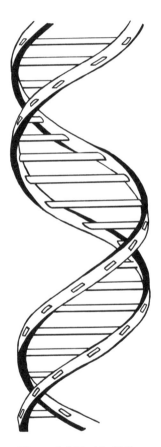

Figure 4.5 Double Helix

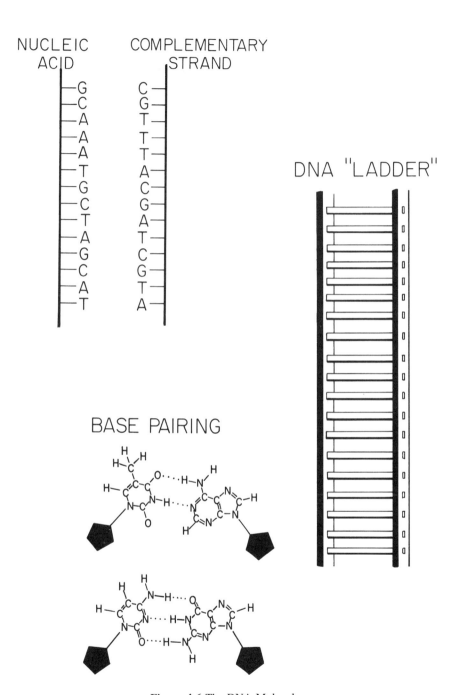

Figure 4.6 The DNA Molecule

iologist Theodor Schwann in 1839, and modified by countless other biologists since then, states that all organisms are composed of cells and the products of cells. Cells contain a complex array of organelles but for our purposes understanding the basic animal cell (figure 4.7) and the basic plant cell (figure 4.8) is adequate. Plant cells are similar to animal cells. One major difference is that plant cells have a nonliving, rigid, cellulose-containing cell wall, which should never be confused with the living cell membrane. The cell membrane is present in both plant and animal cells.

The chromosomes in the nucleus of a cell contain long sequences of DNA. The information encoded into the sequence of bases in the chromosomal DNA must exit from the nucleus into the cytoplasm in order to become functional. The DNA double helix unzips and one of the strands is copied. The bases, phosphate groups, and sugars required to construct the new nucleic acid strand are constituents of the organism's diet and are also synthesized by the organism. The new nucleic acid called messenger RNA (mRNA or messenger ribonucleic acid) is, as mandated by the rules of base pairing, complementary to its DNA template. There are two changes: the sugar in RNA is ribose (formula 7) and the base thymine is replaced by the base uracil (C, formula 8). The function of mRNA is to bring the message encoded in nuclear DNA out into the cytoplasm. mRNA is a short-lived molecule; after it does "its work" it is decomposed into its original components which may be used again. DNA is long-lived and is protected from destruction by its nuclear environment.

PROTEIN SYNTHESIS

What is the "work" of this mRNA which has taken its instructions from DNA? Simply to make proteins! Proteins in turn endow the organism with a specific structure and a precise set of functions. Proteins are long chains of amino acids, as depicted in formula 9. The R group may be one of twenty different chemical

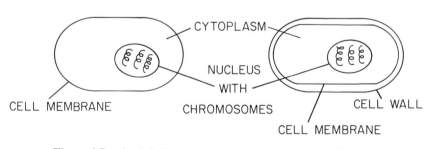

Figure 4.7 Animal Cell   Figure 4.8 Plant Cell

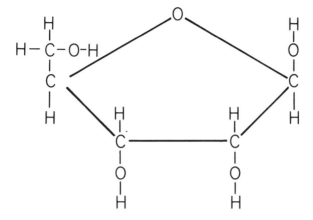

Formula 7 Ribose

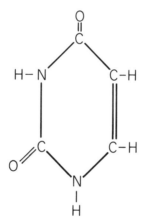

Formula 8 Uracil

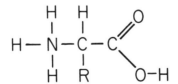

Formula 9 Amino Acid

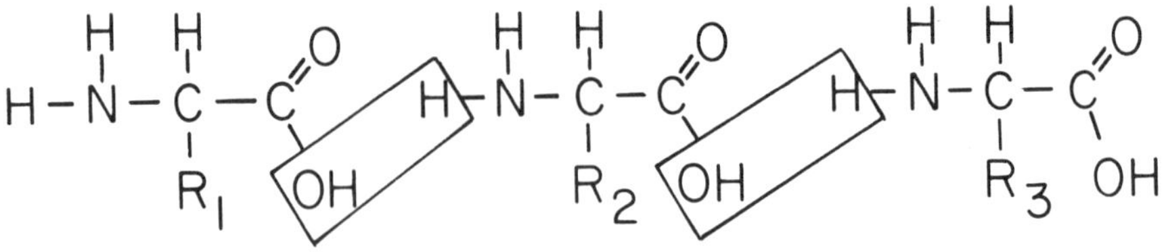

Figure 4.9 Amino Acids

groups, and so there are twenty different amino acids. Amino acids link together to form proteins—dozens to thousands of amino acids (figure 4.9).

When the chemical constituents interact and are removed as water OH and H, peptide bonds are formed between the amino acid pairs (figure 4.10). A chain of three amino acids (as in the figure) is not enough to be labelled a protein; usually a minimum of eight residues are required. The sequence of the amino acids in a protein is precisely determined. Most of the time when one amino acid is substituted for another, even in a sequence of several thousand, the result is nonsense. The amino acid sequence (i.e., the order of the twenty "words" that constitute a protein) is ultimately determined by the precise sequences of the bases in mRNA, which is itself complementary to the precise sequence of the four bases (the entire code of life is written in the sequence of the four "letters") in the DNA in the nucleus. Each three bases in mRNA code for a particular amino acid.

Protein synthesis occurs in the cytoplasm of plant or animal cells (figure 4.11). In the example, the DNA triplet (codon) CAT codes for a particular amino acid, the sequence GCA codes for a different amino acid, the codon TTC codes for its amino acid, and the codon ATG codes for the fourth amino acid in this sequence. The result is a chain four residues long. If a DNA sequence contained three

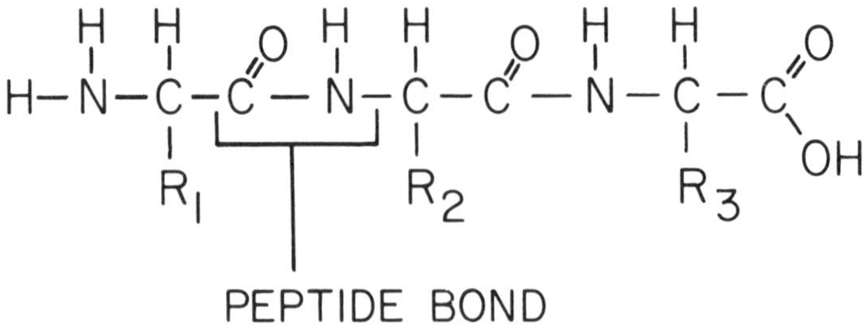

Figure 4.10 Amino Acids (bonded)

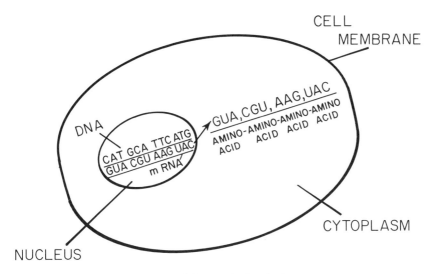

Figure 4.11 Protein Synthesis

thousand bases, the protein would have one thousand amino acids. A precise sequence of bases in DNA, which codes for one polypeptide chain, is called a gene. Organisms have many thousands of genes along the length of their chromosomes. The genes determine what proteins the organism will make. The proteins may be structural (muscle, bone, hair, connective tissue, etc.) or functional (enzymes, hormones, antibodies, etc.); it is our proteins (the precise arrangement of twenty amino acids) that determine what we are. Insulin, for example, is a small protein which contains fifty-four amino acids; most are much larger. To summarize, the trilogy of protein synthesis is:

$$DNA \rightarrow RNA \rightarrow protein$$

Genetic engineering, the manipulation of the molecule that contains within its four bases all of the characteristics of an organism, is a powerful tool, but it is not entirely new. Plant and animal breeders have fostered controlled breeding for hundreds of years and have been able to select for traits they have desired. In other words, because each trait is determined by a gene or group of genes (i.e., by particular DNA sequences), breeders, by laborious, time-consuming (years), and often trial-and-error forced matings have caused the desired DNA from each of the selected parents to be transmitted to and expressed in the offspring. Modern genetic engineers are directly manipulating the genetic material at the cellular and molecular levels; they do not have to wait for years for the results of a cross (controlled breeding) between organisms to become apparent.

RECOMBINANT DNA TECHNOLOGY

There are several new biotechnologies used in genetic engineering; one that appears especially promising is recombinant DNA technology or gene splicing, in which selected genes from a donor can be isolated, inserted into a vector's DNA, amplified, and incorporated into the genetic material (genome) of a suitable host. The host, then, will carry and express its own DNA and the donor's DNA.

The first step in gene splicing is to isolate fragments of DNA from a donor with the desired gene. The second step is to select a vector for the desired gene. The most frequently used vector is the *Escherichia coli* (a bacterium that resides in the human intestine) plasmid. *E. coli* is ubiquitous, well known, thoroughly studied, and easily manipulated in the laboratory. A plasmid is a circular DNA molecule not associated with a chromosome (figure 4.12). Assume a plasmid as in figure 4.13. The sequence GAATTC on one strand of DNA binds to the sequence CTTAAG on the complementary strand of the double helix. *X* is any base and *Y* is the base complementary to *X*. The plasmid and the isolated DNA fragment are treated with the same restriction enzyme, an enzyme which cleaves double-stranded DNA at precise locations, that is, at precise sites determined by the base sequence. In the hypothetical case being presented here the restriction enzyme cleaves between G and A. The result from cleaving the plasmid is AATTCXXXXXXXXXXXXXXXXXXG for one chain, while the complementary chain would be GYYYYYYYYYYYYYYYYYYYCTTAA. A staggered cut identical to that created in the plasmid occurs when the isolated DNA fragment is treated with restriction enzyme; restriction enzyme, because of its specificity for cleaving between certain bases (in our example, between G and A), produces DNA strands with termini of AATTC . . . . . . or CTTAA . . . . . Thus, linear dou-

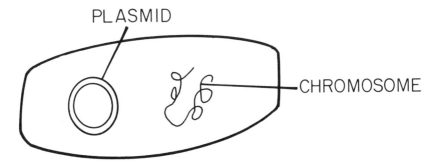

Figure 4.12 *E. coli* Bacterium

Figure 4.13 Plasmid

ble-stranded DNA molecules are produced by both the plasmid and the isolated fragment.

plasmid	fragment
AATTCXXXXXX . . . XXXG	AATTCXXXXX . . . XXXG
GYYYYYY . . . YYYCTTAA	GYYYYY . . . YYYCTTAA

At the end of each double-stranded molecule is a "sticky end," in reality a single-stranded DNA terminus which is available for base pairing with a complementary single-stranded DNA terminus.

An illustrative recapitulation appears in figure 4.14. The joining together (ligation) of the linear DNA molecules into an intact double-stranded molecule is enzymatically mediated by the enzyme DNA ligase. The recombinant (hybrid) DNA molecule need not be comprised of one-half plasmid and one-half fragment. More commonly a smaller section of fragment from the donor, carrying from one to a few genes, is spliced into the plasmid.

Suppose that the isolated fragment incorporated into the plasmid, in the above example, had been the gene for the production of the protein insulin. A method must be found for amplifying the gene for the synthesis of insulin, that is, for propagating the recombinant DNA molecule along with its spliced-in gene for insulin production. The plasmid, with its inserted gene fragment, acts as a

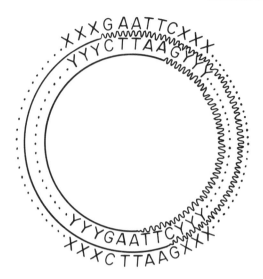

Figure 4.14 Recombinant DNA

vector. It reenters the *E. coli* cell. Subsequent replication of the recombinant DNA is linked to the duplication of the *E. coli* cell (figure 4.15).

Now there are many copies of the gene for insulin production in the *E. coli* cells; when the bacteria are stimulated to commence synthesizing protein, and there are ingenious tricks to get them to do this, insulin is produced by the previously outlined procedure: DNA → mRNA → protein. The synthesis of proteins other than insulin—antibodies, hormones, hemoglobin, vaccines—can also be enhanced.

Let us return to the insulin example and explore one of the tricks used to initiate its production. The gene for the production of insulin is chemically synthesized in the laboratory. Biotechnologists have identified the precise sequence of bases in the insulin gene by one of two ways: (1) They have isolated the gene and chemically determined its sequence of bases—once a laborious process but now readily accomplished with the aid of DNA-sequencing machinery. (2) They have determined the sequence of amino acids in insulin and, knowing what triplet of bases (codon) codes for each amino acid, they have inferred the sequence of bases in the insulin gene.

The gene for insulin is synthesized in the laboratory with sticky ends complementary to those resulting from the staggered cuts caused by restriction enzyme acting on an isolated *E. coli* plasmid (figure 4.16). Some genes may be stimulated to become active when there is a need for their protein product. For example, the gene for lactose (milk sugar) breakdown only becomes active when lactose is available to induce it. If the gene for lactose utilization is synthesized

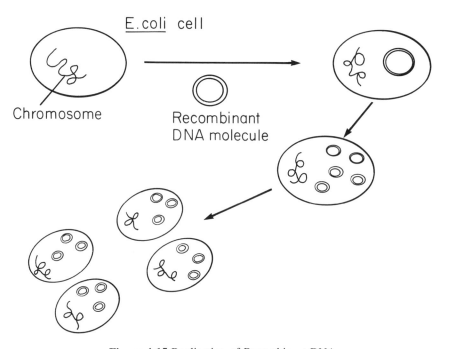

Figure 4.15 Replication of Recombinant DNA

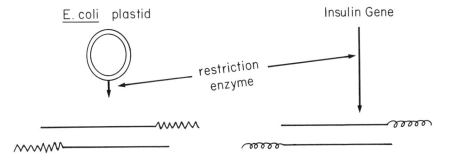

Figure 4.16 Restriction Enzyme Activity

with sticky ends complementary to the protruding sticky ends of the gene for insulin production, then the two genes can be spliced (figure 4.17). The remaining sticky ends, one from the insulin gene and the other from the lactose utilization gene, can now be recombined with the restriction enzyme-treated bacterial plasmid (figure 4.18).

The recombinant DNA is caused to replicate in *E. coli* and by repeated cell divisions many *E. coli* cells with enclosed recombinant DNA molecules are produced. In this manner recombinant DNA molecules are cloned. If one wants to activate the insulin-producing gene one can treat the *E. coli* cells with lactose which turns on the chemically synthesized coding sequence for the proteins of lactose utilization. Since both the lactose gene and the insulin gene are turned on, a protein—part lactose utilization protein, part insulin—is made. Straightforward procedures are available for the cleavage of this mixed protein and the release of the desired insulin. The beauty of all of this is that a genetically engineered plasmid from a bacterium is reinserted into the bacterium which then becomes a biological factory for the fabrication of large quantities of a desired protein. Many genes, natural or synthetic, have been spliced into a plasmid or into some other vector (e.g., into a bacteriophage, a virus that infects a bacterium) to create a recombinant DNA molecule.

In November 1987 the Food and Drug Administration approved tissue plasminogen activator (TPA), a drug designed to be used immediately after heart attacks to dissolve blood clots. TPA is manufactured in the body in minuscule amounts which are insufficient for therapeutic purposes. In 1982 scientists at Genentech, Inc. determined that TPA was comprised of 527 amino acids and they isolated the gene governing its production. Using recombinant DNA techniques that gene was implanted into hamster ovary cells so that the cells produced large amounts of TPA. Pharmaceutical industry analysts expect TPA to become the most successful health product thus far developed by genetic engineering, with annual sales of $35 to 40 million by the end of 1987 alone. TPA, which is being marketed as Activase, is certainly the "millennium" for the more

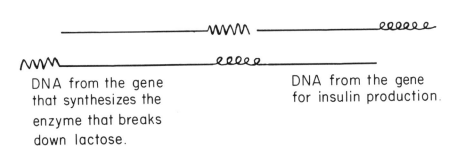

DNA from the gene
that synthesizes the
enzyme that breaks
down lactose.

DNA from the gene
for insulin production.

Figure 4.17 Gene Splicing

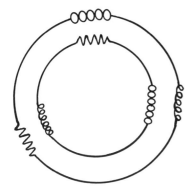

Insulin gene with attached
lactose inducible gene for
lactose utilization spliced
into plasmid DNA

Figure 4.18

than one and a quarter million Americans who each year require emergency treatment of heart attacks. On November 13, 1987, Paine Webber Development Corporation congratulated Genentech, Inc. on the announcement of FDA approval of the revolutionary new heart drug, the development of which they and their investors had participated in.

It is estimated that more than one-half of the new drugs to be developed in the United States in the coming years will be the result of genetic engineering. For example:

- recombinant erythropoietin for anemia patients with kidney disease
- recombinant beta globin, a part of hemoglobin, for the cure of diseases of the blood
- recombinant CD4, a natural protein which may block infection by the virus that causes AIDS
- recombinant Factor IX, a protein needed by some hemophiliacs
- recombinant alpha-1-antitrypsin, a protein which may be used to treat emphysema

GENE SPLICING IN PLANTS

It is not feasible to establish new genes in plants by employing *E. coli* recombinant DNA, because this bacterium does not reside in plants. There is a soil-borne bacterium, *Agrobacterium tumefaciens,* that infects plants at wound sites and causes tumors. *A. tumefaciens,* then, is a natural vector for introducing desired genes into plants and its existence has been central to the explosive growth of plant biotechnology.

The *A. tumefaciens* genes which induce the formation of a tumor are carried on a plasmid, the Ti or *tumor inducing* plasmid. Ti becomes incorporated into the genetic material of the host cell; once incorporated there is no further require-ment for the vector organism, *A. tumefaciens,* for tumor production. Bio-technologists have isolated Ti plasmids and have altered the genes for tumor production so that the plasmids' ability to induce tumors is abolished. The isolated and altered plasmids are treated with restriction enzymes so that sticky ends are formed on linear DNA strands. Natural DNA fragments containing the gene to be spliced into the particular Ti plasmid are treated with the same restriction enzymes so that complementary single-stranded sticky ends are pro-duced. Alternatively, a synthetic gene, with the desired complementary stag-gered bases, is fabricated in the laboratory. The modified Ti plasmid and the gene to be inserted are ligated using the enzyme DNA ligase. The recombinant DNA molecule is forced to infect an *E. coli* cell where amplification (cloning) takes place. One of the cloned recombinant DNA molecules is reinserted into an *A. tumefaciens.* The bacterium, with its newly modified Ti plasmid, infects an isolated plant cell which is growing in a defined nutrient medium under aseptic conditions (tissue culture). The Ti plasmid is incorporated into the host cell's genetic material and a plant with new genes is created.

There are two important attributes which make plants especially suitable orga-nisms for genetic engineering. The first is the ability of researchers to chemically remove the cellulose cell wall of plant cells and to be left with a viable pro-toplast. Protoplasts, plant cells without their cell walls, can be infected by Ti plasmids in tissue culture. The second extraordinary and unique feature of plant cells is their totipotency. Highly specialized plant cells in culture lose their specialized features and revert to an embryonic condition; thus, any isolated plant cell could conceivably give rise to an entire plant. The insertion of new DNA into a plant cell leads to the formation of a hybrid plant, one that exhibits old and new characteristics. For example, the Ti plasmid has been used to transfer (the genes for) herbicide resistance into conifers and tobacco. In the latter case that gene which confers resistance to Roundup® (a herbicide) has been isolated from the bacterium *Salmonella typhinurum,* recombined with the Ti plasmid, and then incorporated into the genetic material of tobacco.

A major barrier to the widespread use of recombinant DNA technology to engineer new cereal crops has been the inability to regenerate cells of these crops from protoplasts and the apparent inability to use *A. tumefaciens* as a vector to transplant genes. Experiments on corn and rice reported in 1987 have successful-ly bypassed these two obstacles and a new era of endowing these major crops with useful characteristics is upon us. For those plants that are not yet susceptible to infection by *A. tumefaciens* other vectors are used, for example, the Ri (*root* *i*nducing) plasmid of *A. rhizogenes* or the cauliflower mosaic virus.

As a result of the biotechnological revolution U.S. farmers can expect to increase their yields, lower their prices, and remain competitive in world mar-kets. There will be:

- leaner pigs
- chickens that lay more eggs
- cows that produce more milk of a more nutritious nature
- plants that produce their own pesticides
- tomato plants that produce a protein lethal to hornworms and other leaf-eating caterpillars
- corn varieties rich in sugar
- trees and shrubs for arid climates
- fruits and vegetables richer in vitamins and other nutrients
- a strain of bacteria designed to prevent frost formation in leaves during the early growing season

SUMMARY

The business of biotechnology has grown rapidly since 1972 and analysts predict that it will become a vast and profitable enterprise in the next two decades, perhaps generating sales of up to thirty billion dollars. In the early stages most of the effort of the biotechnology companies in the United States was devoted to engineering new drugs for humans, but much of the most promising recent advancements have been in agriculture. These advances have proceeded because the process of genetic engineering is complex, time-consuming, and expensive and advancements will be forthcoming primarily in those areas where companies, which exist to make money, can do so.

Biotechnology stocks are given to wild swings on the stock markets. Purchasers are alternatively overly enthusiastic or too pessimistic. In the great bull market of January 1987 13 percent of the rise in value was due to genetic engineering stocks, much of which was given back in the collapse of October 1987. At any rate biotechnology is now here, and products are moving from the laboratory to the marketplace. Major corporations are planning and managing their biotechnology activity so that they may be positioned to earn maximum profit in the coming decades.

It seems clear that biotechnology offers a tremendous opportunity for producing needed products efficiently and without harmful side effects. There is some resistance, even antagonism, to this new technology, which has perhaps been generated by the fear that grave environmental disasters and public health hazards will result. Most of these fears are based on an ignorance of biotechnology, a generalized mistrust of high technology, and the conviction that people should not be creating new forms of life. But the anxiety will recede as the potential is realized. The biotechnological revolution is inexorable and will yield everlasting benefits which can barely be imagined today.

NOTE

1. J. J. Cohrssen, "USA Biotechnology Policy," *American Biotechnology Lab*, January 1988, pp. 22, 24, 26–27; I. H. Miller, "Federal Regulation of Products of the New Biotechnology," *American Biotechnology Lab*, January 1988, pp. 38–43.

REFERENCES

Cohrssen, J. J. "USA Biotechnology Policy," *American Biotechnology Lab*, January 1988, pp. 22, 24, 26–27.
Council of the National Academy of Sciences. *Introduction of Recombinant DNA-Engineered Organisms into the Environment: Key Issues*. Washington, D.C.: National Academy Press, 1987.
Doolittle, Russell F. "Proteins," in *The Molecules of Life*. New York: W. H. Freeman and Co., 1985.
Felsenfeld, Gary. "DNA," in *The Molecules of Life*. New York: W. H. Freeman and Co., 1985.
Miller, I. H. "Federal Regulation of Products of the New Biotechnology," *American Biotechnology Lab*, January 1988, pp. 38–43.
Olsen, Steve. *Biotechnology: An Industry Comes of Age*. Washington, D.C.: National Academy Press, 1986.
Weinberg, Robert A. "The Molecules of Life," in *The Molecules of Life*. New York: W. H. Freeman and Co., 1985.

5

Frontiers in Biophysics: Today's Science for Tomorrow's Technology

Jay Newman

Our understanding of some of the fundamental scientific questions of life has increased dramatically in the recent past primarily because of the rapid development of new methods for studying biological systems. In this chapter we will consider a subset of these questions and in particular show the role laser spectroscopy has played in developing current views. It is hoped that the reader will gain an appreciation not only for the complexity of the living world, but also for the ingenuity of modern science and the possible technological offshoots that are yet to blossom from these efforts.

We will begin with a brief discussion of the nature of visible radiation and its interactions with matter. The basic physical ideas behind several areas of spectroscopy will be described, concentrating on the types of information that can be obtained in the study of biological material. In subsequent sections we will consider a number of areas in modern biophysics. The focus will be on a general view of the current working model of the system, the spectroscopic methods employed, and some representative examples of their application. After our overview of these areas of science, we will discuss various technological realities and possibilities for the future based on current or anticipated research.

INTERACTIONS OF LIGHT WITH MATTER

Visible light is a very small portion of the electromagnetic spectrum of radiation. The modern quantum mechanical view of radiation pictures it to be made of photons, quanta or packets of energy, which travel at the speed of light and can exhibit particle or wave properties depending upon their interactions with matter. Visible photons have energies of a few electron volts (one eV is the energy gained by an electron after acceleration through one volt) which is also a typical energy for a transition of an outer, more weakly bound "valence" electron between two of its possible energy states. It is precisely this fact which is the basis for the use of visible light as a probe of atomic and molecular structure and interactions.

When visible light is incident on a material medium (e.g., a thin section of tissue or a solution of macromolecules), some fraction of the photons interact with the molecules of the medium and are either absorbed or scattered while the remaining photons pass through. The dominant interaction between radiation and matter in the visible region of the spectrum is scattering. Scattering may be thought of as absorption of a photon followed by re-emission of a photon of the same or different energy. The absorbed photon increases the energy of the molecule. The additional energy may or may not correspond to one of the possible excited states of the molecule. If the additional photon energy does not produce a transition to an allowed state, the short-lived excited state is called a "virtual" state and the system rapidly decays back to a lower-energy stable state by one of several modes.

The molecule may emit one photon of the same energy (elastic scattering), returning to its original state. Another possibility is that the molecule returns to a higher or lower energy state with the emission of either a lower (Stokes) or higher (anti-Stokes) energy photon, respectively. This effect is called Raman scattering and, since the intensities or numbers of these emitted photons are much less than for elastic scattering, Raman scattering has only been a useful tool since the advent of high-powered lasers. A third possible mechanism is the absorption of a photon promoting the molecule to a real excited state, followed by some loss of energy via collisions and subsequent emission of a lower-energy photon. This process is called fluorescence (or phosphorescence if the final excited state has a long lifetime) and has become a major tool in biophysical research. A final possibility is that the molecule returns to its ground state without the emission of any photons. Instead, energy is lost via collisions with solvent or other molecules and these result in thermal heating of the sample with an associated rise in temperature. These various interaction mechanisms are summarized schematically in figure 5.1.

We now return to several of the interactions mentioned in order to survey the types of information available from measurements of biological material. Let us begin with the elastic scattering process. If the particles (macromolecules or perhaps small viruses) are small compared to the wavelength of visible light (about five hundred nanometers or five hundred-billionths of a meter), the elastic scattering in the measurement plane will be directionally isotropic. This type of scattering is termed Rayleigh scattering, and was first described by Lord

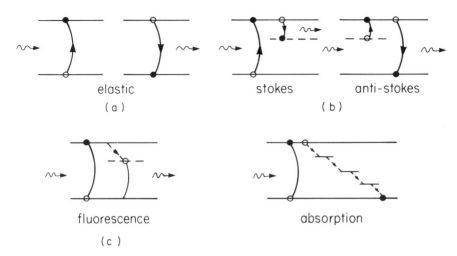

elastic   stokes   anti-stokes

(a)   (b)

fluorescence   absorption

(c)

Figure 5.1 The various interactions of light with matter. Solid curves indicate transitions due to the absorption (upward) or emission (downward) of a photon, while dashed curves indicate loss of energy via collisions with no emission of light. Photons are indicated by wiggly arrows. See the text for a further discussion of each process.

Rayleigh in 1890. The intensity of the scattered light is strongly dependent on the wavelength, varying as the inverse of the wavelength raised to the fourth power. This phenomenon explains the blue color of the sky and the appearance of a brilliant red sunset. Light from the sun is scattered to our eyes from the atmosphere with the shorter blue wavelengths being scattered more. When we observe a sunset, the same scattering occurs leaving the direct rays from the sun with a predominant longer red wavelength. The intensity of the scattered light is also dependent on the molecular weight, size, and the interactions between the scatterers. For larger scatterers, comparable to the wavelength of light, the scattered light is no longer isotropic but will generally be predominantly scattered in the forward direction. Various theories are available to describe the scattering from standard-shaped molecules such as spheres and rods. In general, elastic light scattering measurements of the intensity as a function of the scattering angle and the concentration of macromolecules in suspension can yield information on a scatterer's molecular weight, size, shape, and interactions with other scatterers.

If, instead of simply measuring the average light intensity scattered from a sample, one also measures the time dependence of the fluctuations in the intensity, further information is obtained on the dynamical motions of the scatterers. This technique is called dynamic light scattering or intensity fluctuation spectroscopy. The origin of the intensity fluctuations is the time-varying relation between the light scattered from different scatterers or even from different portions of the same scatterer if it has dimensions comparable to the wavelength of light. The light from different scatterers adds to be brighter or cancels to be darker, depending upon the relative positions of the molecules. Thus, the intensity of light fluctuates as the scatterers move about due to the thermal driving force of Brownian motion. This is the constant random motion produced by collisions with solvent molecules; the time scales of the intensity fluctuations can be analyzed to determine the diffusion coefficients of the scatterers. Information can then be obtained, for example, on the size, shape, and intramolecular motions due to flexibility of the molecule. The technique can be used to monitor changes in these parameters as temperature, solvent, pH, and so on, are varied in a nonperturbative manner. There are many examples of the application of this technique in the study of macromolecules or complex assemblies such as muscle filaments.

The Raman effect has been used mostly in the study of macromolecules in solution to obtain local molecular bonding information. The frequency shifts and intensities of the Stokes lines are characteristic of the types and concentrations of various atomic bonds (e.g., carbon-oxygen, peptide, etc.) present in the sample. These studies have been particularly useful for macromolecules in which there is a chromophore, a particular group in the molecule which can be strongly excited by the incident light. These may be native metal atoms, such as copper or iron (found in many proteins), or they may be added colored enzymes or dyes that bind to specific groups on the macromolecule and absorb much light. Changes in the Raman spectra can be correlated with local environmental changes in the region of the strong absorber and can be used to monitor the local conformation of the macromolecule.

Fluorescence is a more specific type of interaction than elastic scattering. With monochromatic light illuminating a sample, only those molecules which can absorb the photon energy and end up in a real excited state will be involved in generating fluorescence. In naturally occurring biological materials, the major fluorescent molecules are limited to those which have a ring-structure, such as the amino acids tryptophan and tyrosine which are natural building blocks in many proteins. The amount of fluorescence obtained from such ''intrinsic fluorophores'' contained in a larger macromolecular structure depends strongly on the local chemical environment, including factors such as pH and the electrical charge of neighboring groups of the molecule; and the degree of ''quenching,'' or diminishing of the fluorescent signal, can be used as a probe of the local environment of the fluorophore.

To make the fluorescence technique applicable when no fluorescent group is present in the native molecule, extrinsic fluorophores may be attached to a molecule of interest at a particular site in order to probe the local environment. A large catalog of such fluorescent molecules has been developed with recipes for attachment at various binding sites. In the discussion so far we have implicitly assumed that the fluorophore which absorbed a photon was the same group that emitted the fluorescent photon. It is also possible for an excited fluorophore to transfer its energy to a second nearby fluor (up to ten nanometers or so apart) which then emits a fluorescent photon. This resonant transfer of energy can be used as a meter stick to measure distances between these groups since the interaction is a strong function of the separation distance (inverse sixth power). Other studies make use of the polarization direction of the light (the direction in which the electric field oscillates) to gain information about the rotational motions of fluorescent groups. Typically fluors are rigidly attached to a portion of a macromolecule, and the time dependence of the fluorescent signal in two polarization directions is used to deduce the rotational motion of that segment of the molecule. We will later see applications of fluorescence techniques in the study of muscle proteins, membrane composition, and dynamics and cell motility.

NUCLEIC ACIDS AND PROTEINS

Modern biophysical research has two complementary approaches to the study of biological materials. One approach has been to study native *in vivo* biological systems, including entire organisms, organs, or complex functional assemblies, such as nerve or muscle cells. In recent years new methods of isolating individual component macromolecules in highly purified form have allowed rapid progress in the second approach, the study of *in vitro* systems. The assumed working philosophy of much *in vitro* research has been that a detailed understanding of the structure and function of the component parts and the control mechanisms which regulate the functioning should allow one to more easily understand the whole. In fact, many model systems, simple representations of the whole, have been used quite successfully. As an example, one can single out artificial membranes that have been studied for their electrical, osmotic, and hydrodynamic properties under controlled conditions and which have been used to make artificial cells (vesicles). It should be pointed out initially that even the simplest system in biology can be extremely complex and that many independent approaches using different experimental techniques are clearly desirable. In this section we will discuss aspects of the basic building blocks of all biomaterials— proteins and nucleic acids.

Recent progress in macromolecular studies probably had its origin in new biochemical techniques in chromatography and electrophoresis which have enabled researchers to isolate a protein or nucleic acid in its functional state and to characterize its purity and activity (functionality). Chromatography is used to separate different molecules based on their size or molecular weight, electric charge, or interactions with other specific molecules. For large macromolecules, gel chromatography has become a standard method of purification. It works by a sieving process in which the macromolecules flow, under gravity or pressure, through a gel matrix with the larger molecules flowing faster since the smaller ones follow a more tortuous path, entering the pores of the gel not accessible to the larger molecules. The process is a graded one and, in fact, one can empirically determine molecular weights to within a few percent. A large number of gels made from either agarose, dextran, or polyacrylamide are available with different ranges of pore sizes. They may be used to fractionate and characterize proteins and other macromolecules with molecular weights ranging up to over several hundred million atomic mass units.

Perhaps the most significant addition to the arsenal of preparative techniques is affinity chromatography. In this method one uses the specific interaction between two molecules (e.g., the antibody-antigen interaction) in order to purify a molecule. One of the molecules is bound to the column matrix material and when a mixture of molecules (e.g., whole cell extracts) are passed through the column, only the second specifically recognized molecule is bound to the matrix. The column is then washed by flowing copious amounts of solvent through it in order to remove all other material, and the specific molecule is then recovered.

Electrophoresis is the forced migration of a charged molecule in an electric field. The technique has become very sophisticated in its ability to separate molecules based on their size. Migration is usually through a gel network of agarose or polyacrylamide with either the native molecule or a molecule coated with SDS (sodium dodecyl sulfate) as the sample. All SDS-coated proteins have the same charge per unit length and therefore move in an electric field according to their size or molecular weight. This is a very fast, cheap, and relatively accurate method to determine molecular weights for proteins. New variations of electrophoresis using complex arrays of pulsed electric fields have been used to successfully separate very large DNA molecules with molecular weights of several billion.

Proteins and nucleic acids are formed from a small number of basic building blocks. An ordered linear sequence of covalently bound amino acids, of which there are about twenty with molecular weights of about one-hundred (in units of the weight of a hydrogen atom), form all of the proteins. Similarly, for DNA (deoxyribonucleic acid) and RNA (ribonucleic acid) there are four bases which form the backbone of each of the two strands of the double helical polymer. The term *primary structure* is used to indicate the linear sequence of the subunits in these structures. *Secondary structure* refers to the regular repeating array along the backbone or axis of each chain. Thus, for example, in the case of the B-form of DNA the secondary structure refers to the Watson-Crick helix. The term *tertiary structure* refers to the folding in space of the backbone chain and the bonding which holds it in shape. A further hierarchy of structural characterization, *quaternary,* is reserved for molecules which have more than one independent chain subunit, as, for example, in hemoglobin.

For DNA the main information content resides in the primary structure, the specific sequence of bases along either one of the strands. The general mechanism for coding the information needed to manufacture proteins has been known since the mid-1960s. Three consecutive bases code for a particular amino acid and have been aptly termed a "codon." Since there are 3^4 or sixty-four possible permutations of the four bases to form a codon, there is some degeneracy in the code as well as some codons which indicate terminations.

In proteins, the primary sequence leads to folding of the backbone of the molecule into specific secondary and tertiary structures which play a role in the functioning of the protein. Structure may affect protein function by determining protein strength (as, for example, in collagen of tendons and bone matrix, a triple helix), or simply by determining a unique characteristic shape which may be recognized by other proteins (as, for example, in enzymes or antibodies). Some proteins, such as actin, are extremely well designed and have had very little evolutionary change over hundreds of millions of years. The overall three-dimensional structure of the proteins is therefore of great importance in understanding their functioning. Similar questions on the tertiary structure of DNA are also important in understanding the packaging of DNA inside the confines of the nucleus of a cell.

As typical examples of the application of laser spectroscopic techniques to the study of macromolecules, we will consider two separate areas: the muscle proteins actin and myosin, and the conformation and dynamics of DNA.

Actin and Myosin. These are the two major protein constituents of muscle; it is the interaction between actin and myosin which is responsible for generating force in a muscle. Filamentous actin, composed of about four hundred identical globular actin subunits, together with several other proteins, forms a thin filament. These interdigitate with thicker myosin-containing filaments. An array of thin and thick filaments form the basic building block, called the sarcomere, which is repeated throughout the many myofibrils which make up a muscle.

One of the key problems in muscle research is to understand the detailed mechanism of force generation. A better understanding of the ability of a muscle cell to exert force will greatly aid our thinking about various diseased states of muscle. It has been known for some time that the globular sections of the myosin molecule which protrude from the axis of the thick filaments (myosin "heads") make attachments with the actin molecules on the thin filaments and produce a relative "sliding" of the thick and thin filaments, thus shortening the muscle fiber (see figure 5.2). The problem is a very complex one, involving the binding of several ions and small regulating molecules. The detailed array of the actin and myosin molecules on their filaments, the location of the actin-actin and myosin-myosin binding sites, the binding sites for calcium and magnesium ions, the ATP (adenosine triphosphate, the ubiquitous energy-storing molecule) binding sites, and the relation between the kinetics of the complex chemical cycle and the mechanical force generation have all been studied. Several models have been

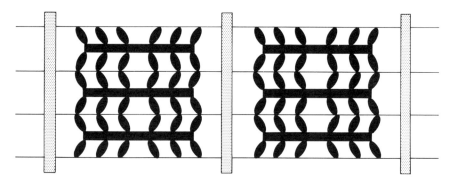

Figure 5.2 Schematic representation of a muscle fiber showing two repeating subunits or sarcomeres. The interdigitating thick and thin filaments interact via the myosin heads (cross-bridges), here shown as ovals.

developed for the origin of the molecular force, including one in which a spring-like hinge region of the myosin molecule has its stiffness regulated by conformational changes in that region. Such theories have their basis in a large array of data on the physical structure of actin and myosin and on their dynamics and interactions both *in vitro* and in a muscle fiber.

Fluorescent studies of myosin, in particular, have provided much of the data on its structure. Probes rigidly attached at specific sites have been used as orientation markers in the molecule. This can be done by measuring the fluorescence intensity at a 90-degree scattering angle for two orthogonal polarization directions after excitation along one of these. If during the fluorescence lifetime of the probe significant orientational motion has occurred, the fluorescence signal will be depolarized, that is, will decrease along the original axis and increase along the second. The degree of depolarization, determined with continuous or pulsed laser light, can be related to the degree of rotational mobility of the fluor on the time scale of its fluorescence lifetime (at most on the order of milliseconds). Since the fluor is rigidly attached, it is likely that the connected portion of the molecule has the same rotational mobility. This type of measurement has been used to investigate the degree of rotational flexibility of myosin heads under resting, contracting, or rigor solvent conditions. Only under rigor are the heads immobilized, indicating that the attachment time is short compared to the lifetime of the probe.

Deoxyribonucleic Acid. Mammalian cells have typically about 6 picograms (10^{-12} g or one-millionth of a millionth of a gram) of DNA corresponding to about 5.5 billion nucleotides, or bases, which if stretched out would be about two meters long. A typical nuclear dimension is less than one-millionth this size so one can immediately appreciate the packaging problem. Chromosomal DNA is actually a complex of DNA with (histone) proteins. These proteins are positively charged and serve to shield the high negative charge on the DNA and allow it to fold up in a characteristic compact state. Studies on the flexibility, conformation, and charge interactions of DNA *in vitro* have revealed many interesting properties.

Dynamic light scattering can determine diffusion coefficients of molecules rapidly without perturbing them. Studies of the diffusion of DNA as a function of the ionic conditions have shown that as the salt concentration is decreased an abrupt collapse of the DNA occurs. The DNA appears to form a toroidal shape which is very compact. An accepted theoretical explanation has emerged in terms of a condensation of the excess counterion charge from the solvent, producing a collapsed molecule, once the average interaction energy between ions becomes greater than the thermal energy. Other studies have examined the stiffness of DNA which is characterized by a parameter called the persistence length, related to the bending rigidity. The dependence of DNA stiffness on ionic environment and the size of the DNA has been studied by light scattering (dynamic and static), and more sophisticated theoretical models have been developed which include the twisting as well as the bending rigidity. These studies have benefited greatly from the ability to make samples of precisely uniform length DNA fragments from larger DNA molecules using restriction enzymes which cut DNA at only specific sequences of nucleotides.

As a final example of DNA studies, we mention dynamic light scattering measurements on supercoiled (superhelical) DNA. These are covalently closed circles of the usual double-helical DNA which are torsionally strained due to a net number of twists that partially unwind the double-helical structure. Such plasmid DNA molecules are found in bacteria, viruses, and mitochondria, and evidence for superhelical turns in various stages of the production and transcription of DNA have been reported, so that there is general interest in the conformation of these DNAs. Different equilibrium conformations have been observed with several distinct properties, including varying torsional rigidities, when immersed in different buffer ions. Cooperative conversions between such configurations provide a mechanism for long-distance communication between a bound regulatory protein and a site along the DNA. Various fluorescent molecules have been used as intercalating agents which bind to the supercoiled DNAs and produce additional winding or unwinding of the supercoil. These reagents have allowed such detailed studies as the separation of DNAs with different degrees of supercoiling with a variant of gel electrophoresis and the physical study of the effect of unwinding on the overall conformation. Native enzymes, DNA-gyrase and nicking-closing enzyme, isolated from various sources, have been found to interact with DNA in a complex manner to nick or cut a single strand of the

DNA, introduce a rotation of one strand about the other, and to reanneal the strands resulting in a net change to the superhelical winding. These amazing enzymes appear to be involved in the decoding process.

Such detailed studies of proteins and DNA result in a more complete knowledge of what we know as life. They allow us to understand the mechanisms that lead to disease and provide the framework in which to develop vaccines and other preventative or curative measures.

MOLECULAR PHOTOBIOLOGY: CHLOROPHYLL

In this section we shall see an overview of the highly efficient and complex molecular mechanisms involved in the conversion of solar energy into chemical forms of stored energy. Our fundamental understanding of these processes of energy conversion has, and will undoubtedly further, play a major role in improving the efficiency and design of various solar energy sources. These, collectively, have been called *in vitro* photosynthetic processes since they do not involve living matter.

Photosynthesis functions to combine carbon dioxide and water, utilizing chlorophyll and light, in order to generate oxygen and carbohydrates with an overall efficiency of 30 to 40 percent. In plants and most algae, photosynthesis occurs in organelles called chloroplasts, flattened vesicles with dimensions of $2-4 \times 5-10$ micrometers, in which folded membrane regions containing chlorophyll ($5-10$ percent) and other pigments are the photosynthetic centers. Several forms of chlorophyll exist, all of which contain a large ring structure similar to that in hemoglobin, but containing magnesium in place of iron. Several hundred chlorophyll molecules together form the basic reaction centers at which chemical transformations occur. The primary reactions in photosynthesis involve the production, in the presence of light, of a reductant or electron donor, the molecule NADPH (the reduced form of NADP or nicotinamide adenine dinucleotide phosphate) in green plants, and the subsequent utilization of this reductant, in the absence of light, to synthesize carbohydrates by the reduction of carbon dioxide.

In green plants two primary reactions are needed to produce NADPH, and the series of reactions and molecules involved are termed Photosystems I and II. Each of these photosystems consists of a number of so-called accessory pigments (including carotenoids, secondary forms of chlorophyll, and, in algae, phycobilins) and reaction centers (consisting of chlorophyll a in green plants and bacteriochlorophyll in photosynthetic bacteria). One form of accessory pigment, the antenna molecules, absorb photons of light and transfer their energy to the reaction centers with a remarkable efficiency of over 90 percent. There are typically several hundred antenna molecules per reaction center in plants and up to several thousand per reaction center in certain green bacteria. The details of the energy transmission from these molecules to the reaction centers has been studied in great detail, particularly in certain bacterial systems for which large quantities of these antenna molecules can be purified, although the physical details are still poorly understood. The extremely high efficiency of photosynthesis, including regulatory mechanisms that respond to light intensity and spectral distribution changes, is largely due to the antenna molecules. These are held in proteins with orientations and separations that enhance the rapid energy transfer process. A detailed understanding of this process could lead to significant new methods to harness solar energy more efficiently.

The two photosystems of green plants each have a separate function which is coupled through an electron transport chain of events called the "Z" scheme. Photosystem II's role in the overall photosynthesis process is to produce both a strong oxidant or electron acceptor named Z, which chemically oxidizes water to molecular oxygen, and a relatively weak reductant named Q. Photosystem I's function is to produce a strong reductant, named X, which can reduce NADP to NADPH, and a weak oxidant, named $P700$. The weak products Q and $P700$ interact via an electron transport scheme which produces ATP while NADPH goes on, in the dark reactions which follow, to produce carbohydrates from carbon dioxide. These are the bare outlines of a very complex chain of events involving many different molecules; some of the details of kinetic rates and conformations have been emerging from recent spectroscopic studies. However, relatively few primary molecular studies have been carried out on green plant photosystems because of their complexity and because of the difficulty in purifying the reaction centers without any antenna molecules.

The bulk of the studies on the primary mechanisms of photosynthesis have been carried out on bacterial systems because there is only one photosystem present with one type of reaction center. The reaction centers include four molecules of bacteriochlorophyll and a handful of other proteins. In these photosynthetic bacteria, water is not oxidized to produce oxygen but the single photosystem present is quite similar to Photosystem I in green plants. An advantage in the use of bacteria to study photosynthesis is that, unlike the green plants, bacteria can use other sources of energy to survive and mutant strains can be produced and studied which lack certain facets of the photosynthetic function. In 1983 the three-dimensional structure of an entire bacterial reaction center was determined by X-ray diffraction from crystals of the proteins. This achievement represents the first (and as yet only) atomic structural determination of an integral membrane protein. Various spectroscopic techniques have elucidated the conformational changes that occur after interaction with a photon and the time scales involved, ranging from subpicoseconds to milliseconds. These steps are quite complex and remarkable in that over 98 percent of the energy present in the photons absorbed by the reaction centers is captured, and about 50 percent of it is "stored" in the electric charge separations which result. An understanding of the detailed physics involved in photosynthesis will undoubtedly lead to developments in the broad areas of *in vitro* photosynthetic processes. It will also provide new tools in areas such as genetic engineering manipulations to incorporate features of photosynthesis into nonphotosynthetic organisms, or in areas of modern technological instrumentation which require fast, high-efficiency light detection.

BIOLOGICAL MEMBRANES

Biological membranes have three general functions: (1) they form the boundary of cells and cell organelles, creating and maintaining definite concentrations of chemical components by both passive (diffusion) and active (energy-requiring) transport; (2) they act as a substrate for many chemical reactions that involve the enzymes incorporated in or bound to the membrane surface, including those which govern ion transport across the membrane; and (3) they serve other specific functions, such as providing electrical insulation around nerve cells or the large surface areas needed for the grana of chloroplasts and the outer segments of rod cells. Membranes make up from a few percent to as much as 80 percent of the dry cell mass in some eukaryotic (nucleus-containing) cells. Information on various aspects of the structure and functioning of membranes will lead to a large array of technological applications both in nonbiological membrane technology and in other areas which will benefit from improved measurement techniques. Specifically, one important area is the development of biodegradable packaging materials with important properties such as strength, porosity, and flexibility. Some of these applications will be discussed in the final section of this chapter.

The picture of membrane structure has changed dramatically in the past fifteen years, from a static picture of a cell boundary with proteins and other molecules stuck to the surface to a dynamic picture of proteins floating in a viscous medium (with viscosity about 100 times that of water, similar to that of olive oil) and able to diffuse distances of about 10 micrometers per minute. The basic unit of the membrane is a double sheet or bilayer composed of lipids with hydrophilic (water-seeking) polar heads and long hydrophobic (water-repelling) hydrocarbon tails (see figure 5.3). The polar heads orient in two parallel planes exposed to the water environment both inside and outside the cell and shield the hydrocarbon tails sandwiched in the bilayer. A test tube mixture of these phospholipid molecules will, in fact, spontaneously form a closed vesicle or hollow sphere with a bilayer wall. The overall thickness of a membrane is roughly eight nanometers and the composition is typically 40 percent lipid and 60 percent protein but may vary quite a bit from 20 percent protein in myelin sheath with its high fat content serving as an electrical insulator to 75 percent protein in the purple membrane of the halobacteria in which the protein is used as a proton pump to generate energy. About 70 percent of the membrane protein is intrinsic; that is, these proteins either span across the bilayer (sometimes more than once) or are embedded on

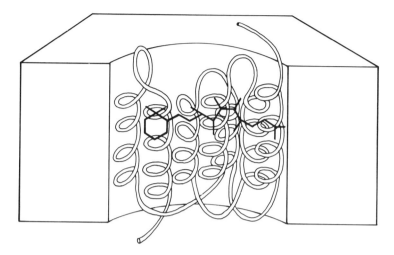

Figure 5.3 The cross-section of a typical membrane in cartoon form. The basic structural bilayer of phospholipids with water-seeking polar heads (shown as spheres) and long hydrocarbon chains is shown together with typical membrane proteins.

either side. These membrane proteins are either alpha-helical or globular in shape, and the former may extend well out into the surrounding medium functioning typically as receptors for sequestering certain types of molecules. The globular proteins are typically those required in defining a spatially organized portion of the membrane, as, for example, in an ion channel, described below, through which selective ions may enter or leave the cell. A typical cell may have several million proteins of which several thousand types are membrane-bound.

The preceding picture is a dynamic one. The proteins of the cell are constantly being broken down and rebuilt, and the membrane is primarily responsible for controlling the flow of needed building blocks into the cell. Even the phospholipid molecules themselves move about within the two-dimensional surface, always having the polar heads exposed to water and the hydrocarbon tails internal to the membrane. Measurements using fluorescent-labeled molecules indicate that neighboring phospholipids exchange positions roughly every microsecond. However, the two layers of the bilayer exchange molecules much less often as there is a high energy barrier to exposing the hydrophobic tails to water. In fact, the type of phospholipids in the two layers is usually different although the reason for this is not yet clear. Molecular associations in a membrane are tightly controlled and long-range lateral motions are usually restricted.

A variety of fluorescence techniques have been used to measure the apparent microviscosity of the membrane and to compare different states of the membrane in terms of the dynamical motions allowed. One such dynamic fluorescence method, fluorescence photobleaching recovery (FPR), has been used to measure the lateral diffusion of lipids and proteins on a membrane surface. In one version, the technique involves pulsing a high-intensity laser on a small spot (typically two micrometers in diameter, using a focused laser beam through a modified microscope) on the membrane, which has been labeled with a fluorescent probe on either a lipid or protein component. The molecules in this region will no longer fluoresce and are said to be bleached. Subsequent fluorescence from the bleached region is monitored by a low-intensity continuous laser beam. The return of the fluorescence to the prebleached level occurs by transport of unbleached fluors into the spot by flow or lateral diffusion. By measuring the time course of the fluorescence recovery, one can calculate the diffusion coefficient of the labeled molecule in the absence of bulk flow.

The FPR method has been used to probe lipid diffusion in the bilayer as functions of lipid composition, temperature, added agents such as cholesterol, and the portion of the cell membrane which is bleached. Much effort has gone into finding lipid fluors which bind only to the membrane, do so in a relatively benign way so as to not perturb the membrane properties being probed, and do not aggregate themselves on the membrane.

Diffusion coefficients of proteins in cell membranes vary by a factor of more than 1,000 in contrast to lipid diffusion, which varies by a factor of less than 10 even including diffusion in artificial membranes. A second contrast is that while most or all of the lipids are mobile, only a small fraction (20–50 percent) of the proteins have been found mobile. The fraction of mobile labels may be determined by measuring the fractional recovery of the fluorescence to the original prebleached value. These results clearly indicate that certain proteins are restricted in their membrane diffusion, and several sources for this have been suggested.

Filamentous proteins of the cytoplasm have been found to have ends attached to membranes. Associations of membrane-bound protein to these filament arrays might account for their apparent immobilization or decreased diffusion rates. These interactions suggest mechanisms for transmission of information between the cell exterior and interior. The effects of various drugs on the interactions of the proteins and on the structures of the filamentous networks have been monitored by their indirect effect on the diffusion of membrane proteins. Changes in transmembrane electrical polarization by direct electrical stimulation or by changes in ion fluxes have also been shown to affect the mobility of membrane proteins. Another source of restricted diffusion is the formation of crystalline or nonbilayer domains within a region of the membrane which may prevent proteins from diffusing outside the domain.

Increased knowledge of the dynamic properties of membranes will aid our ability to provide cures for many diseases which involve the loss of normal membrane functioning. This knowledge will also lead to the development of new types of artificial membranes which can be designed for specific purposes, such as strength or flexibility.

CYTOPLASMIC STRUCTURE AND MOTILITY

In the early twentieth century the cell was pictured as a bag of fluid with a nucleus and several other organelles floating therein. By the 1940s the picture had changed to one in which the cell was thought to be a much more organized structure in which membranes, fibers, and many more organelles were embedded. In the 1970s the first evidence of the detailed fibrous substructure of the cell emerged and with it the realization that this network of skeletal elements had a dynamic behavior. Of all the areas we have considered here, this is perhaps the least well understood because of its greater complexity and because of the variety of different cells which exhibit various forms of motility. However, an initial understanding of the interactions between the skeletal lattice and the membrane and organelles has emerged and will be described in this section. Applications of these studies are mainly in medicine—specifically in those diseases which affect the structural integrity of cells.

There are at least three basic structural filamentous systems in cells: the microtubules, the microfilaments, and the intermediate filaments. These were initially characterized by their appearances in electron microscope photographs, but their chemical composition and structure are now known. Much of our information on the localization of these filaments within a cell has come from visualization of the filaments using fluorescent antibody techniques and optical microscopy. This method originated in 1974 when antibodies to the protein actin were first prepared. Antibodies to one of the basic component proteins of the filaments are introduced into a cell by injection through the plasma membrane. A second antibody, which is specific to the first and has a fluorescent group attached to it, is then injected into the cell. This second antibody binds specifically to the first antibody which in turn has bound to the filament protein of interest. When illuminated, the now-labeled filaments fluoresce and can be seen directly in a specially adapted light microscope. In fact, by using fluorescent groups with diverse emission spectra one can simultaneously label a cell for each of the three filament systems and visualize all three sets of filaments within the same cell.

These pictures of the specific locations of various filaments have led to a better understanding of the structure-function relationships in cell architecture. The cellular cytoplasm can be pictured as being composed of two phases: a dynamic protein-rich cytoskeletal network (the microtrabecular lattice), and a water-rich phase with small molecules such as sugars and amino acids. Maintaining the overall structural integrity of the cell, the cytoskeletal network has several other purposes. It provides a mechanism for linkage with the various membranes of the cell, compartmentalizes the interior of the cell, determines the consistency and ease of diffusion of small molecules through its pores, and provides a mechanism for generating force within the cell for locomotion or shape changes.

The microfilaments are 6–nanometer-diameter filaments of the protein actin and associated actin-binding proteins. Often these filaments aggregate side-by-side to form bundles which lie just inside and parallel to the plasma membrane of a cell. They have also been shown to organize in annular rings around the entire cell or parts of the cell and in loose bundles of filaments near the leading edge of a motile cell. A large majority of these filaments are relatively short and form an isotropic structural mesh throughout the cytoplasm called the microfilament network. This network probably accounts, in part, for the consistency of the cytoplasm and the regulation of diffusion of smaller molecules. During various stages of the life-cycle of the cell, this network is disrupted to allow flow of the cytoplasm, as for example, during mitosis or cell division.

There are a large number of actin-binding proteins which are divided into several classes based on their functional interaction with actin. Myosin, spectrin, and others can cross-link different actin filaments together to form networks. Myosin filaments may also interact with actin to produce force by a relative shortening of the interacting filament complex. Other classes of actin-binding molecules include a variety of aptly named small proteins: those which prevent actin monomers from polymerizing (profilin, . . .), those which sever or cap the actin-preventing growth (fragmin, severin, . . .), those which inhibit actin fragmentation (tropomyosins), as well as a large class which link actin to other proteins (spectrin, microtubule-associated proteins, . . .). Some of the interactions of these filaments depend upon local pH or calcium ion concentration in *in vitro* experiments.

The microtubules are thick (22–nanometer-diameter) filaments made from tubulin and associated proteins. These play a role in cell division, forming the mitotic spindle. Antibodies to tubulin have shown that the microtubules originate from an organelle called the centrosome, usually found near the nucleus of cells, in a polar fashion with the same ends of the tubule radiating out into the cytoplasm. Kinetic studies have shown that the microtubules grow or lose subunits at the end outside the centrosome, and it is thought that the centrosome blocks the other end and regulates both the growth and orientation of the microtubules using MAPs (microtubule-associated proteins), thus acting as a microtubule-organizing center within the cell. The major function of the microtubules appears to be in determining the shape of the cell and in providing a framework for transport processes both within the cell and for the cell proper.

Intermediate filaments, named because of their diameters of 7 to 11 nanometers, have a varied composition depending upon cell type. At least five classes of intermediate filaments can be distinguished with different proteins. The three filament systems form the cytoskeletal network of the cell. Most cell motions couple this network to the membrane as, for example, in phagocytosis (in which cells engulf external molecules) or retraction (elongation of surface projections from a cell).

The linkage of cytoskeletal filaments to membrane has been studied in several model systems, the most popular being perhaps the red blood cell "ghost," an intact red cell in which the hemoglobin contents have been removed. In this system the detailed arrangement of anchorage sites and proteins is being mapped out and includes several proteins (e.g., ankyrin) which link the membrane and filament systems. This system serves as a useful prototype for more complex membranes.

Spectroscopy has been used in two primary ways in the study of cytoplasmic motility. It has been used to characterize cellular flow in amoeboid motion and other types of protoplasmic streaming as well as directed flagellar swimming in bacteria or sperm. Dynamic light scattering has been used to measure the streaming velocity distribution, a measurement which was previously only possible by microscopic cinematography and laborious visual analysis. A second and perhaps more important application has been in tracer diffusion measurements on labeled proteins within a cell. In large living amoeba cells, the diffusive properties of labeled actin have been studied using fluorescence photobleaching recovery methods. It was found that only about 10 percent of the actin was immobile, presumably as a filament network, and that the remaining actin diffused more slowly than *in vitro,* being bound in a complex with another protein, presumably profilin or a similar actin-binding protein which inhibits polymerization of the actin. The injection of the drug phalloidin, a stimulator of polymerization, led to a large increase in the immobilized fraction of actin, in accord with the working model.

As the revolution in our understanding of cellular processes continues, extensive applications, particularly in medicine, will abound. One can also expect the design of new materials will benefit from a deeper knowledge of the structure-function relations for various types of cells, such as muscle or bone.

GELS

A gel has often been loosely defined as a diluted system which, when inverted in its container, does not flow. It is a material which is intermediate between a solid and a liquid. We are probably most familiar with its form as the dessert Jello. The polymer gel structure is usually a moderately dilute cross-linked solution in which the polymer strands are linked, typically by chemical bonds, and the solvent is trapped in the interstices. For example, in Jello only a few percent of the volume consists of animal protein which forms the cross-linked network while the rest is sweetened water.

We have seen in the previous section the gel-like nature of the cytoplasm and some techniques for studying its porosity and structure. In this section we will focus on some recent general findings on the structure and interactions of gels. In fact this entire area of research essentially originated in the mid-1970s and is still in its infancy. Many possible technological applications for this new science will be discussed in the next section. Our discussion will be based more on the physics and the physical chemistry of gel systems with few components and will be at least initially somewhat removed from a specific biological problem. It should be mentioned, however, that many other examples of biologically relevant gels exist such as the vitreous humor of the eye and the lubricating fluid of the joints. In all cases the fluid component allows diffusion of small ions, nutrients, proteins, and the like, while the polymer matrix supplies the structural backbone.

In the late 1970s it was discovered that, under specific external conditions, a gel can undergo drastic changes in its state as a result of very small changes in, for example, temperature. A clear gel of polyacrylamide at room temperature will become opaque at lower temperatures. This is due to large fluctuations in the local concentration of the polyacrylamide network. The polymer strands continually form regions of much higher or lower concentration than the average bulk concentration in the macroscopic gel and therefore scatter mugh light. As the temperature approaches a specific "critical" limit, which depends on the sample conditions of concentration, solvent, pH, and so on, these fluctuations increase and the pores in the gel approach macroscopic size. Correspondingly, the elasticity of the gel, its resistance to stretch or compression, goes to zero and the gel can reversibly swell or shrink by factors of over one hundred when the temperature is slightly varied. This type of behavior near a critical point can be described in a mathematical form which is the same as for all other "critical phenomena." These include such varied physical phenomena as phase transitions between liquid and gas, magnetic systems, mixtures of immiscible fluids, and many others. Previous to the late 1970s, gels had been studied in only one state and the phase transition was unknown. This situation is akin to one in which water is studied only in the vapor state without realizing that it may condense to form a liquid.

Light scattering, both dynamic and static, can be used to study these properties of gels. Measurement of the scattered intensity from a gel as a function of the temperature shows a tremendous increase as the temperature is cooled toward the critical level. At the same time, dynamic light scattering measurements of the rate at which concentration fluctuations in the sample relax back toward the average bulk concentration show that this rate goes to zero at the critical temperature. Thus, one pictures an increasingly aggregated set of polymer cross-links with larger and larger pores which form and dissolve more and more slowly as the temperature is cooled toward its critical value (see figure 5.4). The specific mathematical dependence of these variations in scattering and relaxation rates on temperature follows a universal curve which is predicted by critical phenomena theory.

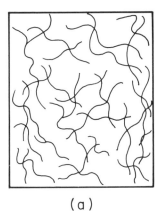
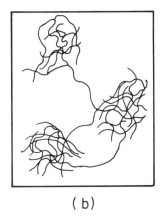

(a)   (b)

Figure 5.4 A polymer network shown before (a) and after (b) a discontinuous phase change. As discussed in the text, this change may be produced by a small change in any of a variety of parameters, such as temperature or pH.

Measurements have shown that various ionic polymer gels can undergo this reversible discontinuous volume change when the temperature is slightly varied and has led to the prediction that this is a universal phenomenon in gels. Both negatively and positively charged gels exhibit this effect, which can be imagined as a phase transition between the shrunken and swollen gel states. The transition is governed by the osmotic, or internal, pressure of the gel. This pressure has three basic components: the interaction between the polymer networks as mediated by the solvent, the thermal motions of the ions of the solvent, and the elasticity of the polymer. The polymer-solvent interactions can be either attractive or repulsive; if attractive, the polymer surrounds itself with a layer of bound solvent, while if repulsive, the solvent is excluded and the polymers tend to aggregate. Thermal motions of the ions in the gel create a pressure just as when a gas is confined to a bottle. The polymer in the gel is in the form of a network throughout the volume of the gel and can exert either positive or negative pressure, corresponding to repulsive or attractive forces, depending upon the volume of the gel. This is similar to a spring which exerts a positive force when it is compressed and a negative force when it is stretched. It should be clear that there are a variety of parameters which could be used to control the balance of these interactions and thus control the abrupt volume transition.

Recent studies have investigated gels in which both positive and negative ions are present in the same network and have shown a "re-entrant volume transition," one in which the gels swell, shrink abruptly, and then swell again as the temperature is continually lowered.

In the above discussion we have mentioned only the dependence of the gel properties on temperature. In fact, the gel volume can be controlled in a variety of other ways, many of them much more significant for future technologies. Discontinuous volume changes have been observed to occur in response to small changes in solvent composition, pH or hydrogen ion concentration, ionic composition, and the presence of a small external electric field.

PROGNOSIS FOR THE FUTURE

Biophysics is a fast-growing science which has made extensive use of frontier experimental methods. The next decade should provide answers to a number of as yet unresolved fundamental questions on the functioning of important biomolecules and biomolecular complexes. There will also be steady progress in utilizing current measurement technology to probe shorter time events and more detailed kinetic processes *in vivo*. Applications of femtosecond (10^{-15} s or one-millionth of a billionth of a second) technology in biological areas are beginning to develop. The use of X-rays and neutron beams from accelerators and reactors has and will continue to expand research in many areas which probe structural changes on atomic dimensions, such as in muscle research. Biological studies using the new scanning tunneling electron microscope (1986 Nobel Prize in physics) to study surfaces and molecular details at very high resolution will emerge. New areas in nonlinear optics and multiphoton processes will have an impact on biophysical research. Other types of measurement techniques may be forthcoming, such as an X-ray laser which would allow monitoring of detailed molecular structure in living cells.

In the next decade we will also begin to see many more technological fruits from basic biophysical research. The detailed structural sequences of events which have been mapped out for certain molecules, as for rhodopsin, will allow new types of applied studies. One area, using genetic engineering, will attempt to modify specific steps in the sequences. This type of research will lead to methods for correcting defects in the process and should have direct medical benefits. Such methods have already been used to alter and improve the functioning of certain molecules; for example, improved strains of vegetables and fruits have been developed which are better adapted for certain climates or are more immune to certain diseases. Several diseases in humans have recently been shown to arise from defects in specific, now located, genes. Developments in genetic engineering should point the way to ''cures'' for these diseases. As our understanding of virus assembly and infection improves, more effective and less invasive methods of immunization will be developed. In fact, rapid advances in the control of many diseases can be expected.

Another direction for new structural studies will be to develop new materials. One such area is the synthesis of new drug molecules, an area which has become a real science based on creating structural analogs to mimic the body's naturally produced defense molecules. Specially designed molecules can bind to invasive agents and render them impotent. On a larger scale, redesigned bacteria have been produced which ingest oil and convert it to nontoxic substances, an application of profound ecological importance. Strains of bacteria are being developed to sequester other toxic agents. Bacteria are also used to concentrate minerals and are currently used in several mining operations.

The area of new materials also includes the design of new artificial membranes with specific properties. Such membranes will allow large surface areas for a variety of more efficient processes including *in vitro* photosynthesis to produce electricity from solar energy more efficiently. Selectively permeable membranes would also have major applications in the electronic industry.

Gels promise to be a major new material for many applications. This new technology is entirely based on the recently discovered phenomena discussed in the previous section. While the kinetics of gel shrinkage are slow for large volumes, for small sections (a few micrometers), relatively large volume changes can occur in the millisecond time scale. Such large, rapid, reversible length changes suggest applications as artificial muscles. Indeed, these length changes may be controlled by low voltage electrical signals, an ideal situation for such an application. Currently, the rapid volume change in gels can be used to locally concentrate chemical substances by a factor of over a thousand. Other future applications range from memory cells in computer devices, using electrically conducting gels whose conductance switches rapidly, to controlled release of drugs or uptake of specific antigens.

As always there will be many unforeseen technological developments. The potential to extend life, to control disease, to produce adequate food for the world's population, and to make life more comfortable and meaningful in this modern age is all inherent in basic science, particularly in biophysics. With this increased knowledge comes also the potential for destruction. Biological warfare and misuse of genetic engineering are two particular areas which society must guard against. Moral questions never considered before are emerging from genetic engineering experiments and we must, as a society, be prepared to make fundamental choices in the near future. Only a scientifically literate public will be able to wisely choose our future course.

BIBLIOGRAPHY

GENERAL

For further general reading in the areas of this chapter and many others, I recommend *Biophysics,* edited by W. Hoppe, W. Lohmann, H. Markl, and H. Ziegler, published by Springer-Verlag, New York, 1983. At a somewhat lower and, unfortunately, more outdated level are the second edition of *Biophysical Science* by E. Ackerman, L. Ellis, and L. Williams, Prentice-Hall, New Jersey, 1979, and *An Introduction to Biophysics* by C. Sybesma, Academic Press, New York, 1977.

Alfano, R. R. ed. *Biological Events Probed by Ultrafast Laser Spectroscopy*. New York: Academic Press, 1982. Studies on the primary events in photosynthesis as well as other topics.

Campbell, I. D., and R. A. Dwek. *Biological Spectroscopy*. Menlo Park, Calif.: Benjamin Cummings, 1984. Good introductory treatment of spectroscopy. *Cold Spring Harbor Symposia on Quantitative Biology*. Vol. 43. New York: CSH, 1978. A compendium of work on DNA.

Govindjee, ed. *Photosynthesis*. New York: Academic Press, 1982. *Scientific American*. October 1985 issue devoted to new developments in biology.

Shay, J. W. ed. *Cell and Muscle Motility, The Cytoskeleton*. Vol. 5. New York: Plenum, 1984. A collection of articles on the cytoplasm.

Stieve, H. "The Biophysics of Photoreception: Molecular Basis," in *Biophysics* ed. W. Hoppe, W. Lohmann, H. Markl, and H. Ziegler (New York: Springer-Verlag, 1983).

Tanaka, T., "Gels," in *Scientific American* (Jan. 1981), pp. 124–136, 138.

Taylor, D. L., et al., eds. *Applications of Fluorescence in the Biomedical Sciences*. Alan R. Liss, 1986. Papers on membrane dynamics.

Weber, K., and M. Osborn. "Molecules of the Cell Matrix," *Scientific American* (Oct. 1985), pp. 110–121.

Wilkie, D. R., and F. D. Carlson. *Muscle Physiology*. N.J.: Prentice-Hall, 1974.

Volkenstein, M. V. *Molecules and Life*. New York: Plenum, 1970. A general reference on nucleic acids and proteins.

6

The Grand System: Telecommunications in the United States

Part I. The Bell Story

> I believe, in the future, wires will unite the head offices of the Telephone Company in different cities, and a man in one part of the country may communicate by word of mouth with another in a distant place.
>
> ALEXANDER GRAHAM BELL, *March 5, 1878*[1]

When Alexander Graham Bell first uttered those words, the telephone was in its infancy and viewed by many with fear and suspicion. Despite this, Bell had a vision—a vision of a "grand system" that would enable people in distant places to communicate with one another by speaking into a telephone. He called his vision the "grand system" because he believed that one day telephone wires would stretch across the country and the telephone would be used by virtually everyone. Today, in the United States, Bell's vision is a reality. His grand system is now known as universal service, making telephone communication available and affordable to all. Over 95 percent of U.S. households have telephone service today.

The U.S. telecommunications industry was born in 1835 when Samuel Morse, Professor of Literature of Arts and Design at New York University, invented the electric telegraph. His invention, consisting of an electromagnet holding a pen to mark a moving strip of paper with dots and dashes, launched long-distance communications. Morse's invention was quite extraordinary at the time, providing the fastest, most sophisticated method of sending messages over long distances.

The next stage in the development of the telecommunications industry occurred in 1895 when Alexander Graham Bell, a Scottish immigrant and speech professor, invented the telephone in his Boston laboratory. He filed patent applications in 1876 which described two general methods of transmission: the magneto-induction principle and the variable-resistance principle. Bell filed in the patent office in Washington, D.C. only hours before Elisha Gray, a Chicago inventor, also filed a patent application on the variable-resistance method of transmitting speech. This led to a series of disputes over patent rights that went on for many years and resulted in hundreds of lawsuits.

Commercial telephone service began in the United States with the formation of the Bell Telephone Company in 1877. In those days, however, telephone service was a far cry from the sophisticated service we use today. Telephone lines only extended short distances. The service itself was poor, with static, cross-conversation, and fade-outs being the norm rather than the exception. Nevertheless, by 1878, businessmen in New York, Boston, and Chicago were beginning to use the telephone for business transactions.

As use of the telephone grew, Western Union purchased Elisha Gray's patent rights in 1878 and entered the telephone business by establishing the American Speaking Telephone Company and the Gold & Stock Telephone Company. The Bell Telephone Company responded with a patent infringement suit against Western Union. Indeed, Bell had reason to be concerned since Western Union, with existing equipment, facilities, and a network connecting its offices throughout the country, was well positioned to enter the telephone business.

Later that year, the Bell Telephone Company, requiring capital to expand and compete with the more powerful Western Union, was reorganized into two companies—the New England Telephone Company and the new Bell Telephone Company. Also during this period, the effectiveness of the telephone was improved by the invention of a "workable exchange," enabling calls to be switched among a number of subscribers. Western Union quickly installed these new exchanges where it had existing facilities. The Bell companies, at a competitive disadvantage without existing facilities, attempted to compete by placing new facilities in the same geographical areas. The result was the development of two unconnected telephone systems in the same locations.

In an effort to strengthen its position against Western Union, Bell Telephone and New England Telephone joined forces again in 1879 to become the National Bell Telephone Company.

NATIONAL BELL BECOMES A LEGAL MONOPOLY (1879–1892)

On November 10, 1879, Western Union and National Bell settled their patent infringement suit out of court. The settlement came at a time when Western Union had a significant financial lead over Bell. But during that year, Western Union, then controlled by financier William H. Vanderbilt, came under attack from financier Jay Gould, who was trying to gain control of the company.

Eventually he would succeed. Through a series of stock manipulations and heavy competition from Atlantic and Pacific, a rival telegraph company established by Gould, Western Union's business had declined by some $2 million that year. With business declining, Western Union agreed to settle with National Bell.

Under their settlement, Bell purchased Western Union's telephone equipment consisting of approximately 56,000 telephones in 55 cities. The company also agreed to pay Western Union a small royalty and promised not to enter the telegraph business until the expiration of the disputed patents in 1893 and 1894. Western Union, in turn, agreed to stay out of the telephone business for the same period. Thus the National Bell Telephone Company—then the predominant voice carrier in the United States—became a legal monopoly. National Bell became the American Bell Telephone Company the following year.

Another important step in the development of the Bell monopoly came in 1881 when the company purchased a major interest in the Western Electric Company from Western Union. In 1882, Western Electric became the sole manufacturer of telephone equipment for American Bell. The purchase was the brainchild of Theodore Vail, general manager of American Bell, who was concerned with the company's position after the Bell patents expired. Vail's strategy was to put the company in the dominant position regardless of patents.

Prior to the purchase of Western Electric, the company's equipment came principally from the Charles Williams, Jr., plant in Boston and the Ezra T. Gilliland plant in Indianapolis. These small companies, however, could not satisfy the equipment needs of the expanding telephone company.

From its beginning, Western Electric made significant technological contributions. Originally founded in 1869 as Gray and Barton, the company played an important role in manufacturing the world's first commercial typewriters, as well as a significant part in Thomas Edison's invention of the incandescent lamp. Later, as the Western Electric Company, it would manufacture almost all of the Bell System's telephone equipment, thus standardizing telephone facilities.

Western's scientists made coast-to-coast telephone service a reality by developing the high-vacuum electronic amplifying tube. During World War II, the company provided U.S. armed forces with half of all the radar used. It later contributed to the country's defense by building the Nike missile system.

Shortly after the formation of the Bell monopoly, the first long-distance line was stretched 45 miles between Boston, Massachusetts, and Providence, Rhode Island. However, calls between the two points were disrupted by such severe interference that the project was considered a failure. Three years later, long-distance service began between Boston and New York, a distance of 292 miles. Despite the poor transmission quality, the service became a success because of the lack of an alternative.

Construction of a long-distance network was espoused by Vail, who was still thinking ahead to the expiration of the Bell patents. He said the development of a long-distance network would give the company a competitive advantage over newly developing telephone companies.

EXPIRATION OF THE BELL PATENTS RESULTS IN COMPETITION (1893–1906)

When the Bell patents expired in 1893 and 1894, entrepreneurs eager to get a share of the highly profitable telecommunication market quickly established independent telephone companies. The market was ripe. In its rush to expand its long-distance network, the Bell monopoly had failed to correct the poor transmission quality of the long lines. The public was unhappy with poor service and welcomed the independent telephone companies.

The independents began operation in rural areas where American Bell did not provide service. But as these areas dwindled, the independents began moving into Bell territory. Thus, for the second time in the industry's history, there were two and sometimes three unconnected telephone systems operating in the same area. Users who wanted access to all telephones had to subscribe to several telephone companies—an expensive proposition.

The independent telephone companies competed with Bell by reducing their rates. But Bell had the upper hand. As Vail planned, American Bell owned most of the long-distance lines. Lacking the capital needed for long-distance expansion, the independents were forced to concentrate on supplying local service; so if customers wanted long-distance service, they had to subscribe to Bell facilities.

Understandably discontent with this arrangement, the independents petitioned their government representatives for connection rights. Beginning in 1904, various state legislatures mandated interconnection between telephone companies. Bell was successful in having these laws revoked because a public-utility concept of the telephone business did not yet exist.

Despite Bell's competitive advantage, the independents continued to move forward. While Bell had 1,514 main telephone exchanges and some 1,278,000 subscribers in 1903, the independents led with 6,150 exchanges and approximately 2,000,000 subscribers.[2]

While American Bell's expansion during the peak years of competition brought increased revenue and profits, it eventually became a financial drain on the company.

As a Massachusetts corporation, American Bell's authorized capitalization was limited by the state legislature to $10 million. Because of this restriction, the company transferred its assets to its fully owned subsidiary in New York, the American Telephone and Telegraph Company (AT&T). In New York's less restrictive environment, Bell was able to increase its capitalization from $100,000 to $20 million.

With capital of more than $70 million, on December 30, 1899, AT&T became the parent company of what would become a Bell System of companies. The-odore Vail, the general manager of American Bell, became president of AT&T.

THE BELL SYSTEM BECOMES A REGULATED
MONOPOLY (1907–1929)

Vail became president at a time when AT&T had a poor public image. It was a time when long-distance calls were noisy, service delays were common, and coast-to-coast service was not yet a reality. Vail's leadership had a profound effect on the structure of the telephone industry.

Under Vail, AT&T was the first large corporation to maintain that maximum private profit was not the primary objective of private industry. He supported the public-utility concept of telephone business, which emphasized service. Vail also believed in the concept of universality and was the first to support the idea of the telephone industry as a regulated monopoly, firmly maintaining that competition was a detriment to good telephone service.

As a result, Vail worked to establish AT&T as the sole supplier of telecom-munications in the United States. He consolidated the company's research and development facilities into a separate company—Bell Telephone Laboratories—jointly owned by AT&T and Western Electric. While the scientists at Bell Labs would develop the technology for the company, Western Electric would be the manufacturer. Some of Vail's other strategies included refusing to connect inde-pendent telephone companies to Bell facilities; purchasing independent tele-phone companies; and gaining control of Western Union Telegraph Company—which was accomplished in 1910. By 1911, AT&T had obtained so many inde-pendent telephone companies that they were consolidated into a smaller number of state and regional companies. The Bell Telephone companies were born.

During Vail's tenure as president of AT&T, the seeds of regulation were planted in the telephone industry. The increasing use of wireless communica-tions, invented by Guglielmo Marconi in 1895, played a significant role in the development of regulation as international concern grew about the potential of monopolistic control of the new technology.

As the Bell System continued to expand, concern grew over the company's size and power. Independent companies and their subscribers were eager to obtain connection rights to Bell facilities and pressured their government repre-sentatives to take action. In 1912, a number of independent telephone companies complained to the Department of Justice that AT&T was violating antitrust laws. As a result, Attorney General George W. Wickersham advised AT&T in January 1913 that it might be in violation of the Sherman Antitrust Act. Shortly there-after, the Interstate Commerce Commission (ICC) began an investigation to determine if AT&T was indeed monopolizing communications in the United States.

AT&T, afraid that an antitrust suit would dismantle the company, responded with the Kingsbury Commitment. The commitment was a reversal of Vail's policies. It stated that the company would relinquish control of Western Union, refrain from purchasing independent telephone companies (except with the approval of the ICC), and allow independent telephone companies to interconnect to Bell facilities.

THE BEGINNING OF RIGOROUS FEDERAL REGULATION (1930–1956)

By the 1930s, the telephone was an important part of American life. The telephone business was then recognized as a natural monopoly and the concept of universal service was widely accepted. Concern, however, was mounting over Bell's control of such an important technology. Many users believed more stringent regulation was needed.

Congress responded by passing the Communications Act of 1934, which still defines national communications policy in this country. Section 1 of the act states the purpose of the legislation: "To make available, so far as possible, to all the people of the United States a rapid, efficient, nation-wide, and world-wide wire and radio communication service with adequate facilities at reasonable charges."[3]

The Communications Act also established the Federal Communications Commission (FCC)—replacing the ICC—and charged it with controlling interstate telephone rates and monitoring the provision of facilities and services. Thus began rigorous regulation of the telephone industry.

In 1934, the newly formed commission began an examination of all telephone companies, including a thorough investigation of AT&T. The FCC released a report in 1938 which denounced AT&T's business operations and focused its attention on Western Electric. It requested the regulation of Western Electric prices. It also requested that AT&T be required to participate in competitive bidding between Western Electric and other manufacturers.

AT&T retaliated with a report stating that arrangements with Western Electric enabled the Bell companies to obtain standardized quality equipment at reasonable prices, benefiting the public.

The commission concluded its examination of the industry with the "Report on the Investigation of the Telephone Industry in the U.S.," released prior to World War II. Since the country's attention was focused mainly on the war, the report received little attention and AT&T remained intact.

In 1949, the Justice Department once again filed suit against AT&T under the Sherman Act. The suit charged that "the absence of effective competition has tended to defeat public regulation of rates charged subscribers for telephone service, since the higher the price charged by Western Electric for telephone apparatus and equipment, the higher the plant investment of which the operating companies are entitled to earn a reasonable return.''[4] This time the Justice Department was not merely seeking regulation of Western Electric's prices, but also its divestiture from AT&T. Intending to create a more competitive environment, it requested Western Electric to split into three independent companies.

The case lingered on for several years, moving from the Democratic administration that initiated the suit to a Republican administration that had a laissez-faire attitude toward the case. The suit was finally resolved by the Consent Decree which stated that Western Electric would limit its operation to producing telephone equipment, excluding defense work, and that the Bell System would engage only in common-carrier communications and incidental operations.

What actually held the company together was the U.S. government's need for an organization with the integrated capabilities of AT&T, Bell Laboratories, and Western Electric. In the midst of the suit, the government was urgently seeking an organization that could operate its atomic bomb laboratory (Sandia Base) and approached Bell Laboratories. Bell Labs refused, citing their policy that defense work could not exceed 15 percent of their total budget. But President Harry Truman interceded and asked that the company undertake this task. This resulted in the creation of the Sandia Corporation as a fully owned subsidiary of Western Union.

COMPETITION RETURNS TO THE TELECOMMUNICATIONS INDUSTRY (1957–1973)

While the 1949–1956 federal antitrust suit was unsuccessful in establishing competition in the telecommunications industry, it was the impetus to reverse the concept of the industry as a natural monopoly. This perceptual change occurred because the United States was shifting from a manufacturing to an information society.

In an information society, the economy is based on the production, processing, and distribution of information. The need arises for faster and more efficient means of managing that information. Thus the business community was seeking more sophisticated technology than the existing telephone network. Specifically, what was needed was an integrated, high-speed network, capable of transporting several forms of information—voice, data, and video image.

The computer also was having a significant influence on the attitudes of regulators. The application of such progressive technologies as the transistor, invented by Bell Laboratories, had greatly increased the efficiency and potential of the computer. Marketplace needs coupled with technological advances led to the convergence of telecommunications and computers, leading to the development of enhanced communication services.

As computers become increasingly essential to telecommunications and vice versa, the FCC initiated its First Computer Inquiry in 1965 to consider what regulatory ground rules should exist for the two converging technologies. The First Computer Inquiry determined that while data processing should not be regulated, separation should be maintained between common carriers and companies providing computer services. Thus, marketplace demands for more sophisticated services resulted in a technological revolution and forced regulators to re-evaluate the monopolistic structure of the U.S. telecommunications industry.

Competition was again introduced to the telephone industry in 1955 when the Hush-a-Phone (a silencing device placed on telephone handsets to prevent telephone conversations from being overheard) became available to consumers from a non-Bell manufacturer.

While the FCC supported AT&T's position against subscribers' use of the device, a U.S. court of appeals ruled that the company had acted unlawfully in protesting its use. The decision was based on the fact that the device was not electrically attached to the telephone network and was not detrimental to the system. During this period, Bell System tariffs said telephone companies had the legal right to refuse service to subscribers who attached foreign equipment to telephone lines.

The 1968 Carterfone decision brought the issue of competition in the customer premise equipment market to the forefront. The Carterfone was a device that enabled private two-way radios to interconnect with the telephone system through a home station. While the Hush-a-Phone did not require electrical connection to the telephone network, the Carterfone did. In this case, the FCC clearly indicated the changing attitudes of regulators by ruling that the Carterfone could be connected to telephone lines without requiring the telephone company to disconnect the line. The telephone company, however, had the right to install protective equipment between the telephone line and the device.

Users and manufacturers protested the Bell System's right to install protective equipment. Their protests led the FCC to consider the elimination of these restrictions. In 1975, the commission adopted a federal registration program for terminal devices allowing FCC "registered devices" to be connected directly to the telephone network. As a result of this decision, the interconnect industry developed in direct competition with the Bell System to sell customer-owned telephone equipment.

Competition struck again in 1970, when the FCC ruled that specialized common carriers could establish microwave relay systems for private leased line telephone users. The ruling also required the Bell System to provide these carriers with access to customers using their facilities. Before the ruling, it had been maintained that these transmission services were best provided in a monopolistic environment—they were only available through telephone companies and Western Union.

As the use of computers continued to grow, a need arose for specialized private line services requiring high-speed digital transmission. Telephone lines, principally suited for voice transmission, were not providing this service. As a result of the FCC ruling, large businesses could construct private microwave systems, bypassing telephone companies and Western Union. But in most cases this was not economically feasible. Therefore, other common carriers like Microwave Communications of America, Inc. (MCI) began to provide services and to compete directly with the Bell System.

AT&T told the government and the public that competition would increase the cost of local telephone service. Historically, the Bell System based its rates for interstate service on nationwide averaging of costs. In other words, the company charged the same price for "lines of like distance," regardless of whether they went over the high-capacity, low-cost routes or over the low-volume, high-cost routes. In contrast, the specialized common carriers, by choosing to serve only customers located along high-volume, low-cost routes, could undercut AT&T's prices.

THE ROAD TO DIVESTITURE (1974–1983)

While the debate over competition in the telecommunications industry continued, AT&T was upgrading its nationwide network, moving it from an analog to a digital system that could provide voice, data, and video services to its customers. Electronic switching systems with digital technology were installed across the country. They could be programmed not only to transmit telephone calls more quickly and economically than the analog system, but could also provide specialized services. And fiber optic cables made up of hair-thin glass tubes were being tested by Bell Laboratories. These cables took up less space while offering greater carrying capacity than the commonly used co-axial cables.

The United States was struggling to develop a clear telecommunications policy as it moved into the information age. While the FCC continued to promote competition in the terminal equipment and intercity private line segments of the business, the Bell System vehemently opposed such competition, believing that it would only result in higher prices for poorer service. AT&T also emphasized that if competition was to continue, it wanted the opportunity to play by the same ground rules as its competitors.

The larger blow to the Bell System came on November 20, 1974, when the Justice Department filed an antitrust suit against AT&T. John DeButts, then AT&T's chairman, vigorously defended the company, stating that it had complied with government mandates regarding competition and was not in violation of antitrust laws.

AT&T asked that the suit be dropped on the grounds that the company was stringently regulated by both state and federal agencies that had the power to settle such issues. The company also stressed that Congress recognized the structure of the company as valid when it passed the Communications Act of 1934 as well as the 1956 Consent Decree.

In November 1976, U.S. District Court Judge Joseph C. Waddy declined dismissal of the case, stating that some issues were within the court's antitrust jurisdiction. Then in 1978, as the pretrial discovery stage of the suit continued, U.S. District Judge Harold H. Greene replaced Judge Waddy. Greene determined that the court, not the FCC, had jurisdiction over the entire case.

As the case progressed, the FCC in 1977 initiated its Second Computer Inquiry. The purpose of the inquiry was to distinguish the range of regulated data communication services provided by common carriers from the data processing services that the commission said it would not regulate in its First Computer Inquiry. AT&T asked the commission not to prohibit the telephone companies from using electronic processing, including data processing, in providing common carrier services. AT&T maintained that such technology had become essential to the provision of service and to the management of the company's facilities.

The final decision, published by the FCC in December 1980, made a clear distinction between basic and enhanced services. It defined basic services as network services that transport information without any alteration. It said a company provided enhanced services when some aspect of the original information is changed or customer interaction occurs with the stored information. The decision also required the Bell System to set up separate subsidiaries to provide terminal equipment and enhanced services on a de-tariffed basis.

Later, the FCC issued a modified order stating that newly manufactured or acquired customer premise equipment could be offered by AT&T only through a fully separate subsidiary. Equipment already in place, however, would remain tariffed and the responsibility of the Bell Telephone companies. The order permitted the Bell System to compete in the terminal equipment market without having to seek regulatory rate approval.

The Justice Department's antitrust suit finally came to trial on January 15, 1981, but was recessed after the court deemed that both sides had made significant progress toward reaching a settlement.

Both parties signed a Consent Decree that put a halt to the trial. Early in 1982, AT&T agreed to divest its 22 local telephone companies. The 1956 Consent Decree was modified and its restrictions confining AT&T to regulated business were eliminated.

Under the settlement, AT&T would retain all the Bell System's interstate facilities, a portion of the intrastate long-distance facilities, and customer premise equipment that was owned by the local telephone companies. In addition, AT&T would retain Western Electric and Bell Laboratories.

The telephone companies would be organized into seven regional holding companies. Each would be able to provide intralata telecommunications, exchange access, printed directory services, and cellular mobile communications.

The regional companies would also be able to establish separate subsidiaries to enter into new ventures, if approved by the court.

AT&T Chairman Charles Brown told shareowners at the time of the settlement: "This is not the solution we sought. Why, then, did we agree to the Decree—this rearrangement of an organizational structure that has served this country so well for so long? Because, when all was said and done, it was obvious that in accepting the agreement we were only acknowledging what already had been decided: not in court, but as a consequence of the vigorous testing over time of contending ideas and proposals within the industry, in government and, most significantly, in the marketplace."[5]

NOTES

1. Letter from Bell, March 5, 1878, cited in Harold S. Osborne, *Biographical Memoir of Alexander Graham Bell* (Washington, D.C: National Academy of Science, 1945), volume 5, number 23, p. 10.
2. Brooks, John, *Telephone* (New York: Harper and Row, 1976), p. 83.
3. *AT&T Annual Report 1976*, p. 21.
4. Brooks, *Telephone*, p. 233.
5. *AT&T Annual Report 1981*, p. 1.

Part II. Telecommunications and Technology
Alan J. Scrime

As we review the socioeconomic history of the U.S. telecommunications industry, we can build vivid mental pictures of the technology in evolution. In sequence, we build a picture of two telephones connected directly by crudely strung wire, as in the days of Alexander Graham Bell and Tom Watson, and can almost hear the poor fidelity such an arrangement would have provided those many years ago. Then our image shifts to one popularized by Lily Tomlin in her characterization of Ernestine, sitting at the switchboard connecting one party to another. Ernestine is the personification of the manual switching era.

Our next picture would depict the arrival of the dial telephone, that marvelous invention which permits connection without human intervention. Dial systems ushered in the electromechanical switching era. Our final visualization, albeit somewhat transparent to the telephone user, is a picture in which the telephone switch is an electronic computer rather than an electromechanical device. Though slightly more difficult to visualize, the user recognizes the added features and functionality made available by electronic switching technology, such as call waiting and call forwarding.

With these four images, we have captured the essence of switched public communications evolution during the period from 1875 to 1975. These changes, coupled with equally impressive improvements in transmission quality and speed (beginning with a single conversation per pair of wires evolving to thousands of simultaneous conversations over a hair-thin optical fiber), provide the base telecommunications platform we employ today in the United States.

To fully appreciate the changes possible during the remainder of the current century and into the next, we must consider both technical and environmental trends. Technology provides the enabling factors and the environment facilitates the deployment of the enabling technology, creating a new platform or springboard from which the next round of evolution can begin. In effect, this is a classic example of technology push and market pull.

But, in order to better understand the impact of change, perhaps we should continue to build a conceptual image of a futuristic telecommunications environment. To begin, let us picture an executive sitting behind a desk in a spacious, modern office, nicely furnished and totally uncluttered. We note two distinct differences in this futuristic image: no telephone and no paper. On his desk, however, is an attractive device which looks something like today's personal computer (which, we shall shortly see, acts as the replacement for both the missing items) and a framed picture of his wife which serves as a reminder of his wedding anniversary the following week. In this scenario, our executive is conducting a conversation with an assistant using the aforementioned terminal which is actually a voice, data, and image input and output device.

During the conversation with his assistant, the executive receives an "alert message" on his terminal's video screen. His digital communications line carried the alert without disturbing his voice conversation. He recognizes the alert as one generated by an information service he employs to analyze news trends of particular interest to him in his business. Without interrupting his current conversation and with only a simple keystroke or two, he retrieves and displays the information which triggered the alert and discovers a change in stock trading patterns which require his immediate attention. Though he has the communications capacity to continue the conversation with his assistant, he prefers to conclude the conversation in order to pursue his trading pattern investigation without distraction.

He begins by using the power of "hypertext" to leaf through the correlated reports in other financial markets. Hypertext is a term used to define the concept of information access in a manner analogous to the way one might read a newspaper. Typically, a newspaper reader may scan the front-page headlines, turn to the business section to review the more important financial events of the day, flip to the sports page to see how the local team fared on the prior day, and finally return to read one or two of the front-page articles in more detail. This form of information access and retrieval is quite sophisticated and much more natural than one which forces the information seeker to follow rigid, structured, first-to-last formats common today in most computerized data bases.

Since our executive uses the hypertext service frequently, the reports he is reviewing are stacked in a local information storage node, a convenience provided by the hypertext service's ability to learn by watching his activities during prior sessions. Having reviewed all necessary information currently available, the executive calls upon two resources, a financial modeling tool and a market projection data base, both available as strategic aids and programmed to consider a complex variety of interactive variables and simulate a business environment based upon current facts and trends. Note that the hypertext information and the analysis tools can act in harmony because they follow international standard formats and protocols finalized in the late 1980s and commonly implemented shortly thereafter.

From the results of this analysis, our executive determines that a specific action is required. He signals his assistant, transfers the results of his brief study to the assistant's terminal, describes the action necessary, and asks to be informed when his instructions have been carried out.

At this juncture, he turns his mind to the pleasant prospect of his upcoming anniversary. After some deliberation, he decides to purchase a necklace and matching earrings as an anniversary gift and that he and his wife shall also dine at their favorite French restaurant. Through his terminal he brings to his display screen the Bloomingdale's catalog, in full color and of a quality that rivals the best 35-mm slide, and selects the perfect necklace for this special occasion. Unfortunately, none of the available earrings please him. He recalls, however, that on a recent trip he saw an advertisement in an issue of *Der Spiegel* magazine, published in Germany, which featured a dazzling set of earrings. With a few keystrokes he retrieves the *Der Spiegel* advertisement and displays the selection of earrings on his terminal screen side-by-side with the picture of the necklace. This combination creates a perfect match and he places an order with both companies instantly from his terminal, an action which triggers automatic payment from his electronic funds account.

Noting that the clock has reached 5:00 P.M., our executive decides to leave for the day. He enters his car, which has a mobile communications system fully integrated with the public telecommunications network, and signals his wife by speaking her name into a hands-free audio dialing unit. When she answers, he predicts his arrival time and suggests that they go for dinner at Chez Henri on the following Wednesday to celebrate their anniversary. She is delighted. He asks whether she has a preferred reservation time or any special request of the chef which might require advance preparation. (Alas, in this day of modern technology, the best food is still prepared the old-fashioned way!) With her on the line, he signals the restaurant and makes the reservation.

During the conversation with his wife and the restaurant, his assistant signals to tell him that the action he requested earlier is now complete. Having received this information and completed the conversation with his wife and the restaurant, he initiates a session with his voice mailbox to review routine messages from the day and to concentrate on voice translations of specific documents he chose to defer to the tranquility of the ride home.

Our example now complete, let us explore some of the underlying technology necessary to bring the dream to fruition. First, we recognize that the executive has neither paper nor telephone. Paper is replaced by easily accessible, readily available, up-to-the-minute, on-line data bases accessible through the public telecommunications network.

The functionality of today's telephone is absorbed into the executive's multimedia terminal. Voice just happens to be one mode of communication, and the "new" terminal is designed to accept voice mode input as easily as keyboard input. One might also assume that this terminal device can accept and generate facsimile copies, still or moving video images, or even handwritten input. The enabling technologies underlying this terminal of the future are derivatives of voice, data, video, and image processing research actively underway in major laboratories around the world.

Next we note that our executive receives an alert message on his video display while in conversation with his assistant. The conceptual framework for an Integrated Services Digital Network (ISDN) was born in the 1970s when it became apparent that technology was driving down the cost of converting analog signals to digital format. If all information could be converted to digital format irrespective of its origin as voice, data, image (like facsimile), or video, great economies could be achieved through the use of common equipment to transport, switch, store, and generally manipulate the information stream. It was also evident that digital information streams could be combined and separated more easily than their analog counterparts making it possible to send information both more efficiently and economically. In simple terms, digital format is simply a series of on and off electrical pulses (commonly known as "bits"), not unlike a sequence of dots and dashes in Morse code.

Thus, following the principles of ISDN and having digitally encoded conversations, or "sessions," on a communications line, makes it relatively simple to intersperse additional messages without interfering with the primary conversation. The term *session* is introduced here because in our new world it is a more general way in which to refer to a communications connection such as the dialog between a terminal and a computer or one between a video camera and a display screen. In effect, in our example, the alert signal just "piggybacks" along with the digitally encoded voice session and the two different signals are separated by the terminal and translated back into sounds or images, as appropriate. Actually, this general technique is useful for several reasons. For instance, multiple conversations, or sessions, can be conducted simultaneously as in our example when the executive carries on a voice conversation and simultaneously manipulates a data base. A more powerful concept, however, is the ability to send and receive signalling information while a voice, data, or video session is underway.

Signalling is the means used to control other sessions. Dialing is the best example of signalling today. The act of dialing generates a series of pulses which provide the switching equipment instructions on where to route the call. With the technology of the 1960s and 1970s, after the dialed party answers, the caller can only signal the telephone exchange in a limited fashion, for example, by depressing the switch hook briefly to answer an incoming "call waiting." ISDN, mentioned earlier, is designed to provide the ability to signal during an active session by incorporating a separate signalling channel on an otherwise ordinary digital communications line. Thus, there is no need to interrupt a conversation to pass simple or complex instructions back and forth between the communications network and its associated devices or users. In a physical sense, having ISDN is like having a telephone with multiple lines connected, one of which is reserved for dialing only. With this arrangement one might dial using the first line and establish a conversation on the second line. Then, without interrupting the conversation dial again on the first line to attach another conversation on the third line, and so on. The underlying technologies embodied in this portion of our visualization are integrated digital transmission and use of a separate signalling channel over a common transmission medium.

Next in sequence is the use of a hypertext service to capture relevant material of interest. Ease of information access and use are the keys to the information age upon which we are embarking. Note, however, that our example incorporates an illustration of both information screening and storage. The hypertext service to which our executive subscribed is intelligent enough to watch his information-gathering activities and to capture and store for ready access information he usually finds of interest. The underlying technologies in this instance are a combination of hypertext for information manipulation and artificial intelligence to provide the capture-and-store function. Artificial intelligence is a growing field of computer science in which the goal is to build computer-based systems which approximate the human ability to reason and learn.

Having gathered information about the problem, our executive enlists the aid of financial programs which may be offered as part of some on-line information service or resident as a program in his desktop terminal or both. He uses these programs to massage the data he gathered. Note that the issue of standards is raised here for the first time. Standards are broad agreements that govern the design of products and services in a fashion that will permit separate but complementary products to work together. A modular telephone jack and its companion outlet are prominent examples of a standard implementation. Standards also govern the audio frequency of touch-tone dialing pulses. In a more complex sense, standards exist that govern the interchange of information between a terminal and a remote computer. As one can see, standards must be tightly coupled with the evolution of communications technology in order to optimize the introduction and use of new products and services. Without standards, we will inevitably design an unlimited variety of "square pegs" and "round holes" and literally build an ungainly array of information islands and processes which will prove expensive and frustrating to the end user, who will ultimately bear the burden of trying to make things work together.

The next series of visual images encompasses the arena of home shopping. Video broadcast home shopping networks made their debut on commercial television in the 1980s. However, the merchandising offered in this mode is designed for high volume and mass appeal, and the audience must passively choose articles from those on display. An extension of this concept addresses an upscale market in which the shopper actively selects the merchandise to be viewed. Publication and distribution of catalogs season after season is a costly undertaking for mass merchandisers. Given a suitable high-quality technology, especially if items from separate pages of a single catalog or articles from different catalogs can be viewed side-by-side, perhaps even in full motion video, whole new marketing approaches can be realized. Just imagine the appeal of animated catalogs when contrasted with today's versions which usually show only one view of an offering. Our executive not only shops electronically, but also matches products from a domestic and an international merchandiser. The underlying technologies in this instance are standards for information interchange, a two-way interactive video display and communications system for high-quality viewing and order generation, and a global electronic funds transfer system to facilitate billing.

In the executive's car, we see wireless technology adapted to the world of ISDN. His car phone employs voice recognition technology to identify his wife's name and automatically generates a digital signal to the local cellular telephone office requesting a connection. Using the same concepts resident in ISDN, he speaks with the restaurant and his wife at the same time and simultaneously receives a message from his office. Indeed, the days of Dick Tracy's wrist radio never seemed closer.

In the final scene, our hero settles back to listen to stored messages or documents deferred or ignored earlier in the day. Future technology will make the translation from voice to text and vice versa commonplace.

Let us now summarize the application of technology in telecommunications. First, as defined in our example, the switch to an all-digital environment can prove attractive because it will simplify the interface for all communications equipment. In effect, only one communications outlet will be necessary. It will accept a "universal plug"; it will not matter whether the device attached to the plug is voice-oriented as is today's telephone, keyboard-based like a modern-day terminal or computer, or video-based like a television or facsimile machine. Today we expect our refrigerator, toaster, and hair dryer to use the same electrical outlet. We should expect the same to be true in the future for the communications outlet.

The second part of access is the medium used to transport the communications content to and from the network. Today we can use twisted-pair copper wire, coaxial cable, or fiber optic strands as a physical medium or utilize various portions of the frequency spectrum (cellular, microwave, satellite, etc.) to transmit information. The most significant factor regardless of the medium, wire-based or wireless, is the fact that technology has paved the way for an exponential increase in the carrying capacity of the transmission medium and the handling capacity of the sending, receiving, and switching systems connecting them. This trend has characteristics of the "turnpike effect," in that whatever we build will saturate, and saturate quickly. The real challenge is to identify needs early enough to place appropriate capacity where and when demand warrants.

The third and final part of access technology that is worthy of note is the ability of a communications link to carry multiple sessions simultaneously. Current definitions of ISDN call for a rather structured allocation of the communications medium which will initially place some practical limits on the numbers of simultaneous sessions available to the end user. A glimpse of the future suggests, however, that a more fluid arrangement will emerge as technologists better understand techniques for the utilization of the extremely high carrying capacities of fiber cables and optical switches. In effect, we may be allowed to have as many sessions as we wish and are willing to pay for.

Now let us leave access and turn to the future evolution of switching technology. We discussed the transition of the public switched network from its manual beginning, through the electromechanical era, to the electronic-based systems of today. The next generation of switching systems rely heavily on R&D underway in optical switching technology. Today optical signals transported along a fiber must be converted to an electrical form, switched, then converted back to optical form for further transmission, and so on. Optical switches will make this constant conversion unnecessary.

Beyond access, transport, and basic switching, however, lies the real power of a futuristic telecommunications network. This concept is sometimes referred to as the "intelligent network." In simple terms, one can view the communications switch as two pieces, one for control and another for switching. Conceptually, this is Ernestine (control) and her switchboard (switching). The signalling channel, used frequently in the example with our executive, is the end user's means of communicating with tomorrow's Ernestine, who will in fact be nothing more than a computer system equipped with features based on artificial intelligence, speech recognition, speech synthesis technology, and the like. The signalling channel need not be limited to simple dialing information, but can include all the things Ernestine might possibly do: locating someone, delivering a message later, holding all except certain calls, identifying who is calling before completing the connection, and forwarding specific calls.

With a moderate amount of imagination one can envision a data base like the one which holds calling card numbers today, but different in that it contains voice prints rather than calling card numbers. Given that capability, we can see a weary traveler pick up a public telephone in an airport, identify himself by name, and initiate a call by simply saying, "Phone home." The data base may have many added pieces of information, such as preferred long-distance carrier, personal directory, and other imaginative conveniences providing quasi-intelligent, Ernestine-like services.

Let us conclude our technology wrap-up with a focus on the equipment available to the consumer for use in his home or business location. "Intelligence" need not be limited to the public network. Microprocesser technology has multiplied the amount of functionality available to the telecommunications user several-fold. Indeed, there is little reason to believe that this trend will diminish in the near future. For instance, there are already modern versions of a video phone, available for under $500, which uses ordinary telephone lines to transmit images between calling parties.

Despite the nature of the intelligence resident "inside" or "outside" the public network, the most important issue is that both kinds of equipment be designed in a manner in which they can complement each other. Only in this fashion can an accommodation be negotiated to determine which portion of the "call handling" will be delegated to each participant: the call-originating equipment, the call-receiving equipment, and the intervening telecommunications network. Of paramount importance is that all of this be accomplished in such a way that the user of the service need not concern himself with the details of how or where final functionality is resident.

We have crossed the threshold to the information age. Processing devices have entered every corner of our lives, from home and office personal computers, to controllers in our cars and even in our dishwashers, refrigerators, and toasters. Sophisticated data bases are available for both private and public use. News services, encyclopedias, and even games are offered "on-line" for modest fees. Witness the fact that financial market swings have become somewhat less predictable given the advent of "program trading." All of this makes one fact abundantly clear: in order to compete successfully internationally, nationally, in a large or small business, or even in our own personal lives, ready access to information is no longer an option. Without timely information we will surely lose our competitive edge.

Clearly, a most critical resource in this age of technology is a modern, reliable, economical, easy-to-use telecommunications infrastructure. Nations, corporations, and individuals who fail to recognize the importance of this asset may find prosperity is but a fleeting memory. The telecommunications resource is the key to rapid flow and use of available information.

At the same time, technology, like fire, is both friend and foe. Unless we work to package technology in a usable form, we will never be able to capitalize on its full potential. To be considered successful, our evolution in communications technology should foster a system no more difficult to use than that simple, old-fashioned request to Ernestine, "Please connect me to my wife."

Our challenge is to listen to, and understand, the needs of the consumer, both large and small, and to harness the power of technology in a partnership which leads to successful products and services in the world marketplace. The critical path of technology evolution continues to accelerate at an ever-increasing rate—so much so, that breakthroughs in hardware technology have begun to almost outstrip our ability to cope. Indeed, in the remainder of this century and beyond, we will need to achieve greater strides in the art of information handling and especially in the human interface to complicated and powerful systems technology.

For the United States to remain a world leader, we must maintain the most functional telecommunications infrastructure available to any modern nation. To accomplish this, we must have:

- Support for cooperative standards initiatives in order to foster portable functionality of telecommunications features across national and international borders and between the public and private telecommunications domains.

- Encouragement for research and development efforts through proactive tax policies and continuing promotion of cooperative research consortiums like those which have proved so successful elsewhere in the world.

- Creation of an executive, legislative, judicial, and regulatory environment which inspires technical progress and imposes no arbitrary limitations on the use of emerging technology.

Given these supportive factors, the burden will fall to industry and the marketplace to build the human element of usability into future telecommunications product and service offerings. And then, we may awake one day, activate our telecommunications service, and hear the nasal tones of an electronic Ernestine utter, "Good morning, and how may I help you today?"

BIBLIOGRAPHY

Bell, Trudy E. "Technology '88: Communications," *IEEE Spectrum* (Jan. 1988), pp. 41–43.
Foley, John. "At the Speed of Light," *Communications Week* (Feb. 8, 1988), p. 6.

Hawkins, Williams J. "For-Your-Home Video Phones," *Popular Science* (Mar. 1988), pp. 60–62.

High Technology Business. "Fiber Optics: The Rewiring of America" (Feb. 1988), pp. 34–38.

Schreiber, Paul. "Phone Service at Gate of Information Age," *New York Newsday* (Jan. 31, 1988), p. 78.

Schwartz, Mischa. *Telecommunication Networks: Protocols, Modeling and Analysis.* Reading, Mass.: Addison-Wesley, 1987.

Skrzypczak, Casimir S. "The Intelligent Home of 2010," *IEEE Communications Magazine* (Dec. 1987), pp. 81–84.

Stamper, David A. *Business Data Communications.* Menlo Park, Calif.: Benjamin Cummings, 1986.

von Auw, Alvin. *Heritage & Destiny: Reflections on the Bell System in Transition.* New York: Praeger, 1983.

7

The Revolution in Manufacturing

I. M. Hymes

THE EXPONENTIAL CURVE

The exponential curve can be described as the effort to generate know-how over time. The change depicted results principally from the basic geometric population growth further compounded by the level of knowledge retained through time.

This curve can be divided into three parts: (1) an initial portion (relatively flat) representing the early know-how of thousands of years; (2) a fairly linear portion of hundreds of years; and (3) a rapidly changing portion of tens of years. Many parameters correlating with generated know-how can be represented this way. This curve has often been used to depict the "progress of man" (see figure 7.1).

The Phases

0A. In the *A* portion (figure 7.2), little change took place over long periods of time. This implies that looking backward would give fairly reliable indications of the future. This is why "experience is the best teacher" had great meaning in the "old" days.

0B. Even during *B* times, this adage was appropriate for predicting the future. Looking forward could be extrapolated from the past using the slope of the "linear" rise.

0C. The degree of uncertainty grew rapidly in the *C* portion of the curve. There is an increasingly limited ability to accurately project forward. Experience is still a good teacher, but not the only teacher. This uncertainty is due to the rapidly increasing interactivity of growing complexity(ies).

Let us assume the *A* phase covered the period from the beginning of time to the industrial period (1600–1700s) while phase *B* went up to World War I. Phase *C* represents the contemporary situation.

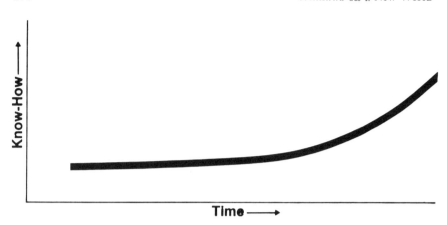

Figure 7.1 The Exponential Curve

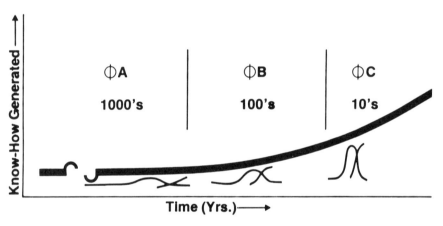

Figure 7.2 Phases in the Manufacturing Revolution

Life-Cycles

Since this curve is the vehicle for the discussion which follows, the recognition of technological life-cycles (which are the elements of this curve) associated with these periods of time can be described as follows:

0A. 1. Long or indefinite lifetime
     2. Stable design of product/process
     3. Relatively low activity to generate know-how

0B. 1. Finite lifetime
    2. Expectation still indefinite in some cases
    3. Design of product/process change
       beginning/growing
    4. Increased activity to generate production and development know-how

0C. 1. Shortening lifetime, rapid obsolescence
    2. Rapid design change
    3. Growing technological displacement
    4. Very rapid growth in know-how development

TECHNOLOGICAL DISPLACEMENT

Bronze over stone, steel over bronze, and gun powder over manual weaponry represent some examples of technological displacement. While these basic technologies are very old, they are still with us. Many improvements have been made but the basic ideas persist. Partial displacement by superior technology occurs, but total replacement only happens occasionally.

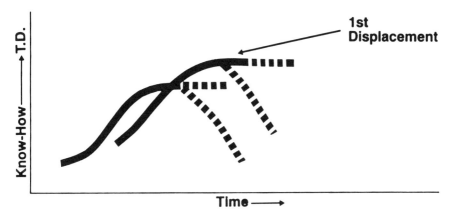

Figure 7.3 Technological Displacement

In a few hundreds of years (0B) the classical industrial relationship of marketing to product design (development) to manufacturing brought about the transition to modern times. Emphasis moved from the physical exploration *for,* to the development *of* natural resources. From there highly competitive industries drained farm labor and set the stage for education of the masses and the beginning of what is now the latest and probably the greatest transition—0C.

A NEW ERA

OC has been leading into the "postindustrial era"—"the computer and/or automation era" to some, and the "service industry" era to others. It is the time, for example, where venture capital seeks the chance to capitalize on any opportunity. This search occurs increasingly at higher levels, that is, single company to conglomerate corporations to multinational corporations to nation/state "corporations." The conflict in political systems is increasing in the area of socioeconomic planning in various nations. There is little doubt that in OC we are entering the most competitive era man has ever known. We also run head-on into the increasingly significant paradox of the growing difficulty to plan versus the need for planning.

Planning

Some segments of industry have rationalized this by separating strategic planning from tactical planning (i.e., "operations"). The increasing complexity of everything around us creates a "demand" (for strategic planning) for which we do not have an adequate "supply." Computers, mathematical modeling, and statistical concepts will be the tools, but the systems are in their infancy.

Worldwide Concept

Through the technological breakthroughs of recent years we are truly entering a total world environment. A broadening range of essentially instantaneous communications are now available. They have been enhanced by stationary satellites and digitalization of information transmitted worldwide through sophisticated military and business networks at the "high" end, and by the handheld transistor radio at the "low" end. Unfortunately this close-neighbor pressure will take many years to sort out before the conflicts and tensions are relieved with a grand scheme for accommodating the world's population pressures. The day when an individual, company, or state can foul the turf without affecting neighbors is long gone.

Supply-Demand Balance

Another critical concept is the generalized idea of "supply and demand," which is not only applicable to commodities, in a marketing sense, but also to other parameters such as competence.

Intuitively we sense that when the supply-demand balance is out of whack conflict occurs. Under-supply can cause expansion, while under-demand can cause depression. The longer the imbalance or the imperturbability of imbalance,

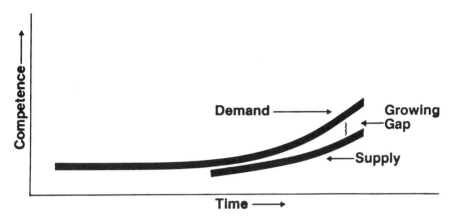

Figure 7.4 The Competence Gap

the more serious the consequences. On the other hand, in the Western world the demand for talent because of the rapid expansion of know-how due to ever-growing complexity is producing a critical competence gap. "Competence" here is not only human talent/education/experience but also the means to utilize these through tools/equipment as well as methods and procedures which "manage" all this, and permit the concept of "competent" systems.

The competence gap can be thought of as a supply-and-demand situation in which change toward threshold technology generates an industry demand which at best can only be met with a significant time lag. A significant contribution may be a more universal education, deeper but less applied, for those in the technological forefront.

One of the sources of competence in the past which has resulted from the struggle of people to keep pace with the technological evolution has been the migration of many people downstream on the path from R&D to manufacturing and/or the "field." With equilibration of the areas from a complexity point of view, this migration will no longer be a valid concept. All functions will require sophisticated levels, though not necessarily the same disciplines of education and experience.

Upstream Trend—Manufacturing

Another result of the "exponential" has been the shift of manufacturing upstream (i.e., earlier in the lifetime of a technology). Graphically this can be depicted as shown in figure 7.5.

This is a reflection of the increase in complexity, the shorter technological lifetimes, the "competence" gap, and so on, and must be recognized.

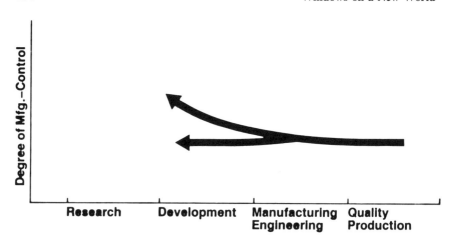

Figure 7.5 Upstream Manufacturing Trend

SCIENCE VERSUS ART

It is time to reconsider the way in which we prepare our students for the rapidly increasing technical complexity of our society. First, we should understand that "technical" things are not limited to engineering. Most everything has had an increasing technical content over the years. The arts have significant technical content but certainly more than that: the relation of music and mathematics and pigment/vehicle technology as well as the metrology of color are all increasingly recognized as technical. The social sciences not only depend on statistics but are opening to acquisition of technical knowledge about the meaning of the statistics. Knowledge in terms of the function of the human brain and its body sensors relative to physical health, motivation, well-being, and so on, is growing rapidly. In fact, most disciplines have a major technical element that is more and more apparent as we increase our specific understanding of these areas (see figure 7.6).

COMPUTERS/COMMUNICATION

The avalanche of information/technical data/know-how being generated to address the exploding complexity of society has already facilitated the emergence of the computer. With the extension of the computer's calculating ability, memory data bases, and communication systems, computers will permit modeling for a great many purposes. In some cases the algorithms have already been generated and will be improved for controlling machines, processes, production lines, airport and road traffic systems, railroads, and so on. In the future a "handle"

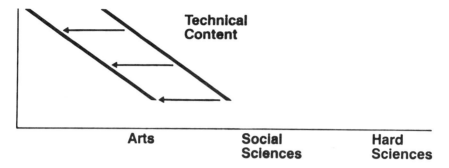

Figure 7.6 Technical Content of Major Disciplines

will be put on the exceptional circumstances through so-called inferential systems.

For our purposes here the ''computer'' is mentioned as a tool, the advent of which is both a cause and result of the information explosion in 0C.

NEW RELATIONSHIPS

For those technologies on the leading edge, unlimited by direct human interference or accommodation, innovation will continue to accelerate. The implication of this is tremendous. For colleges and universities where the leadership role has given way to industry, new relationships are evolving. For example, research corporations contain both industry and university participation in several formats: network linkups (university-university, university-industry); increased spe-

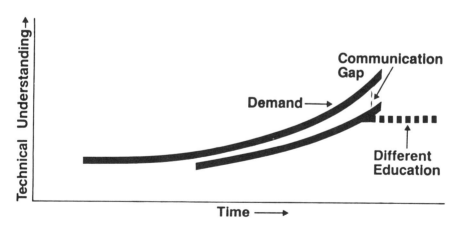

Figure 7.7

cialization of application; on-going skill renewal of professors; the recognition of systems engineering (systems which broadly cover any "process" including tools, methods, and human participation); and the recognition of the complex engineering areas.

TECHNOLOGICAL EVOLUTION/REVOLUTION

If we again refer to 0A in figure 7.1, we can follow in figure 7.8 the evolution of "shovel" technology as an example. In place of a shovel, Hercules cleaned the Augean stables by diverting a river. Power shovels partially displaced manual shovels, which in turn were superseded by a more direct application of power. Serious proposals for atomic/nuclear excavation have even been made.

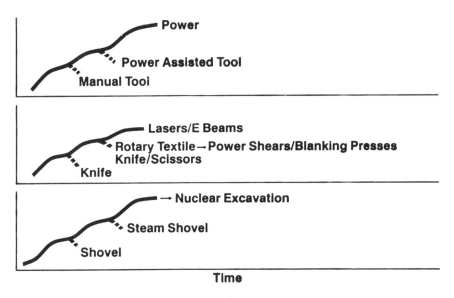

Figure 7.8 The Evolution of "Shovel" Technology

Similarly, in many technological areas evolution has taken place or is taking place.

These illustrations are not exhaustively researched progressions. They are "quick" diagrams which permit the following observations:

1. Manual activities become power-assisted as power becomes available.
2. More exotic technologies challenge the *type* of progression but not the progression itself by more directly applied power rather than "power-assisted" mechanics.

3. The new technologies only partially displace the existing ones usually at the high end, expanding the technological spectra covered.

4. Generations of technological evolution are required to eliminate a technology totally.

TECHNOLOGICAL CONVERSION

If we refer to 0A we can characterize the precursor to manufacturing as the smithy fabricating an agricultural tool, for example, "our shovel." The general design was known and stable for many years (and, as a matter of fact, still is). The manufactured cost had no product/development/engineering content. The cost concerned labor and materials only—for example, obtaining and manipulating a piece of a straight tree for the handle and steel for the blade.

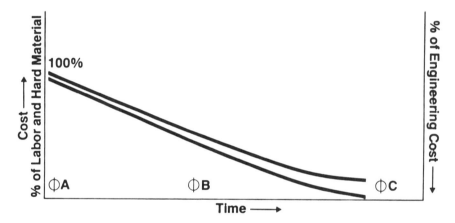

Figure 7.9 Technological Conversion Curve

In 0A and a significant portion of 0B, no engineering contribution was made to products. This is because processes produce products, and products are used in processes. This is an ongoing sequence, that is, someone's product is used in the next one's process; therefore, no differentiation is made here for the different engineerings. Fabricated costs were essentially due only to labor and materials. Product design was simple, known, and stable. Product technologies were long-lived, in fact, indefinite. Capital was very difficult to obtain.

In 0C—today and more so in the future—the engineering content in products will continue to increase and become dominant. The labor and materials content will greatly diminish because of more advanced technologies and methods which produce greater function with less labor and materials; sometimes with entirely new approaches. For example, consider computer logic in figure 7.10 below.

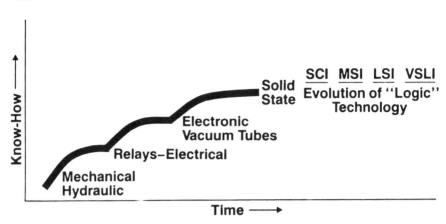

Figure 7.10 Evolution of Computer Logic

HARD TO SOFT CONVERSION

Probably the most interesting implication of figure 7.9 is that the curve becomes asymptotic to, or reaches zero, for a particular product technology. This shape implies that the process is at least as significant as the product it produces. If one could assume a process sufficiently flexible to produce more than one generation of product technology, then the conclusion could be drawn that the process of producing (i.e., the manufacturing process) may challenge/surpass the product it produces.

As the ratio of engineering content to labor and materials becomes dominant, the product becomes "softer," that is, as the material content approaches zero (in value), there is a de facto conversion from hard(ware) to soft(ware).

Concurrent with this change is the shortening of product life, that is, the time before displacement product technologies become available. For companies that wish to lead their industries, there is no choice but to center on the leading edge and drive for technological advantage.

ORDER INVERSION

In order to more fully understand this point, it is important to take a look at the relationship of marketing, product development, manufacturing, and formal business management control which includes quality/excellence, information systems programs, and organizations ("control" for short reference). We can assume the classical relationship of marketing, product development, manufacturing, and the "control" curve (see figure 7.11).

For most of history the sequential relationship of marketing creating a demand

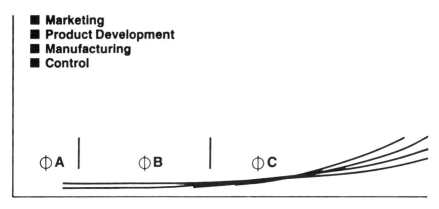

Figure 7.11 The "Control" Curve

for the development of a subsequent product has been generally accepted as permanent. Three observations can be made:

1. The relationship is moving toward a reversed sequence of control: manufacturing-product development-marketing.
2. The fourth factor, "control," is becoming dominant.
3. We are in transition toward the "new" relationship. More simply stated, we are moving toward the following sequence: (1) understanding the type of "control" desired; (2) determining the type of manufacturing (degree of automation); (3) recognizing an increasing constraint on and/or stimulus to product development; (4) the making of a market. "Flexible manufacturing" is normally flexible only within the chosen limits and quite inflexible beyond that.

Although on a national scale redistribution of wealth through taxation is not new, the international equivalent of substituting "blackmail" for ability to pay is being broadly applied. The exploitation of this "demand" by worldwide political blocs, such as the developing countries, is truly creating a new worldwide demand *without* the ability to pay.

We are witnessing an irreversible change of relationship with profound implications for the size of companies and the number of companies accepting the need for strategic thinking and planning.

If we examine the exponential during the three phases previously described, we can see that a delay in decision making will have the following consequences in phase:

0A: only the time is lost but technological advantage is not

0B: delay causes the need for rapid catch-up learning and a capacity overshoot

0C: increasingly, delay will threaten the ability to ever catch up

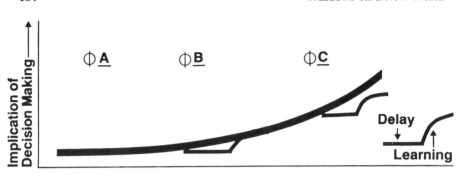

Figure 7.12 Effects of Delayed Decision Making

Herein lies the technological development treadmill. One cannot afford to "get off" since it is beginning to go too fast to "get back on." With worldwide instant understanding now available through modern communications (and these will also improve at an exponential rate), with companies formally doing competitive analysis to assure that planning has relevance to the anticipated future environment, with venture capital companies always ready to take advantage of any opportunity, shortsightedness or delay will be deadly. Indeed, this treadmill is one in which industry leaders will be forced to develop innovation in a steady stream to maintain their position; planned invention will apply increasing pressure not only for leadership but for survival.

Remember that the exponential is the envelope of a carrier—individual technology lifetime curves—whose amplitude and frequency are increasing. Figure 7.13 illustrates the key observations which can be made relative to shortened lifetime and increasing activity.

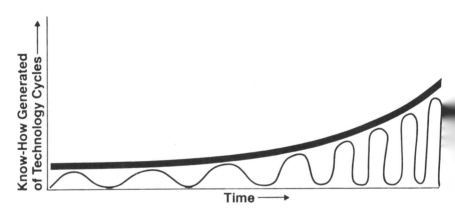

Figure 7.13 Lifetime/Activity Curve

1. Rapid obsolescence—wear-out will be less a factor, in that limited lifetime (rather than indefinite lifetime) will be the design point.

2. Increasing complexity—shorter lifetime incurs greater risks to increasing expenditure for know-how/equipment/facilities.

3. Functional enhancement will increase personalization and ''optionality.'' This choice will cause broader and broader function to be offered as standard/easily programmable.

4. The world of ''used'' may be equal to, or better than, new. New will be more understood in terms of debugged machines, cars, homes, and experienced people.

THE SIMPLE LEARNING CURVE

In order to examine the technology life-cycle we can consider the initial learning curve.

Learning from a zero base as shown in figure 7.14 implies revolution rather than evolution. The tremendous increase of complexity, today's ''evolution,'' is comparable in some cases to yesterday's revolution; this radical shift is also partially caused by the shorter technology life times.

Learning requires, for highly complex threshold technologies, a base which is for manufacturing a sophisticated set of complementary talents, educations, and relationships/methods. Zero base implies the lack of a manufacturing base or working manufacturing system which can successfully undergo a major technology change and therefore would require a significant time (incubation period) to gather the necessary talents to be ''educatable.''

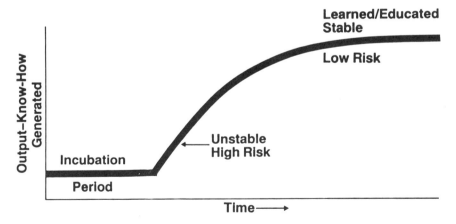

Figure 7.14 The Learning Curve

Minor loop changes imply that the learnable base exists—they are the evolutionary changes of today, and relate to follow-on products of similar technology.

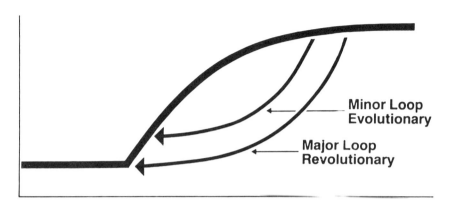

Figure 7.15 Minor Loop Changes

The characteristics of the beginning of the learning curve are instability, need of know-how, and high risk. The slope of the curve of such a time versus expenditure curve is risk. An interesting exercise is to superimpose on this learning curve a grid representing the extremes of the "normal" modes of organization (figure 7.16).

Programs requiring significant learning follow a path of multitalent program dedication migrating with increased learning toward the classical functional or-

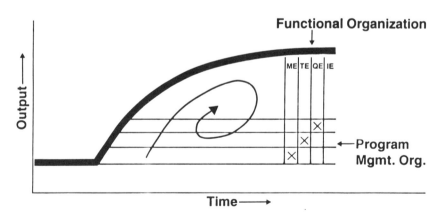

Figure 7.16 Extreme Organizational Modes

ganization. The latter organization implies efficient resource application but is suitable only during technologically stable periods. The conclusion then is that there is no one organization for all times. Organization is cyclic, a function of where manufacturing systems are on the technology learning curve. How many times have we seen an organization changed to what it should have been, but not what was currently appropriate? "Organization" must be capable of going through the learning curve in a timely manner.

FUTURE EDUCATION

The preparation/education of future key technical leaders/management for high-technology industries raises key questions. Certainly more complex technologies require more profound technical understanding. Longer, better, more current applied curricula could conceivably meet this need.

On the other hand, a different and better approach to education will be required for key leadership. Eventually this wave of new leaders must migrate throughout the company's R&D, manufacturing, and other technical areas.

Certainly we will also need many more increasingly sophisticated technicians as complexity rises. However, much complexity arises from the continuing increase of function being offered to customers. Therefore, the powerful integration and simplification toward "user friendliness" required for direct practical human utilization results in increasing product complexity, especially the complexity of the process to produce it.

The education we propose is something of a throwback to the broadly educated person of the Renaissance. Specifically, we see the need for courses in mathematics, physics, chemistry, law, sociology, psychology, biology, economics, and philosophy—all unapplied, over five or six years! The graduate would be not only a worldly generalist but also one technically powerful enough to learn applied areas rapidly. This ability is especially important if rapid change makes applied learning of limited value because of rapid technological obsolescence. This recognition is another example of the growth of importance in the "process itself" rather than a "particular product" of the process (or the "how" rather than the "what"). Without this broad background, there will be a widening gap between the top administration and the operating level of high-technology enterprises.

TECHNOLOGICAL COMPLEXITY

Increased complexity in all technologies—product, process, maintenance, and support systems—is an increasing dilemma for industries who have to face more expensive and riskier technology introductions with shorter lead times and lifetimes.

Technologies are know-how—technical data which demand adequate pre-
paratory work. The only logical way to do more work of a more complex nature
is to start earlier with higher competence and efficient management. The alternative to thoughtful strategy is total flexibility which is extremely expensive but
the only alternative to a poor or nonexistent strategy.

Figure 7.17 gives four product/process variables for an electronic box family.

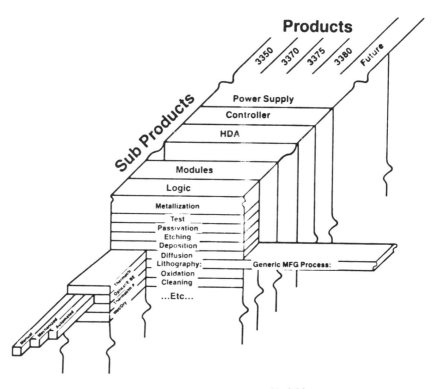

Figure 7.17 Product/Process Variables

Pressure

The growing competition for international markets will apply greater and
greater pressure on participants in the technology race.

Even without the additional complexity of the international aspects of the
technology race, each individual company will be faced with increasing pressure. With all factors driving in this direction and the stakes so high, increasing
ethical conduct will be necessary. From the technician who is careless about the

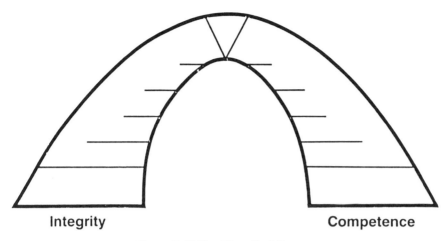

Figure 7.18 The "Legs" of Success

integrity of his data to the manager who makes a blind decision because of his inability to admit lack of adequate competence, there are increasing dangers. These basic pressures are not new but there are now additional factors with higher stakes.

Since the potential of rewards is higher for leadership, the risks to a company are even greater and more unforgetable because of increasing power competition, a more educated/knowledgeable customer and public, and an increasing number of government regulations. Therefore, continuing emphasis on integrity by top management will be a must.

AUTOMATION

Tremendous progress has been made in recent years in the area of process control, a major area of application for automation. The meaning of the term *automation* has become unclear. Initially it reflected the advance of process, test, or tool design beyond "mechanization." We understand it to be closed-loop, adaptive feedback control. With the advent of "office automation" and "programmable robots," automation has become a much looser term encompassing many others (i.e., computerization, computer integrated manufacturing [CIM], CAD-CAM, line integration, etc.).

As the drive toward the automatic factory gathers momentum and the manufacturing system engineering discipline comes to the forefront to meet this need, the implications are that:

1. The ability to control in time sequence has surpassed the ability to control geographically (batch). Batch will increasingly give way to single element processing for highly process-oriented products. The single element will at times have a "batch" nature as know-how is developed.
2. As engineering displaces labor and material, miniaturization of product and process will be emphasized.
3. With improved design and process control and process flexibility, individual product customization will approach the cost of noncustomized production and individual taste will prevail.

While batch size growth will not be eliminated, the batch will be treated as one single element, such as single wafer processing. More production will go toward single element processing and where these products are not limited by a human interface, the elements will be made smaller and smaller until they approach zero material content and therefore become "soft." At this time, the particular manufacturing industry approaches a service industry.

Planning is an absolute necessity. In a complex process, getting better in process yield than the planned yield does not help because the insufficient downstream processing capacity of a balanced line cannot use the "bonus." In fact, the instability of production, either better or worse than planned, is a cause for alarm.

Bad planning is worse than no planning. Poor planning implies that flexibility (in lieu of planning) is not necessary but this strategy gives disastrous results.

Decisions are also an absolute necessity. When compared with no decisions and, under the assumption that there are checks and balances to give competent alternatives, any alternative is often better than *no* decision. Decisions are often fulfilling prophecies; for strategic direction there is no substitute for competence and vision.

SUMMARY

Japanese approaches to manufacturing, which have been recognized as very successful, are essential to our discussion.

Consideration of the government-industry relationship and Japanese versus Western business methods is beyond the scope of this chapter; however, manufacturing areas within that environment show no mystery—just the imaginative application of principles which have been known and available for a long time and were similar to the criteria for the master craftsman in the guild system.

The so-called "just in time" relationship to the so-called "total quality control" philosophy represents a good mix.

Major strengths of this system are:

* The minimization of work in process (WIP) inventory;
* The use of people to assure perfection of the independent operations;
* No time lost between operations;
* The prevention of a defective operation;
* The constant striving for improvement.

The direct application of this mentality is appropriate for classical assembly operations, where part value is heavily material- and labor-oriented. Where there is little labor and materials cost in the product, that is, where the dominant cost is overhead/engineering, only the accounting system gives an appearance of WIP saving by stopping production since the same costs are distributed over the parts whether there are few or many.

On the other hand, process-oriented production—especially of threshold technologies—is more subject to wide swings of yield, yield "busts," and minimal rework capability; therefore, the need for perfection is absolute.

Integrity of specifications—function

Quality—reliability of product

Quality—reliability of process

Productivity of resources

Schedule—timeliness

Costs—the result of, and minimization by, the efficient exercise of the above sequence.

The principal advantage of the Japanese approach is its degree of long-range consideration. Industry is an investment, continually increased and funded by earned profitability.

BIBLIOGRAPHY

Galbraith, John Kenneth. *The New Industrial State*. Boston: Houghton Mifflin, 1985.
Schlosstein, Steven. *Trade War*. New York: Congdon & Weed, 1984.
Schonberger, Richard J. *Japanese Manufacturing Techniques*. New York: Free Press, 1982.
Wolf, Marvin J. *Japanese Conspiracy, A Plot to Dominate Industry Worldwide and How To Deal with It*. New York: Harper & Row, 1983.

8

Management During the Third Industrial Revolution

Allan Doyle

The "gale of creative destruction," as Joseph Schumpeter described the process of revitalization of the capitalistic economy, has been buffeting the Western industrial world for the past decade.[1] The winds are, in fact, jet streams encompassing the entire world and creating a single world economy. Hundreds of books, articles, and speeches remind us that industrial leadership in automobiles, steel, consumer electronics, and even high-technology components such as 256K RAMs has passed from the United States to Japan and East Asia. The emergence of a truly global economy was the product of the technologies of the Second Industrial Revolution such as communications and transportation. Now new technologies are emerging which are identified with the beginning of the Third Industrial Revolution, and destabilizing change is again revitalizing industrial economies.

The economic, social, and political environment in which managers in the United States, Europe, and Japan will be operating will be quite different from that which existed until recently. The basic responsibility of management for the success and perpetuation of their organizations remains unchanged, but the way in which they carry out this responsibility will be quite different twenty years from now. The shapes and structures of business organizations will be different and the way that people work is already changing. The goal of this chapter is to speculate about how successful Third Industrial Revolution companies will be managed and how the structure of these organizations will differ from today's businesses. Prototypes of these future organizations exist today among the high-technology companies that are helping to create the Third Industrial Revolution.

THE ROLE OF TOP MANAGEMENT

Peter Drucker has described the federal system of decentralized management as the best functioning of all systems if top management understands its job and does it well. The job of top management as he sees it is first to think through "what our business is and what it should be," and then to "accept the responsibility for setting the objectives for the entire company and for working out the strategies for obtaining those objectives."[2] In discussing the decisions that must be reserved to top management Drucker states: "Top management, and top management alone, can make the decision what technologies, markets, and products to go into; what businesses to start and what businesses to abandon; and also what the basic values, beliefs, and principles of the company are."[3] He also believes that top management should control the allocation of the key resource of capital and that "both the supply of capital and its investment are top-management responsibilities which cannot be turned over to the autonomous units of a federal organization."[4] Drucker also believes that top management has to play a strong role in decisions related to key people in the company.

The role of successful top managers in the new organizations of the Third Industrial Revolution will be to do some of these tasks very well, but to be very careful not to do others of them at all. These organizations will follow the principles of federal decentralization, but will carry the concept well beyond what Drucker envisioned. The operating units will assume responsibility for most of the decisions related to technologies, products, and markets and will redirect resources from mature technologies into new areas. The role of top management will be to unify, direct, and focus the energies of the highly autonomous business units. In this role top management's responsibilities will be:

1. To become leaders instead of professional managers. They will have to provide a vision of the future that will be exciting to employees. This vision must answer the key questions of *what* business the company is really in and *why* the organization will be able to survive in that business.
2. To create and nourish a strong culture that will support the vision and unify the efforts of people. This culture must guarantee people a high degree of personal freedom without fear of coercion.
3. To develop structures that support the culture and make it real.
4. To attract, nurture, train, and evaluate the performance of the managers of the decentralized business units.
5. To establish basic policies about how capital will be invested by the company and define what returns it intends to earn on those investments.
6. To interface with other constituencies and with the social and political environment.

These tasks pose a formidable challenge to managers—a challenge which most will find much more difficult than the action-oriented "doing" tasks that they have been used to performing, and which they have done well.

VISION/CULTURE/STRUCTURE

The three most important responsibilities of management relate to people. The vision, the culture, and the structure constitute a "people triangle" which will determine the success of the organization.

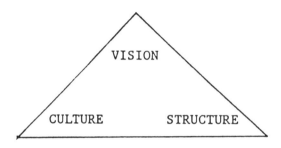

The vision must satisfy basic individual and collective needs of people; the culture provides them with a constitution and states the organization's beliefs about people; and the structure reinforces and interacts with the culture and breathes life into its statements.

LEADERSHIP AND THE VISION

The primary role of top managers is to lead, not to manage. The quality of leadership has always been important in the success or failure of organizations. For tomorrow's corporations it will be even more important because central managers will be doing fewer of the tasks currently associated with managing an organization. The top-down flow of orders, policies, and instructions is being replaced by the delegation of authority and responsibility to the decentralized operating units. The job of leadership is how to keep these decentralized independent and entrepreneurial managers focused on attaining the goals of the organization. The paths that are taken toward these goals will not be controllable by central managers who must be very sure that a common understanding exists as to where the separate parts are heading.

Leaders must provide a vision of the future that will be both exciting and psychologically rewarding to the people who make up the organization. This is the only way that they will have a focused organization rather than many small decentralized business units achieving random results. The belief that "small is beautiful'' is gaining support from many sources, and it will be the basis for structuring the successful company of the Third Industrial Revolution. The positive forces unleashed by this revolution are apparent to many people, especially in those high-technology businesses which actually practice this concept. How to effectively focus the resulting power and energy without destroying its source is the challenge managers are facing. Traditional concepts of planning and control from a central corporate headquarters will not be widely applicable to the highly decentralized organizations which are evolving. Daily decisions will be made relating to technologies and market directions which cannot be funneled up the organization to central staffs. This fact is becoming apparent to companies which are not necessarily thought of as technology companies, but also depend on new products for their success. A major consumer goods company, General Foods, has seen the need to restructure its organization to allow product managers more freedom in getting new products into the market without having to get approvals from multiple layers of management. The role of corporate staff departments is being reduced and responsibility and accountability are being transferred to the operating managers.[5] The complexity created by new technical directions and the increasingly short product life-cycles of new products dictate that managers who are close to their markets and understand these technical forces will be the ones making the decisions. Their intuitive understanding of what is going on, supported by the availability of relevant information through their own decentralized computer capabilities, will be the strength of the companies. CEOs of these companies will lose a lot of sleep unless they have a high degree of confidence that most of these decisions are moving the overall company toward its objectives and goals. Probably the most comforting knowledge is that the managers and other employees of these small decentralized units share the same vision of where the company wants to go and what it wants to become. This knowledge will replace reliance upon today's systems of management control.

The vision of the founder of a business may have to change over time as the enterprise grows and becomes successful. Entrepreneurs generally have a single-minded purpose or commitment to achieving a relatively limited number of goals. A founder's vision may be a personal conviction about what product or service the world needs and it may not be based on any market research. His conviction and his competence persuade others to join his team and to share his vision. Success often complicates the situation. The founder is forced to broaden his vision and to find ways to accommodate the desires of the market as competition provides his customers with a wider range of choices which go far beyond his original view of what they ought to want. No matter how brilliant the founding genius of a company may be, he will be unable to keep up with all of the changing technologies that will affect the future of his business. He will be forced to rely on the skills and talents of others, many of whom may well be of lesser brilliance. In many cases the founder may not be able or willing to adapt his view of the world to the realities of the market or the needs of his growing organization. It has become quite common to see the founders of technology companies either share leadership with outside managers brought in by the board of directors or to leave companies completely to start another business. Some may act as independent contractors to the companies they founded and still provide the technical direction for new product activities.

The history of Apple Computer offers many fascinating insights into the transition from the vision of the founder to a broader vision imposed by the competitive marketplace. In an interview published in the October 1987 issue of *INC* magazine, John Sculley, the CEO of Apple, discusses the need for a founder to grow and change as his company grows, and he describes how the larger business may require skills which in many ways are quite different from those that enabled the founder to create the business. In particular, he talks about the founder's conviction of invincibility and need to make the major decisions, which tend to limit his ability to retain the leadership of a large company that must be flexible in a fast-growth industry. In Sculley's view, the CEO of a third-wave company must be able to "climb down off his perch and wander around inside the bowels of his organization, whether it's a small company or a large one, and figure out how to glean from it the ideas and creativity that can make the company better" (p. 58).[6]

The vision of the leadership of a highly decentralized company of the future must reflect the realities of the competitive market which the company serves, and must be communicated in a way that permits discussion and modification when those realities change. It must also provide answers to the questions of *what* business the company is really in and *why* the company will be successful in that business. Answers such as "we are in business to make money" or "we have been around for fifty years and we will be here another fifty" do not provide helpful definitions of what business the company is in and why it expects to survive. Schumpeter's gale of creative destruction is blowing too hard during this period of transition for any company to feel good about its future unless it has a clear idea of why it will continue to exist. Leaders at all levels must be able to articulate strategies for survival and success in order that others may follow them.

Success strategies will vary widely from company to company and some will attract a certain group of followers while turning off other types of people. It is becoming increasingly difficult to be all things to everybody. Entire businesses will have to become more focused on what they do well in order to rise above the competition from other countries and from new technologies. The smaller the individual business units the more focused the vision will be. One company may focus on being a technological leader in certain fields while another may want to be the lowest cost producer in a mass market. It is hard to imagine any company today not having quality and superb customer service high on its list of priorities, and the challenge will be to differentiate its approach from everyone else's. Leaders will emphasize the ways in which their business is differentiated from all of the others who will be competing with them, and people who are concerned with achieving their personal goals will be excited by the vision that both they and the company are going to be winners.

A vision, to be constructive, must strike some emotional chords within people. The language to which it is reduced in writing will often be flowery. This is necessary since a corporate vision must be able to include a number of subvisions as it grows. The leaders of the independent decentralized units will be creating visions of where that division or subsidiary wants to go, and it is desirable that product groups or task forces will also have objectives and goals that are consistent with the overall grand vision of the company. The high-sounding phrases of the vision will be a standard against which people measure themselves, and it must keep them stretching. When the goals of the company have been condensed into a statement of purpose then the communication process begins to create a culture which expands upon the statement and supports it. This is how managers sell their goals and objectives to their associates and create the basis for coordinated action.

At Kollmorgen, the corporate officers and division presidents met together for three days a number of years ago and hammered out a relatively concise statement of vision or purpose:

Our purpose is to fulfill our responsibility to Kollmorgen shareholders and employees by creating and supporting an organization of strong and vital business divisions where a spirit of freedom, equality, mutual trust, respect, and even love prevails; and whose members strive together towards an exciting vision of economic, technical and social greatness.

This statement certainly does not define what Kollmorgen's business is, but it provides valuable guidelines as to what qualities the business must possess. It also defines the kind of culture and structure that must exist. The power of a statement such as this is not in the grandeur of its prose or its precise definition of a course of action. The power comes from the ability it gives managers to communicate with people about concepts, philosophies of organization, the requirements for success of a business, people relationships, and so on. Each operating unit of the company has developed its own statement of purpose consistent with the corporate vision while relevant to the particular situation of that unit.

The questions ''What business are we in?'' and ''Why will we survive and be successful?'' are questions which must be answered by businesses other than basic manufacturing and high-technology firms. Service industries, which now provide over half of the total employment in the United States, are currently experiencing at least as much turmoil and change. A glance at the financial services industry indicates the need for these handlers of money to figure out what their business really is. The differentiation between major commercial banks, insurance companies, investment bankers and brokerage firms, savings and loan institutions, and other commercial credit and finance companies is becoming hazier every day. New technologies in communications and computers have effectively eliminated the geographic monopolies which many of these firms used to possess and rely upon. The electronic transfer of money with the instantaneous updating of account balances is only beginning to affect our lives. The "smart" plastic card and automatic teller machines are enabling (forcing?) relatively small regional banks to provide services on a nationwide basis to their customers. The pressure of new technologies has probably contributed more to the current confusion than has deregulation. The rush to become full service suppliers of all possible financial products is under way as the major players acquire and merge with suppliers of other services. How one full service supplier will differentiate itself from another is not at all clear. The costs of providing these services are staggering, and many suppliers may not be able to make the required investments in computers, terminals, software, satellites, and other communications equipment as well as in the training of personnel. Many smaller suppliers will have to think hard about how to find a niche in which they can survive. Specialized opportunities will always be there and may be much more profitable for the business that thinks its way through the problem and executes well than for the commodity supplier who is sitting on a tremendous investment and is trying to cover all the bases.

Professional accounting firms are also asking what business they are in as the staple product of auditing services has become a mass-produced standard product. As major auditing firms have turned to providing services on an international basis in the area of taxes, they find themselves employing more lawyers than many large law firms, and may find that the lawyers someday outnumber accountants. Technology has already affected the providers of health care, but the big dislocations are still to come as biogenetic engineering becomes a reality. Managers of a wide variety of medical service businesses have to start thinking about how they want to position themselves for survival before the wave hits. The impact of change is certainly being felt in these service businesses as strongly as in manufacturing and high technology.

For all of these businesses, then, the creation of a vision which gives credible answers to the "what" and "why" questions is the essential first step in building the "people triangle" which is management's prime responsibility. The strategies of survival and success will have a lot to do with how the company organizes to do business (its structure); what it believes in and how it operates (its culture); and what kind of people work there, the ultimate determinant of success.

DEVELOPING THE CORPORATE CULTURE

The importance of strong corporate cultures to successful organizations is underscored in *In Search of Excellence* by Tom Peters and Robert Waterman and *Corporate Cultures* by Terrence Deal and Allan Kennedy. Both books provide many examples of how the personal values of strong leaders have played significant roles in the development of pervasive cultures within their companies. After many years these cultures can express almost everything that there is to know about a company, and they can provide the answers to most questions involving individual behavior. As such, the culture can be a tremendous unifying force which focuses and motivates the efforts of people, or it can become a set of rules, procedures, and behavioral norms that constrain individuality, prevent creativity and innovation, and keep the organization from adapting to changing conditions. Successful Third Industrial Revolution companies will create cultures which avoid becoming statements of "how things are done around here" or "this is how people in this company behave." Deal and Kennedy state that the business environment which each company faces is the single greatest influence in shaping a corporate culture.[7] Managers who are facing business environments subject to continual change must work hard to avoid any culture that is based on any current business environment because this will only reduce their ability to adapt and survive. The successful company will have a culture which creates and welcomes change rather than resists it. The culture focused on a few statements of values and beliefs that are fundamental to people relationships will be much more effective than the culture that concentrates on how things are done. Definitions of the word *culture* all include the transmitting of information from one generation to another and imply a certain stability as a result. It may become necessary for managers to prevent the spread of their culture beyond basic statements of philosophy and belief. The existence of manuals that cover standard practices and procedures, and a proliferation of administrative guidelines for managers, may all be viewed as necessary for the smooth running of the business, but they are also indications of encroaching rigidity that may restrict the ability of the company to move quickly when faced by change. Thomas J. Watson, Jr., chairman of IBM, said it as well as it can be said:

This, then, is my thesis: I firmly believe that any organization, in order to survive and achieve success, must have a sound set of beliefs on which it premises all its policies and actions. Next, I believe that the most important single factor in corporate success is faithful adherence to those beliefs. And finally, I believe if an organization is to meet the challenges of a changing world, it must be prepared to change everything about itself except those beliefs as it moves through corporate life.[8]

IBM has done a marvelous job of sticking to a few basic beliefs such as "respect for the individual" but it has also generated a large number of rules related to the behavior of employees and the conduct of its business. How these opposing influences will affect IBM's ability to initiate and adapt to change in the future is not clear, but the movement toward decentralization and the recent creation of independent business units to promote new ventures indicate the awareness of the need to promote flexibility and individuality.

The type of culture that will be the most effective for current and future businesses is one which, similar to IBM's, provides employees with a "constitution" complete with a "bill of rights." It will be a statement of basic human values and how the company feels about people.

Cultures will always develop around these basic statements of value, and after a number of years have passed the basic constitution may be submerged and lost beneath a proliferation of standard practice and administrative manuals. The folklore, heroes, and rituals that tell how things are done and reward people for doing them in approved fashion ultimately threaten to become more important and visible than the constitutional values. The processes of change are forcing many companies to deal with making changes in their cultures in order to survive or maintain leadership positions. IBM is dealing with the increasing complexity of its world by purchasing more equipment and software from outside vendors, and is distributing products such as its popular personal computers through third parties. IBM managers who have been immersed in a culture that says "IBM means service" are having to adapt to new conditions. Eastman Kodak has held a dominant position in light-sensitive films by being the best in the field of silver-halide chemistry, but today it has to change the way in which it looks at itself because electronics have drastically changed its marketplace. The basic people values of these companies have not changed, but substantial changes are taking place in their cultures.

The transition of AT&T is another clear example of how outside forces (in this case the courts) have changed the business environment of a company in such a way that its culture must also undergo radical change. The cultural norms of a regulated utility are very different from those of a competitive marketplace, and it may well be that some basic people values will also be different as the new entities discover what kinds of people and attitudes they need in order to be competitive. In all cases the costs of achieving major changes in the culture of a large firm are staggering. Many older employees may be unable or unwilling to adapt to the new environment, and the organization will suffer when uncertainty replaces confidence as new methods replace the tried and true ways of doing business. To the extent that the culture can keep the emphasis on constitutional values about the rights of people, changes in the business environment will be handled with less stress on the organization.

The hierarchical structure of many companies has been blamed for much of the unresponsiveness, inflexibility, and resistance to change that has led to our being "noncompetitive" in world markets. How will business organizations exist and function without this type of structure in the future? Not many satisfactory answers have been given to this question, but one critical element in reducing hierarchy is the creation of a strong cultural basis for relationships. The power of a common culture to enable independent groups of people to collectively attain a common goal has been demonstrated by the Japanese. Companies involved in the development of new technologies may find that strong cultures will provide them with better control of their business than is provided today by the detailed systems so common in excessively organized companies. The Japanese have had this cultural basis and it has helped them operate with fewer levels of supervision and staff with resultant cost savings. Americans do not have a common culture that tends to make them work together smoothly and to trust each other. In fact, our culture leads us in the opposite direction, where the emphasis is on individualism and looking out for our own interests. This culture is our strength, and corporate cultures must build upon this heritage. U.S. Third Industrial Revolution companies will have a common emphasis on qualities of innovation, flexibility, teamwork, and individual freedom.

The role of a culture is to support the vision of the organization's future as articulated by the leadership. Kollmorgen has focused on the need for individuals in the company to know that they are free from arbitrary coercion. A key phrase in its culture states that "the conviction among Kollmorgen management is that freedom and respect for the individual are the best motivators of man, especially when innovation and growth are the objectives. For without innovation and growth Kollmorgen cannot achieve its goals." These statements form the basis of a corporate constitution.

In a world of increasing complexity where the design of a product as small as a microprocessor may be beyond the capabilities of a single engineer, the need for each member of a team to make the fullest use of his knowledge is extremely important. Corporate constitutions which provide a high degree of personal freedom to talented people will make a valuable contribution to the success of those companies.

Corporate cultures must be disseminated throughout the organization and they must be believable. Many employees will view the visions and values as being idealistic, unreal, and manipulative. The ultimate test of how believable these statements will be to employees is how consistently managers behave in accordance with the principles they expound. A management which allows its values to be violated faces a loss of credibility. Actions, not words, are the key. When a company is trying to create a culture from scratch or make significant changes in an existing set of values, it will take a number of years to gain credibility. People will want to see if management will behave in the same manner in difficult times as they did in good times. Values and beliefs must be experienced and tested under a variety of conditions and circumstances before they will be accepted as real and become a part of people's lives.

Atari brought in a new chief executive after a very difficult first half of 1983. One of his objectives was to "build a corporate culture." This was viewed as "more valuable than bringing out a hot new product or finding an exploitable market niche."[9] However, it will take time to gain the confidence of employees who have lived through periods of high turnover and internal functional conflicts.

Distinctive cultures have been important to major technology companies such as IBM, Texas Instruments, and Hewlett-Packard, and to smaller growth companies like Analog Devices, Tandem Computers, and Kollmorgen. Strong positive values do not prevent market or technical disasters, but they do make dealing with adversity easier. Problem-solving task forces, interdivisional cooperation, and multifunctional teams will all be most effective if they are perceived as nonthreatening by those who are experiencing problems. Cultures which stress the rights and responsibilities of individuals will develop ways for people to work together toward a common goal.

The technologies of today, which are less complex than those of tomorrow, require cooperative action; and when all parties recognize that such action is consistent with their personal goals, it will be most productive. Highly independent organizational units, which will be the basis of tomorrow's businesses, will have to form a variety of temporary alliances, teams, and task forces to solve new problems and market demands. These partnerships will be dissolved when the jobs are done, and new relationships will be formed to take advantage of the next opportunity. Concepts of structure are of lesser importance and should be easily changeable to meet new market and technical requirements. This flexibility will be essential for survival during the Third Industrial Revolution. The most basic moral beliefs and ethical principles of the company will not change, but the structure and form must be flexible and bend before the gale of change.

Cultures of successful high-technology businesses will be more tolerant of risk and uncertainty than were their predecessors of the mass-production era. The process of innovation should only be entered into by those who enjoy risk taking and who are willing to experience failure in some of their efforts. Cultures which promote individualism and personal freedom will lack the predictability that authoritarian managers at least felt existed in their organizations. Americans seem to be more comfortable with risk taking than the people of many other countries and this cultural strength can help us in the future. The heady excitement of high-technology ventures and the entrepreneurial drive of our individualism can combine to strengthen our industrial leadership position. Trying to copy and instill cultural patterns alien to our native culture cannot be a good road to travel. It is wise to see why other nations can compete so effectively, and to learn from them, but we must integrate only those elements which are compatible with our own traditions. The risks of creativity may well be less than the risks being assumed by some other nations who are over-investing in today's technologies. The risks being incurred by these countries may become more apparent as the pace of technological change increases, particularly if innovation does not take place in these countries.

DESIGNING THE STRUCTURE

The structure of an organization enables it to do business and work toward its vision. Structure interacts very closely with the culture and must be compatible with articulated beliefs and principles. The way in which most employees experience the culture is on a daily basis through the structure of the organization. A compatible structure shows that the organization practices what it preaches. A culture that talks about respect for individuals, personal freedom, creativity, and taking risks had better structure itself so that these things can happen. If it designs a structure that is filled with tight controls, long approval chains, narrow position descriptions, centralized responsibilities, and the like, it will not have a chance to become what it says it wants to be.

Organizations of the Third Industrial Revolution will tend to be long and flat instead of pyramids; there will be few tiers of management. The culture and the vision will provide the proverbial glue that keeps the organization on course, rather than a plethora of sophisticated monitoring and control procedures. Companies will go beyond the "decentralized federal system" described by Drucker as more of the responsibilities reserved for top management are performed by the decentralized units. (From this point on, we will use the term *central management* when talking about corporate-level managers rather than the term *top management*. The responsibilities of the managers of the decentralized units are of equal importance to the business entity, and the only real difference will lie in the nature of the tasks which each group performs.) Decisions about products and technologies will be made close to the markets by those responsible for results rather than by central management and staff. Decisions about the key resources of capital investment and professional talent will be made by operating managers. All of these decisions will be made within the scope of the vision of the organization and a few basic policies related to areas such as capital investment. (The responsibilities of central managers for the raising and investing of capital will be discussed in a later section.) These decisions will have to be made at the operating levels because of the pressure of rapid change. The principles of distributed processing of relevant information will be applied and the responsibility for action will also be placed close to where events are taking place. A corollary is that central managers will not be able to keep up with advances in technologies, and organizations will not be able to afford the burden of central staffs who try to keep up. So technical and product-market decisions will have to be made where people have the requisite knowledge and that will be at the small decentralized business unit level. This method of operating will be very different from that which was the model twenty years ago, but it should be a lot more fun for a lot more people.

Organizations will not be devoid of all monitoring and control functions since the central managers will need to know how the various parts of the whole are doing, and the performance of decentralized managers will still be appraised. Central managers and boards of directors will still be responsible to shareholders for the overall performance of companies, and the need to interact with the political and regulatory scene will continue. The business scene will be changing much more rapidly than will social perceptions of business, and there is great danger that businesses will not be able to adapt as rapidly as they should because of the slower rate of change in other institutions. The challenge to central management will be to know what is happening that is important within the company without restricting the freedom of the people who are making it happen. Advances in communications technology and the "information float collapse" of John Naisbitt in *Megatrends* offer central management the tools to know what they need to know about decentralized operating results; in fact, they will be able to know much more than is necessary. Herein lies a major threat to the ability of flat organizations to remain lean, flexible, and competitive. The natural tendency of central managers has always been to do something with information, and the availability of a tremendous data base makes the possibility of central interference very real. Groups of MBAs, fresh out of top schools and highly computer literate, will inevitably want to demonstrate their brilliance with intricate models of operating businesses and recommended strategies to make good businesses better. The potential for the proliferation of central staffs is only limited by the amount of available data. Third Industrial Revolution managers will have to discipline themselves to avoid these attractive rational pitfalls. Staffs will function in the decentralized units to the extent that they are considered productive by the operating managers. Their relevance and effectiveness will be judged on the basis of their contribution to the performance of the business unit, not by the elegance of their analyses. The ability to be selective about the data employed will limit the number of analyses performed, and the proximity to actual markets will help insure their relevance. Central staff activities will become limited to those needed to support the "people triangle" of vision, culture, and structure; and to perform the necessary corporate tasks related to accounting and shareholder reporting, investor relations, finance, and legal services.

Creative design of corporate structures will be necessary to assure investors that the central management is aware of what is happening in all parts of the business so that no major unfavorable surprises will appear in the next quarterly earnings release. Top managements in the past have tried to fill this need through comprehensive reporting systems, analytical staff departments, internal auditing procedures, group vice presidents, and other control mechanisms. These techniques have proved to be costly and generally detrimental to the effort to motivate poeple to be creative and entrepreneurial. Control systems build structures which tend to immobilize the organization and reduce its ability to react quickly to changes in its business environment. Central managers of tomorrow will use these control mechanisms sparingly and reluctantly. They will try to accomplish the same thing through structures and cultures which promote open communications about problems instead of creating defensive reactions. When decentralized managers truly believe that they are running their own show and are not subject to arbitrary intervention from some higher power, they will communicate more openly within the organization about their business. Most of the surprises which create shock waves with investors result from the attempts of managers to solve their problems themselves before admitting to others that problems exist. This reaction is based on a high level of distrust of the organization's ability to support managerial efforts to work out the solutions. Most traditional control systems and mechanisms are viewed as being concrete evidence of distrust of the individual and as enemies to be circumvented in times of difficulty. One very important ingredient in moving from traditional control-oriented structures to more open and trusting structures is the creation of a feeling of real ownership. Past attitudes have generally been that the employee is just a hired hand who will do what he or she is told to do by those who represent the owners. In the evolving organization, this downward flow of direction will not exist and the success of the decentralized units will be proportional to the perception of real control and responsibility that the unit managers possess. If they perceive that it is their business then the game becomes very real and the results may be exceptional.

The creation of a feeling of ownership, with the associated increase in personal commitment, has been an ideal of many management theorists and has led to a number of experiments in the real world. Since the early work of behavioral scientists and the growth of the human relations function, there have been many efforts to improve productivity through participative management. Practices such as job enrichment, team manufacturing, Scanlon plans, suggestion boxes, productivity meetings, and recently imported quality circles have all been tried with mixed results. The major problem with many of these programs is that both employees and employers have viewed them as being manipulative. The cultures and structures of many companies have not been supportive of attempts to involve employees more creatively in their jobs.

Ownership by a large number of employees is not in any way a utopian socialistic concept. Rather, it may well be a market capitalism concept that will help U.S. business retain its world economic leadership. The alienation of workers and the adversarial relationship between labor and management in most mature U.S. industries has negatively affected both productivity and cost competitiveness compared to Japan and the developing nations. Cultural differences are a part of the answer, but the identification of employees with their company because of economic factors such as lifetime employment, bonuses, and retirement benefits is also very important. If the U.S. market-based system is to survive in its present mixed form, companies will have to recognize that employees do acquire an equity in their jobs over a period of time. The forces of change, which will continue to increase as the Third Industrial Revolution progresses, have already raised the issue of how employees who have lost their jobs in smokestack industries can be included in the new technology-based industries. No easy answers have appeared to this troublesome question, and the fact that the public sector will undoubtedly have to provide the major initiative underscores the inability of the private sector to deal with problems it has created. Employees who have devoted all of their working lives to a single employer have not acquired any sweat equity in those businesses that is of worth to them. Employee ownership or lifetime employment are not panaceas which will prevent companies from failure or bankruptcy, but they do represent concepts of responsibility of businesses to employees as well as to financial investors. Third Industrial Revolution firms will have to address this issue which is, in reality, an opportunity, and actual shared equity ownership may be an attractive solution.

There are a multitude of examples of entrepreneurs spinning off from larger high-technology firms with small groups of engineers and founding their own new businesses. This is standard Silicon Valley procedure. Employee ownership is the norm of these start-up ventures and is the motivating force behind them. The founders start with total ownership, quickly give up a substantial part to venture capitalists who provide most of the initial funding, and then grant meaningful stock options to attract key employees during the initial growth phase. Assuming that the new high-technology venture is a success (not always a necessity in frothy stock markets), it then goes public and creates a number of paper millionaires. While this goal has been in front of them, the spirit, dedication, and creative energy of the team has been tremendous and they have achieved impressive results. What does this growth company do now as its sales first cross $50 million, then $100 million, and then head for a billion dollars or so in five years or less? The demands of the Third Industrial Revolution will be such that the company must retain the spirit, dedication, and enthusiasm that it possessed during its initial growth phase. Assuming that an exciting vision of the future still exists (past successes make this likely) and that a positive culture is forming, then the job of management is to put into place a structure that recreates the conditions which encouraged the initial growth and success of the company.

The flat organization which grows in a cellular manner and provides real ownership potential offers a positive solution. As the company continues its rapid growth, it can form new operating subsidiaries built around entrepreneurial teams with new technical ideas and products. This ''small is beautiful'' philosophy exists in many companies today, but future companies will take this spinning-off concept further by adding the element of real equity ownership to the process. The new entrepreneurial team can be in a similar situation to the founders of the parent company if they own a reasonable piece of the equity of the new subsidiary unit. The company, in effect, plays the role of venture capitalist by providing the necessary financial resources, and should be able to retain two-thirds to three-quarters of the total equity for a reasonable period of time. The equity ownership of the new management team may be in the form of initial founders shares or simply stock options exercisable in three to five years at a price related to the parent company's initial investment. The stock option route would seem to be the easiest, and it provides strong incentives as well as a golden handcuff element which ties the management team to the overall organization for many years. Further options will be made available to attract additional technical, marketing, and production talent to the new subsidiary as it grows. The parent company may agree to go public with the shares of the new unit after certain performance levels have been reached, or it may negotiate formulas which determine the prices at which the parent company will repurchase the shares acquired by the employees. The game is now very real and actual ownership can be spread quite widely throughout each subsidiary. Profit-sharing bonuses may be paid in shares of the subsidiary conserving cash and further increasing real ownership.

Many companies have gone public with shares of subsidiary companies and most of these issues have been 20 to 30 percent of the shares of the subsidiary and have not been related to employee ownership in any way. Most efforts seem to be directed toward raising the price of the parent company's stock. The subsidiaries taken public have generally had higher technology images and more rapid growth rates than their parents, and have been issued into public markets at substantially higher price-to-earnings (P/E) ratios than those accorded to the parent. The new and successful Third Industrial Revolution firm will approach public markets with a very different motivation. It will already possess a decent P/E ratio and may not be able to obtain quite as high an evaluation of the subsidiary's shares. Its purpose in selling a part of its holding in the new venture subsidiary is not to improve its own share price, but to create a real public market where the performance of the management of the new unit will be independently measured. Stock markets are imperfect but highly efficient in their judgments, and the managers of the subsidiary will be involved in a very real game with their own chips squarely on the line.

The parent firm should receive several real gains from adopting this structure and growth policy: its investment in over half of the shares of the new publicly owned unit should increase in value as the managers and employees work hard to increase its value; a new access to public capital has been created for financing the growth of the new unit or the parent company itself without diluting the shareholders of the parent; the equity ownership by employees may help finance their own retirements; and talented entrepreneurs will have a way of staying with the company instead of having to form separate and possibly competing businesses. The cost to the parent company and its shareholders of making 20 to 30 percent of the ownership of parts of its business available to employees may well be zero or negative.

Established companies with several operating divisions may want to consider creating separate subsidiaries and selling 20 to 30 percent to the public while reserving another 15 to 20 percent for employees in the form of stock options. Such options, granted at the same price that the public paid for their shares, should enhance the future value of the subsidiary and the parent. The creative energy likely to be released by employees who now perceive that they are involved in a real game, which can have a significant impact upon their standard of living and upon their ability to gain personal recognition, is likely to breathe new vitality into many fairly dull divisions. The short-term reason for the public sale is to motivate people and the longer term result may be an improvement in the value of the parent company's own shares.

Managers of publicly owned companies report to boards of directors and there are a number of reasons why managers of divisions and subsidiaries, whether publicly owned or not, should report to similar boards. The operating units of decentralized organizations which will be operating without reporting hierarchies are expected to run complete businesses in every sense. Reporting to a board of directors rather than to an individual will make this independence even more real, and will emphasize the true scope of unit management's responsibilities. Boards of directors perform several functions with the most important being their responsibility for assessing the performance of the chief executive officer and his top management team. In addition, they must review and critique the long-range plan of the business and also act as a supportive resource to management. It may be possible to attract outsiders to join an internal board and in this way make experience and expertise available to managers. A board of directors should keep completely out of the daily operations of the business and must avoid making any operating decisions. In a flat decentralized organization an internal board of directors can provide needed communication links between the business units and the central management group.

The flexible organization of the future will rely on teamwork for its survival. It will be able to bring many diverse talents together for a period of time to meet the challenges which arise, and it will have evolved ways to eliminate the adversarial relationships characteristic of our present organizations. The vision, the culture, and the structure will all work toward the goal of unity of the organization. The single-mindedness of purpose which has been a basic cause of the success of so many new ventures is what is desired of these teams and of the overall business unit. Adversarial relationships create a great deal of frictional waste and are very costly to the organization in many ways. In order to be competitive in world markets, we will have to face this question and solve it by eliminating the major sources of conflict. The elimination of one-on-one authoritarian reporting hierarchies is one helpful structural change. Minimizing functional divisions within business units will also reduce structural conflict and friction. The team ideal is to have each and every member of the group feel a personal responsibility for getting the entire task accomplished. Members of operating teams do not carry the legal responsibilities of partners, but should feel the same obligations to each other. Team members will share responsibilities in whatever manner moves the group towards success. Formalized administrative practices such as job descriptions tend to get in the way and will be discarded. Functional organizational structures will also tend to disappear. It is hard to imagine how more friction could be created within an organization than is generated by the very common structure where the sales department negotiates a price (too low, but that is what it took to get the job) and accepts technical specifications which are too tight (the same as offered by our toughest competitor); the engineering department proceeds to design a product which cannot be manufactured at a reasonable cost (blame the sale department and the idiots in manufacturing who can't make it like the drawings) and incurs a large budget overrun in the process; and then the manufacturing department tries to adapt the design to the skills and equipment which it has available and produces something which does not meet specifications or cost and delivery goals (if they had only asked us earlier we could have told them how to design something that worked). On top of this the accounting department provides cost records which everyone agrees are wrong and too late to be useful. Teamwork is nonexistent in this traditional functional structure, and attempting to conceive, design, produce, and sell new products in a fast-moving competitive market environment is generally disastrous. Nobody is really responsible for the overall result except the division president, and he is usually thoroughly insulated from what is actually happening. High-technology companies have become team-oriented to avoid these problems and in response to the complexity of the new technologies with which they are dealing. Organizations which cannot find the way to promote teamwork and continue to operate with a high level of internal friction will not have the necessary flexibility required for survival.

Unions will not readily fit in these flexible companies. U.S. trade unions grew out of a history of adversarial relationships between workers and managers and have helped institutionalize this conflict. The union effectively stands between management and the employees and justifies its existence by maintaining we versus they relationships. It is very difficult for individuals to be members of two teams at the same time, particularly when the goals are different. In the United

States, companies have created large labor relations departments to administer labor contracts and handle on-going grievances, arbitrations, promotions, transfers, terminations, and the like. The ability of managers, supervisors, and workers to be flexible has been substantially decreased as labor-management agreements have become more detailed and restrictive under the excuse of protecting the parties. These large overhead costs and the rigidity that has been created have undoubtedly had a major impact on our much publicized loss of international competitiveness. A number of our competitors in the Far East are working from a cultural base which does not include these adversarial positions and have been able to avoid the associated costs. U.S. and European managers are being challenged to create positive teamwork in order to compete. They will have to build "people triangles" of vision, culture, and structure which satisfy the needs of employees and create atmospheres of sufficient trust so that a single team can exist. Management must be respected for its leadership and support and must not be viewed as an adversary.

MANAGEMENT AND PEOPLE

The organization cannot be better than the people who are its parts. The people triangle provides the means of enabling the people within a company to utilize their talents to the fullest degree possible. It is important to recognize that we have been talking about an ideal situation, and that the existence of an exciting vision, supported by a positive culture and structure, will not create a successful business. The most important ingredient, people, must still be added. The new flat decentralized organization will need a population of managers who are more competent than their predecessors in the hierarchical organizations. And there will have to be more of them to lead the larger number of smaller units. They will have to be more competent because more is expected of them; they will be required to assume far greater responsibilities and will receive less direction and guidance. Management's greatest challenge will continue to be in the area of attracting, training, and nurturing other managers who are competent to handle these greater responsibilities. From our childhood we have been told that the flip side of freedom is responsibility and this applies in spades to the world of management. The most important function of central management will be to ensure that the decentralized operating units are led by managers who have demonstrated their competence and ability to handle responsibility. Companies which are not successful in meeting this challenge will either fail quickly or will revert to a top-down functional organization which is likely to fail gradually.

After managers have been selected for the decentralized units, the job of central management has only begun. The measurement of the performance of these business unit managers is a continuing process, and very difficult decisions about what to do with managers whose performance is less than desired must be made. It is interesting that Allan Kennedy, after coming close to disaster in a new business where the creation of a nearly ideal culture was a guiding principle, opined that "if the manuscript of *Corporate Cultures* were before him today, he would include a section on performance standards, measurement systems, and accountability sanctions."[10] How to set standards, measure results, and apply sanctions without being perceived to be acting in an "anticultural" manner will test the skills of central managers, but they will have to be able to do so in order to succeed.

The positive feelings engendered by visions and cultures are wonderful, but they do not manage businesses. Managers must, as always, be tough-minded, and will have to make tough decisions. If they make these decisions with concern for the "constitutional" rights of others, and with a shared vision of the future in mind, then the "people triangle" will be a positive force and the organization will move ahead. When competent managers are in place in the Third Industrial Revolution companies, and when they own a piece of the decentralized business unit for which they have almost complete operating responsibility, then the positive aspects of the vision, the culture, and the structure will improve the companies' ability to retain those managers and to attract others. In this environment competent managers and their teams will have the maximum opportunity to succeed and to get the maximum satisfaction from their efforts.

THE INVESTMENT OF CAPITAL RESOURCES

After management has created the key elements of its people-oriented vision, culture, and structure, it must turn its attention to the formulation of a policy of capital resource investment. Capital, like talented individuals, is and will remain an economically scarce resource. Part of the process of thinking through the fundamental questions of corporate survival involves considerations of returns on capital investment and sources of future capital investment. Ignoring the importance of capital while setting goals and strategies on the assumption that future growth can be easily financed has become an increasingly dangerous practice. Capital investment in new equipment incorporating current technologies will be quickly rendered obsolete by newer and more productive equipment. A new semiconductor manufacturing facility which requires up to five years to construct and hundreds of millions of dollars to equip may have a relatively short life as the lowest cost, most efficient producer. The newer technologies create and require very expensive capital equipment to compete at a "state-of-the-art" level. Many businesses are having a difficult time financing their growth internally as taxes, inflation, and dividends reduce real retained earnings to very low and sometimes negative levels. It is impossible to see how external capital markets will be other than highly volatile over the next several decades in the face of high government deficits and international unrest. It is unlikely that government policies favoring consumption over investment will change rapidly. In addition to all of these forces which will make capital investment more risky and less predictable, we are faced with foreign competitors in Japan and the developing nations of Asia who are investing heavily in highly automated production facilities on which little or no return seems to be demanded or expected. Manufacturing firms in the United States must think their way through the financing implications of various strategies before settling on any definition of how they will be doing business in ten or twenty years.

Concern about the ability to raise large amounts of capital to invest in making products may seem out of place in years such as 1983 or 1986 when record amounts were raised in the new issue markets. A new company that has yet to earn a profit may have a warped idea about how easy it will be to raise capital in the future when its initial public offering is fought over by institutional investors clamoring to pay twenty or more times next year's forecasted sales revenues for the privilege of buying the new shares. This was not the case in 1984 or late 1987 as the cycles dampened investor enthusiasm. The entry fees to be part of the new technologies are high and the next refills of financing may not come so easily or be available when needed. Managers of new companies in high-technology fields and traditional businesses alike must carefully examine how much money they actually want to invest in facilities to manufacture the products they intend to market. Managers of service businesses may be aghast at the magnitude of capital investment required to stay competitive in their fields when they look at the costs of upgrading computers, terminals, and telecommunications equipment, all of which must be supported by systems and software capabilities. Decisions to subcontract significant portions of activities will be wise for many companies.

Some of the trends which exist today in the assembly of high-volume consumer electronics will become more widespread during the Third Industrial Revolution. A U.S. manufacturer of video games, color television sets, or personal computers will probably stuff printed circuit boards with components in a factory located in Taiwan, Hong Kong, Korea, Malaysia, Mexico, or Singapore because costs are 30 percent below those of domestic facilities. For the same reason, almost all of the semiconductor chips made in the United States have been packaged into DIPs (dual in-line packages) or other carriers in offshore locations. Some of the most efficient and lowest cost offshore facilities utilize a high degree of subcontracting themselves and only perform final testing and inspection in their own plants. This base of subcontractors is being supported by major firms who are encouraging employees to go out on their own by assisting them in financing capital equipment and giving them long-term production contracts. A strategy of nonownership of the increasingly automated assembly lines for electronic products may be key to maintaining the flexibility needed to take advantage of tomorrow's opportunities. Nations which started out as low labor cost producers have seen wages rise and capital investment increase to the point where manufacturers are having high labor content assembly operations performed in other less developed areas. Where will these areas be in five, ten, or twenty years? Those who remain flexible will be able to move with these tides.

During the 1980s we have seen large cyclical swings in relative labor costs between the United States and other countries whose currencies float against the dollar. As the dollar has weakened against other currencies some manufacturing and assembly activities have returned to the United States, while Japanese companies export from the United States. Decisions on where to invest capital and how to structure a firm's manufacturing and assembly operations cannot be made on short-term relationships but must look at more basic long-term problems in the United States, such as a low savings rate, tax policies which favor consumption at the expense of investment, overhead structures which reflect the adversarial relationships between groups in our society, and a social ethic which places hard work at a lower level relative to immediate personal gratification. Flexibility is the key to success, and the ability to avoid large investments in long-lived fixed assets is at the heart of flexibility.

This trend toward increasing capital investment in the automation of manufacturing and assembly facilities is raising significant strategic planning questions for managers today. Investment in automation is often being justified in the name of improved quality rather than reduced costs, but the end result is less per unit labor content in the final product. A visitor to VTR or TV assembly plants in Japan or Singapore has to be impressed by the large capital investment which has been made in automatic component insertion equipment, automatic on-line testing, and materials handling. In a number of places, material handling robotics are employed where manual operations would appear to be perfectly adequate. The automation of electronic assembly lines is proceeding to the point where it is easy to envision identical lines being constructed anywhere in the world capable of producing the same product at exactly the same unit cost. Once the direct labor content is reduced to insignificance, where will those products be assembled? Once many companies can produce the same product at the same cost, how can a return be earned on the capital invested? Are there other competitors who will be satisfied with earning lower (nonexistent) returns on the capital they have invested? The answers to these questions will have substantial impact on the strategic planning of companies who intend to obtain large shares of markets such as the worldwide consumer electronics market. Managers will have to take a stance in this area and decide how they intend to invest their capital resources.

In developing and implementing capital investment strategies, corporate leaders will have to become more comfortable with the concept of capital cost as it relates to their business. Economists and academics have been very successful in creating a veil of mystery around this concept, and most businessmen's eyes glaze over quickly when questioned about cost of capital. The realities of differences in the cost of capital will, however, become very important in areas where capital investment replaces labor costs in the production process. The automation of electronic assembly and the high equipment cost necessary to be in a number of information-based businesses tomorrow require that management has an appreciation of its own cost of capital as well as the costs that its competitors are facing. A 1983 study concluded that the high cost of capital in the United States is the largest problem that U.S. manufacturers face in competing against the Japanese, and that the burden is most heavily felt by young technology firms who must devote several years to research and development before generating profits.[11] This report has received a great deal of attention in the political arena in the consideration of the relative competitiveness of U.S. industry.

Much of the mystique associated with the cost of capital to a business is derived from the difficulties involved in trying to measure it precisely. A businessman only needs to have an understanding of what the investors in his company expect in the way of returns on their investment. The expectations of lenders are fairly clear—interest payments at stated rates and the repayment of principal. Equity owners are harder to calibrate and elaborate cash flow or dividend payment models probably will not add enlightenment. The best way a manager can understand the expectations of shareholders is to go out and talk with major investors. For young growth companies, these investors may be represented on the board of directors and there may be a very clear understanding of what is expected and when. A look at competitors in other parts of the world is important because some of them may be using capital provided by investors with very different expectations. Some foreign investors may require lower returns if they perceive that they are operating in an environment that is less risky. If governments are the providers of capital, then rational concepts of returns no longer apply since motives are no longer economic in nature. Governments can also affect the ability of companies to earn returns on capital through tax policies, subsidies, and other measures. Some understanding of these factors and how foreign competitors are likely to price their products is essential for those managements who want to view the entire world as their potential market.

When international companies raise capital in world markets, there is little reason to expect that one company will be able to raise funds at lower rates than another whose prospects are similarly regarded. In the past, Japanese companies have been able to employ capital in large quantities at lower than world rates because they have been able to operate with high debt-to-equity ratios. Their debt funds were often supplied by large banks who were affiliated with the company as part of a large group of companies, and these relationships created a perception of less than market risk to the lenders. These arrangements are now changing. Japanese companies are raising more equity capital in international markets at world rates, and the perception of risk is changing as the realities of global competition and the destabilizing forces of the Third Industrial Revolution are being felt in Japan, much as they are in the United States. The unique cultural emphasis on stability which has helped Japan achieve its impressive economic growth since World War II will be under increasing stress as this revolution continues.

OTHER CONSTITUENCIES

We have discussed some of the ways that the role of the CEO and central management in the Third Industrial Revolution company will differ from what it has been over the past fifty years or more. The problems which founders of new businesses will face as those businesses grow and assume a new and more decentralized form have also been discussed. There will be a switch from active day-to-day decision making in areas related to technologies, products, and markets to a role which focuses primarily on the motivation of others and decisions related to the performance of others. Many entrepreneurs may not get the same thrills of accomplishment from their new roles as they did from active involvement in doing and building. Luckily there are other constituencies that have to be dealt with, and the challenges which they pose ought to provide adequate stimulation to all but the narrowest of managers.

One constituency which deserves a substantial part of the time of central management are investors. It is extremely important that this relationship not be delegated exclusively to an investor relations department. In a world that is undergoing rapid change. investors need direct contacts with the people who are responsible for the consolidated company. A high degree of decentralization makes it more difficult for outside investors to understand how the whole entity is positioned competitively and how the varied strategies of individual small business units are affecting the parent company in which they have invested. Central management must act as the communications link to the investment community.

Decentralization poses the same problem for the board of directors, and, again, it will be the CEO who has the primary responsibility for keeping them informed. The position of directors will be a more difficult one if the current trend toward legal liability continues unabated. In recent years there have been strong pressures to expand and strengthen traditional central control systems in order to reduce the probability of operational surprises, unauthorized actions, and other events which might be used as grounds for suits against officers and directors of companies. The diligence requirement for directors has been expanded to the point where it has become very difficult for outside directors to feel comfortable about many of the management decisions they are asked to approve or disapprove. At the point where the directors require as much information as was available to the management, the differentiation between management and outside directors disappears, and the independent oversight of those directors becomes nonexistent. The problems which directors face are only a symptom of the much larger problem of distrust and adversarial relationships which separate major segments of our society. The competitive forces creating the new world of the Third Industrial Revolution will not tolerate the costs of structural rigidity. The current situation could easily worsen as new technologies such as biogenetic engineering blossom and create such rapid change that extensive public protection will be demanded.

Being internationally competitive as a nation requires much more than legislating protective quotas, subsidizing perceived growth industries, or reducing the tax bias against savings and capital investment. We are in competition with nations who have not developed our costly adversarial relations between business, labor, and government. The avoidance of the overhead and tax costs required to fight domestic adversaries could improve our ability to sell at lower prices in world markets. U.S. business and government must arrive at least at a state of unarmed neutrality if we are going to be competitive in most world markets. All of the burden of competitiveness cannot be placed on the back of new technologies or upon niche markets. We do not have to cede all of our high-volume standard product industries over to the developing nations. As previously discussed, low labor costs may not be a compelling factor where a high degree of process automation is utilized. The costs of raw materials, transportation, and marketing may provide an adequate advantage for many products within our domestic markets. The cultural costs imposed by adversarial relationships may be compelling in these cases, and at this stage of the contest foreign competitors may have a clear advantage.

The solution of these long-term cultural attitude problems will not come easily, but the current focus on some form of national economic planning is more likely to make the problem worse than to offer solutions.

The challenge is there for successful business leaders, and for most of them it will be a more difficult challenge than any they have faced previously. They will be communicating with groups who perceive the world very differently, and who have different motivations and views of success. They will be faced with trying to change institutions and cultures which resist and abhor change. However, these managers will have something that none of the others possess—a knowledge of what actually works in the real world.

NOTES

1. Joseph A. Schumpeter, *Capitalism, Socialism and Democracy,* 3d ed. (New York: Harper & Brothers, 1950), 81–87.

2. Peter F. Drucker, *Management* (New York: Harper & Row, 1974), 577.

3. Ibid., 578.

4. Ibid.

5. "GF Tries the Old Restructure Ploy," *Business Month* (Nov. 1987):37–39.

6. "Corporate Antihero, John Sculley" [interview] Oct. 1978, p. 58.

7. Terrence E. Deal and Allan A. Kennedy, *Corporate Cultures* (Reading, Mass.: Addison-Wesley, 1982), 13.

8. Thomas J. Watson, Jr., *A Business and Its Beliefs* (New York: McGraw-Hill, 1963), 5.

9. "Atari's New Game Plan," *Fortune* (Aug. 8, 1983):46–52.

10. Lucien Rhodes, "That's Easy for You to Say," *INC* (June 1986), p. 63.

11. George Hatsopoulos, *High Cost of Capital: Handicap of American Industry*, American Business Conference, 1983.

9

The Third Industrial Revolution

Joseph Finkelstein and David Newman

We have entered into a Third Industrial Revolution that is reshaping our industrial processes and dramatically changing the bases of industrial and technological growth.[1] It is not at all certain that the United States is well positioned to take advantage of what is happening.[2] Other nations are touted as potential winners, and the challenge is global. The shifts in products and markets are already in evidence: microchips, computer-aided design and computer-aided manufacturing (CAD/CAM), fiber optics, lasers, holography, biogenetics, word processors, robotics, engineered materials, space exploration—the list grows.[3]

This Third Industrial Revolution brings with it the reality of engineered materials as well as engineered life and drugs. For most of history we have been constrained by the materials produced by nature, modified by our intelligence and artifice. We are now able to select the properties we desire in a material and have it engineered to order. The industrial world has never before known this freedom; henceforth engineers and entrepreneurs will have the imaginative range of expression that only poets and artists held.

We know that we are living in ''interesting times.'' New technologies appear; long-established businesses fall on hard times; the economic order is threatened; and society itself experiences drastic challenges to values and standards of behavior. This pace of change and the condition of uncertainty are facts in our lives. The twenty-first century has already begun, even though the technologies of the nineteenth and the twentieth centuries are still very much with us. Accordingly, we live simultaneously in three centuries.

The impact of the First Industrial Revolution was spread over two centuries. The Second Industrial Revolution featured a much more rapid diffusion of technology and techniques over four or more decades. The impacts of the Third Industrial Revolution, however, are overwhelming. The time available to us to adapt is being dramatically compressed. The pace of change threatens our individual and institutional capacities to cope with change. The stresses we all feel are only one manifestation of what we are living through and attempting to "manage."

SIX MAJOR HIGH-TECHNOLOGY CHANGE AGENTS

The Microprocessor

The microprocessor, it has been said, is as revolutionary an invention as the wheel, the combustion engine and the light bulb. Fourteen years ago, INTEL built an entire central processor unit (CPU) of the digital computer on a single silicon chip. By 1980, VLSIs (very large-scale integrated circuits) with 150,000 components on a single chip were in use. People now conceive of one million components on a chip—dimensions measured in billionths of a meter are feasible.

The microprocessor has become a low-cost item. A complete system with essential peripherals now costs much less than a new car. We have entered an era of "distributed intelligence," in which we cannot even vaguely grasp the enormous possibilities of the computer turned little (though our children can, and will). The microprocessor runs totally counter to the concept of ever more powerful centralized computer systems, a concept prevalent and pervasive in the industry just ten or fifteen years ago. As with other emerging technologies, the microprocessor also poses fundamental challenges to conventional wisdom at the corporate and the nation-state level.[4] The powers of informal networks are being radically enhanced by their access to the new technologies of information processing, storage, and communication, and by their control of much of the new and rapidly evolving know-how. Formal structure and style is being effectively replaced through an inexorable process of internal revolution.

Computer-Aided Design and Manufacturing (CAD/CAM)

CAD/CAM is a further intrusion of the new into the traditional; its main uses are in largely conventional organizations. A single component, highlighted in soft green, can be fitted into an assembly of great complexity. This is more than a new technology. It is also artistry. Its practitioners are artists, and like most artists are beyond the understanding of many traditional managers. CAD/CAM represents a great step forward in economizing the time-design-manufacturing cycle with profound significance. The computer can refer the design directly to the shop floor, where computer-controlled machines carry out the instructions—cutting, shaping, marking, and inventorying. Companies such as Boeing have moved far in CAD/CAM use, and John Welch, president of GE, has promised that GE, a leader in this area, will play a role in the retrofitting of other companies. Data generated by designers and engineers, as they fashion products on a CAD system's video screen, will provide much of what is needed to computerize production. The manufacture of tooling, ordering of materials, scheduling of production runs, programming of robots, and inspection are more than promises. Japanese automobile companies have already shown how to use these devices effectively. Joined to new concepts, systems, and management philosophies, CAD/CAM and robotics have created a massive differential of at least $1,500 in the cost of producing a car, to the disadvantage of Detroit. Increasingly in situations where people refuse to go, robots are taking over jobs that pose risks to health and safety.[5]

Fiber Optics and Telecommunications

Fiber optics has been around for some time. But it now represents a dramatic breakthrough in communications that is just a few years away. We can now make logic chips that use photons of light instead of electrons. This breakthrough vastly improves signal strength and expands the bandwidth. Some engineers suggest that one optical chip can contain 10,000 "gates"—those logical devices that permit unscrambling and encoding of signals. The age of stringing millions of miles of wire and burying miles of cable is quickly passing.

Satellite communication is already well established and is growing exponentially. Many newspapers are printed in several locations, using a master copy transmitted by satellite. Satellite channel television has become one of the hottest plays in town. Telecommunications of all kinds—videotext, teletext, and cellular telephones—are looming close on the horizon. AT&T is only one of the giants entering these new areas. Thompson C.S.F., the French electronics giant, has announced that it is launching a major market thrust to secure the communications potential of our TV screens. The U.S. telecommunications scene has not been so vigorous and volatile since the days of Alexander Graham Bell. But now the actors are global.[6]

Biogenetics and Bioagriculture

We are on the threshold of a biogenetic revolution; we are witnessing the emergence of a kind of scientific awareness that has broken through before perhaps only once or twice in history. The miracle of DNA deciphering is the base for a vast new range of inventions, ranging from new drugs to genetic engineering in plants, animals, and humans. The enormity of this biological cosmos is challenging and frightening. We are already artificially producing strains of interferon purer than that obtained naturally. We have now created synthetic insulin for millions of people who need insulin for life support and who depend on insulin extracted from the pancreas of slaughtered animals. Bacteria are being designed to eat sludge, to transmutate elements, to accelerate chemical and industrial processes, and to replace mechanical and chemical techniques. The implications are unparalleled in human history. Hundreds of firms with emerging technologies are active in biogenetics; some of them are looking forward to becoming part of the new wave of billion-dollar businesses.

The biogenetic impacts on agriculture are perhaps the most startling. In 1982, Secretary of Agriculture John R. Block announced that scientists at the University of Wisconsin had "in a pure research breakthrough, introduced a gene for protein production from a french bean into a sunflower." The "sunbean" may be the forerunner of plants resistant to disease, that can survive drought, capable of growing without fertilizers, that can substitute for oil.

It is within our imaginative grasp to "design and grow a single plant that has edible leaves like spinach, high-protein seeds like beans, a highly nutritive potatolike tuber, nitrogen-fixing roots, and a stalk that yields useful fibre" (*New York Times,* Oct. 25, 1981). Some of the cloning experiments on plants are awesome in their potential, and cloning has already been supplanted by automated gene-splicing machines; CAD/CAM may have uses far beyond the concept of the conventional factory.[7]

Lasers-Holography

Lasers are emerging as versatile and powerful tools. Any device that can be used to both weld a detached retina and bore a tunnel through hard rock has an enormous future. Second-cousin to the laser is holography (three-dimensional

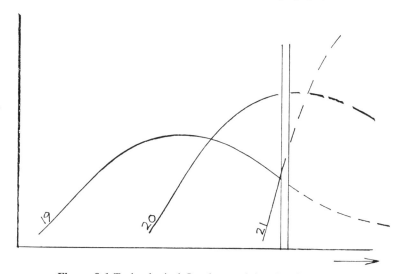

Figure 9.1 Technological Overlaps and Accelerating Change

photography). Holography has established claims in microscopy, especially high-resolution volume images, interferometry, optical memories for storing extremely large amounts of binary data, three-dimensional imagery and advertising, and medicine. Industrial uses are proliferating wherever signal processing is used. Holography has been used to "map" a salt dome as an aid to oil prospecting. Holography is adding to the effectiveness of radar and sonar, and acoustical holography has been used to determine whether a long-sought Leonardo da Vinci fresco is hidden under a more recent one.[8]

IMPLICATIONS FOR MANAGEMENT

Until recently experience has meant something in anticipating the future. Despite change, for much of the 1960s and the early 1970s, things seemed predictable. Long-range strategic planning was often useful, applying rational premises to a logical and sequential planning methodology. Today there is much more need for coherent strategic planning; managers must now adopt a very different attitude and methodology.

What we are living with is discontinuity.[9] The entire structure of business experience and management thought is being transformed. What has already happened to more than a few organizations will eventually happen to many organizations and institutions.

A TYPICAL TRADITIONAL HIGH-TECHNOLOGY COMPANY

The following account describes a large and typical technology-based business that has lived through the 1960s in a traditional and surprise-free way.

Technology in the Product

The technology was totally familiar, long established, and well known in the technical literature. Accordingly, there was a commonality of knowledge and technique. The half-life of the technology-in-use was many years.

Rate of Growth and Change

Growth and change was evolutionary and the pace was appropriate to the firm's financial capacities and management system life-spans. Product innovation was carefully controlled to maintain this gradual pace of change.

Marketing

Demand was tied directly to demography—the need expressed in the marketplace was fundamental and not likely to change much. Since demand was not the driving force, that came from technology (largely under the firm's control).

Management's "Grasp"

The managers had grown up with the technology and with the business. They understood it, and the status quo was a "given." Business-as-usual was the declared corporate mission. Management expected a continuation of the surprise-free business climate that had characterized the previous decades.

Availability of Key People

While individuals with special skills and know-how were important to the business, there was no real dependency.

- There were many more where they came from because the technologies and trades were common to many other organizations and were based upon a long-standing education and experience stream.
- Like many organizations of its era, this business contained numerous redundant capabilities. It was not lean because it had never faced pressures to make it lean.
- The business was not going anywhere in a hurry, and there was nothing like a critical path to compel a squeeze on resources. The key resources in a know-how intensive business are people and money, and there was enough of both. In fact the firm lacked new challenges to allocate them to. There was only "more of the same," and the rate of change of the "more" was known.
- There was little need for aggressive marketing. Accordingly, there was no felt need to develop the extensive product know-how that would have been necessary to support a dynamic and entrepreneurial effort.

THE MAGNITUDE OF PRESENT CHANGES

What has been familiar to us—technology, education, management principles—are all being overtaken by an as yet unpredictable new culture. Because we do not clearly and fully comprehend these changes and their importance either as threats or opportunities, we have to rely on people who do. Accordingly, our uncertainties set up crucial dependencies:

- There are not many such specialists around.
- We do not understand their sciences, and we do not begin to appreciate their expectations and motivations.

- When we bring in "managers" who *can* work with these new kinds of people, we become dependent upon these "managers" as well. Our dependency is as strong as the particular person is effective.
- In some fields we are not even sure what to call the new know-how. It is still emerging. Some of these areas are not yet codified or taught by the universities; these capabilities must be learned on the job.

For many firms, for the first time, resource allocation has become a strategic issue. Both cash flow and availability of the "right" people have become limiting factors. This pressure has been intensified because the product life-cycle has become a tight time frame. Having committed to certain product families, businesses must move from concept to development to production and on to the market on a tight "fast track."[10]

Accordingly, the onus is on a complex assemblage of people in a variety of positions and roles to somehow work together, cutting across all the corporate functions and compartments.

The marketplace has become a new "front end" in not only supporting an existing product but in specifying what comes next in the "need," and in the technology. The "front end" is also internal to the firm—in the predictions and attitudes of key people—and at the "boundaries" with marketing and sales and in the hearts and minds of other kinds of boundary-spanners. The "front end" is definitely not located at the front end of a sequential process of concept, design, and production. The contemporary organization has become highly dependent on those few people who can bring it all together; they should include, but not be restricted to, the top management.

How, then, can organizations be designed to facilitate this "front end" activity? How can a complicated collection of individuals anticipate and respond appropriately to unprecedented demands? How do organizations operate within boundaries of urgent real needs, rather than through evolutionary and long-term processes? Whatever meets these requirements must be innovative![11]

TOWARD A NEW DEFINITION OF PRODUCTIVITY

Competitive advantage in new and uncertain situations derives from innovation based on precedent. Know-how is usually thought of as resident in individuals, in policies, in facilities, and even in organizational structure. The know-how that underpins earlier capital investment and organizational design decisions continues into the future for a time. Thus, know-how, in people and in equipment, is the basis of value-added. Know-how has additional dimensions of great significance for organizations confronting the Third Industrial Revolution:

- Know-how is also a characteristic of a collectivity—of group, team, or organization.

- Know-how is the basis of the feasibility of extending experience to new possibilities (and this is close to Joseph A. Schumpeter's classical definition of entrepreneurship).

- Know-how, as the basis for innovating and for adding value, represents an operational definition of productivity because productivity is itself a measure of value-creating activity.

Productivity accordingly derives from the ways in which special people can work together effectively. Productivity, in the emerging twenty-first century, is equivalent to the know-how of finding, keeping, and building know-how, and of combining know-hows in effective ways.

The following three sections of this chapter (based on actual cases involving several or more business organizations) outline three aspects of organizing for productivity in its more innovative modes:

1. Productivity improvement in production through self-optimization
2. Productivity as effective product "development"—where development spans from concept to marketplace as a highly interactive process
3. Productivity as a corporate strategic process

Self-Optimization

Given the dilemma of managing the unmanageable—of bringing a variety of specializations together toward an open-ended result—one answer is not to attempt to "manage" the situation at all. Rather, the approach is to so set the terms of reference that the group is self-optimizing and self-managing.

This concept is not new. In the mid-nineteenth century, similar schemes were commonplace in U.S. arms factories.[12] Foremen were in fact "contractors" who negotiated with the owners, and were assigned machinery within the factory but left to their own devices both to hire and to get the work done. Since most contracts were firm price, there was a premium on innovation. The benefits, at least in the short term, flowed to the contractor (and to labor that worked under subcontract in much the same way).

The most complete contemporary examples are those in which a special task is contracted out under constraints of cost, quality, and time.

The basic conditions for self-optimization are these:

1. A performance versus payment tradeoff is negotiated in advance with the team.
2. The payment goes to the team as a whole. Individual sharing in the payment is based on peer evaluation.
3. The team leader is perceived by the team members (and by those doing the contracting out) to have special credentials that are indispensable to success.

It is in the interest of each member of the team to ensure that the ensemble contains the minimum number and choice of persons to provide the capacity and the mix needed to perform compatibly and effectively. The team membership, leadership, size, and structure may vary over the course of several contracts, until an optimum is reached. The real limitation in the use of self-optimization is the inability of many managers to acknowledge the full set of enabling conditions. Strongly held assumptions about the nature of individuals and organizations usually go counter to concepts of decentralization and self-management.[13]

A "Right" Set of Policies for Management of "Development"

Some leading high-technology organizations have evolved climates and cultures that include most of the following policies:

1. There are declared corporate fields of interest, and development leaders negotiate their own objectives within this context.

2. Development engineers are sought from among the outstanding students at the leading universities. The qualities that companies look for are these:

    • Applied experience in the firm's core technology so the recruit can make an immediate contribution and feel a sense of worth.

    • Strong theoretical underpinnings so that as the core know-how shifts with discovery and innovation, the individual can make the adjustment.

3. Much of the work is hands-on, and this provides a sense of tangible achievement. (A number of these policies closely fit D. C. McClelland's "need to achieve" model.)

4. A person is hired by the person he or she will work for. Managers do their own recruiting; recruiting is not left to a staff group.

5. A new recruit is assigned immediately to a small team and within that team is given a precise subtask with its own cost-quality-time criteria. Individual performance and team performance become closely complementary.

6. There is frequent and prompt feedback on performance from the people perceived to be important—peers, immediate superiors, and senior management.

7. The members of the team are co-located, and nearly all communication is face-to-face. The working environment is enriched with the best tools available—computers, test equipment, books, access to data, and so on.

8. The team has clear and total responsibility, cutting across all functions from concept to marketplace and beyond. The feedback from the market is the ultimate evaluation of performance, and the main basis of recognition and reward. Accordingly, an assignment that spans from concept to market usually takes less than two years (anything longer would weaken the sense of mission and the feeling of accomplishment).

9. The team "leader" is outstanding technically and, in addition, has considerable

maturity gained within that corporate culture. Leadership is exemplary in the sense of reinforcing the corporate culture and attitudes.

10. The boundary between manager and peer is blurred. It is fairly easy for an individual to move back and forth from being a manager to being a specialist among peers. This design is reflected in a relatively flat organizational structure and few but very broad salary grades.

Not everyone is content in this kind of environment. Some people prefer to work in more traditional organizations. But for those who choose to stay and who are able to gain peer acceptance, the work generally proves highly challenging and rewarding.

Such an organizational scheme, however, has its dangers. Some managers have expressed concern that the turnover is too low to provide an adequate level of renewal and infusion of new ideas. There are, moreover, dangers in perpetuating a task team with a set membership for too many years. Maintenance of the group may become the mission, overshadowing the innovative intention. In other words, there is nothing automatic in the way this, or any other, system of organization works that will ensure the permanence of its desirable features.

Management of Complexity

Those responsible for providing direction to an organization must deal with complexities arising from both external and internal forces. One of the more common ways of bringing complexity under "control" is goal factoring, the process of fragmenting a complex mission into "packets," each designed to match the capacity and know-how of a segment of the formal structure. Eventually, the parts must reassemble into something useful. The connection between the factoring and the assembly comes through trial and feedback into and from the "marketplace." Each unit of the organization attempts to meet its assigned target; performance is measured and used as feedback to the policy level. Targets are revised based on performance and the next phase of effort is launched. This strategy takes an iterative closed-loop mode, using stepwise trial and error to converge on a "best" solution. In this frame of reference, incrementalism means a narrowing of scope and a "one best way" of organizing.[14] There is another kind of incrementalism in an open-system context. There is no convergence, only an expanding range of opportunities. Reality is not only divisible into independent chunks; reality is something that will only emerge with time. Goals are not so much declared as evolved. Goal factoring can be used, but very powerful integrative mechanisms balance the forces of compartmentalization. One of the key mechanisms binding efforts to a common purpose is vision, held by the leadership, and shared by other key players. The corporate culture and mind-set represent this sharing. Thus the legitimacy of the organization in the emerging future takes on new meaning and derives from the integrity of the vision. That integrity, in turn, must come from insight into the underlying systemic reality of both the external and internal "universes" that management must deal with. What counts is not so much form or structure as the pattern or networks of relationships. In satisfying this need, many successful high-technology organizations create very different and idiosyncratic organization designs.

Because reality is dynamic and shifting, the process by which that patterning is evolved and adapted becomes crucial for the organization. This patterning calls for exceptional innovative powers. The act of innovating, then, is that of seeing new possibilities, new patterns, in what to others is the same familiar background. The open-system attitude perceives that the nature of human beings is to search for new insights—to innovate—and that this can be usefully done by people in groups as well as by isolated individuals. An added implication is that collective innovation must operate side-by-side with individual thought and action. Progress then is not something to be measured, but the inevitable by-product of human interaction in an awareness-building frame of reference. Progress is what happens, and progress is "good." Progress is in the process and not in the status; the only limiting factors are the capacities of the shared vision and the willingness to pursue that vision.[15]

CONCLUSION

Long-established enterprises co-exist with radically new technologies. Business-as-usual must continue, in parallel with unprecedented innovation. There are many unknowns. We have entered a zone of uncontrollability, of inherent unmanageability. New rules will apply, though we do not yet know what those rules might be, and "management" takes on new meanings. We have to approach this future experimentally, boldly, and incrementally. We can be guided by our vision of limitless possibilities, but we have to realize that vision by playing upon opportunities as they arise in an open-ended, divergent way. The vision will be reshaped as we do so, and that reshaping will be an enlargement of opportunity at each stage.

Earlier schools of management thought and conventional wisdom have viewed individuals in various ways: as raw units of production; as recalcitrant and incorrigible specimens to be driven and tightly controlled; as necessary components of task forces to be harnessed and motivated by skilled leaders and as such to be manipulated; and as higher beings with an innate capacity for self-control, self-development, and self-motivation. We now recognize the "knowledge worker," and the need for new patterns of interaction and involvement, new forms of recognition and reward, and new types of leadership to respect. And this is only a beginning.

Managers, whether in sunset industries or in the latest and highest "tech," will have to be creative as never before. (The most demanding situations may well be those confronting managers who must simultaneously handle the obsolete and the very new.) Product cycles will, in many instances, be dramatically telescoped because the new technologies will, for years to come, be subject to continuing alteration and elaboration. "New" products will be born before "old" ones reach adolescence. The "life-cycle" may combine the most difficult features of fast track development and simultaneous large-scale production. Little will be neat or follow tried and true formulas.

Most of all, managers will relate to people in ways we do not know and cannot teach. Much will have to be created and learned on the job, as we "develop" managers who can work with these new "knowledge" people and in self-reliant teams. The distributed intelligence of microprocessor technology, for example, may find its organization design arising from the informal networks that individuals bring into being through open-ended self-optimization. The formal organization chart of past and present, with its careful array of boxes representing line and staff hierarchies and linkages, is obsolete. The organization of the future is not likely to look as neat again. It is not long since Keuffel and Esser gave their last slide-rule to the Smithsonian. In like fashion, we will "museum" other ideas. There is an enormous amount of experimentation in organization design going on, as managers and owners search for enhanced productivity and effectiveness as well as survival. One of the things we know from the higher "tech" firms is that there is no "one best way" of organizing. Even the same firm does not look the same as it did; a characteristic of high-tech organization seems to be impermanence. The concept of open-ended innovation in all aspects—product, production, and organization—suggests evident dangers in seizing on panaceas and millennarian solutions. To seek quick salvation in the formulas that worked for a time in other cultures and societies seems at best misguided.

NOTES

An earlier version of this paper appeared in *Organizational Dynamics* (summer 1984), pp. 53–66. Reprinted with the permission of the publisher.

1. Serge Leontiev, "The New Automation," *New York Times,* Feb. 8, 1983, p. 68; John Naisbeth, *Megatrends: Ten New Directions Transforming Our Lives* (N.Y.: Warner Books, 1982).

2. Alfred D. Chandler, Jr., *The Visible Hand* (Cambridge: Belknap Press, 1977); idem. *Strategy and Structure* (Cambridge, Mass.: MIT, 1962); Joseph A. Schumpeter,

Capitalism, Socialism and Democracy 3d ed. (New York: Harper & Row, 1950); *Business and Its Environment: Essays for Thomas C. Cochran,* ed. Harold I. Sharlin (Westport, Conn.: Greenwood Press, 1983).

3. Much of this list was drawn up by international managers at the Administrative Staff College, Henley-on-Thames, 1981, based on a shorter list drawn up that year by Westinghouse scientists. H. Kahn, W. Brown, and L. Martel, *The Next 200 Years* (New York: William Morrow & Co., 1976); Robert B. Reich, *The Next American Frontier* (New York: Times Books, 1983).

4. Dirk Hanson, *The New Alchemists: Silicon Valley and the Microelectronics Revolution* (Boston: Little, Brown, 1982).

5. Hearings before the Subcommittee on Investigations and Oversight of the Committee on Science and Technology, U.S. House of Representatives, Ninety-Seventh Congress, second session, June 2, 23, 1982; Robert J. Miller, ed., *Robotics: Future Factories, Future Workers. The Annals of the American Academy of Political and Social Science,* Vol. 470, Nov. 1983.

6. Martin Mayer, ''Coming Fast: Services Through the TV set,'' *Fortune* (Nov. 14, 1983), pp. 50–56.

7. ''Biotech Comes of Age,'' *Business Week* (Jan. 23, 1984), pp. 85–94.

8. *Applied Science and Technology Index,* March 1982.

9. Kahn, Brown, and Martel, *Next 200 Years,* chaps. VIII, IX.

10. J. William Gotcher, ''Strategic Planning in European Multinationals,'' *Long Range Planning* (Oct. 1977).

11. Mariann Jelinek, *Institutionalizing Innovation* (New York: Praeger, 1979).

12. ''Metalworking: Yesterday & Tomorrow,'' *American Machinist,* 100th anniversary issue, 1978.

13. Warren Benner, ''Conversations with Warren Benner,'' *Organizational Dynamics* (Winter 1974).

14. James Brian Quinn, *Strategies for Change: Logical Incrementalism* (Homewood, Ill.: Richard D. Irwin, 1980).

15. Henry Mintzberg, ''The Manager's Job: Folklore and Fact,'' *Harvard Business Review* (July–Aug. 1975); Joan Woodward, *Industrial Organization: Theory and Practice* 2d ed. (New York: Oxford University Press, 1980), p. 77.

BIBLIOGRAPHY

Bell, Daniel. *The Coming of Post-Industrial Society.* New York: Basic Books, 1973.

Business and Its Environment: Essays for Thomas C. Cochran. Ed. Harold I. Sharlin. Westport, Conn.: Greenwood Press, 1983.

Chandler, Alfred D., Jr., *The Visible Hand: The Managerial Revolution in American Business.* Cambridge: Belknap Press, 1977.

————. *Strategy and Structure.* Cambridge, Mass.: MIT, 1962.

Hanson, Dirk. *The New Alchemists: Silicon Valley and the Microelectronics Revolution.* Boston: Little, Brown, 1982.

Jelinek, Mariann. *Institutionalizing Innovation.* New York: Praeger, 1979.

Kahn, Herman, William Brown, and Leon Martel. *The Next 200 Years*. New York: William Morrow & Co., 1976.

"The Mechanization of Work." *Scientific American,* V. 247, No. 3, Sept. 1982.

Naisbitt, John. *Megatrends: Ten New Directions Transforming Our Lives*. New York: Warner Books, 1982.

Noble, David F. *America by Design: Science, Technology, and the Rise of Corporate Capitalism*. New York: Alfred A. Knopf, 1977.

Quinn, James Brian. *Strategies for Change: Logical Incrementalism*. Homewood, Ill.: Richard D. Irwin, Inc., 1980.

Reich, Robert B. *The Next American Frontier*. New York: Times Books, 1983.

Schumpeter, Joseph A. *Capitalism, Socialism and Democracy*. 3d ed. New York: Harper & Row, 1950.

Thompson, James D. *Organizations in Action*. Hightstown, N.J.: McGraw-Hill, 1967.

Woodward, Joan. *Industrial Organization: Theory and Practice*. 2d ed. New York: Oxford University Press, 1980.

Bibliographic Essay

For those readers interested in the First and Second Industrial Revolutions, classical studies include T. S. Ashton's *The Industrial Revolution, 1760–1830* (New York: Oxford University Press, 1955); Phyllis Deane, *The First Industrial Revolution* (New York: Cambridge University Press, 1965); and David Landes, *Unbound Prometheus: Technological Change and Industrial Development in Western Europe from 1750 to the Present* (New York: Cambridge University Press, 1976). Karl Marx and Friedrich Engels are the most trenchant critics of these changes. See *Manifesto of the Communist Party,* translated by Samuel More, edited and annotated by Friedrich Engels (Chicago: C. H. Kerr & Co., 1946); and Friedrich Engels, *The Condition of the Working Class in England* (New York: Macmillan, 1958).

Although there is no definitive treatment of the Second Industrial Revolution—especially on the dramatic breakthroughs in automobiles, photography, electricity, and organized scientific education and research—some worthwhile studies are Robert Sobel, *The Age of Giant Corporations: A Microeconomic History of American Business, 1914–1970* (Westport, Conn.: Greenwood Press, 1972); Alfred D. Chandler, Jr., *The Visible Hand* (Cambridge, Mass.: Belknap Press, 1977); *Strategy and Structure: Chapters in the History of the American Industrial Enterprise* (Cambridge, Mass.: MIT, 1962); and "The Emergence of Managerial Capitalism," *Bus. Hist. Review* 58 (Winter 1984):473–503. An old but still valuable work is Adolf A. Berle, Jr., and Gardiner C. Means, *The Modern Corporation and Private Property,* (New York: Macmillan, 1932). Three critics of this revolution are Mathew Josephsen, *Robber Barons* (New York: Harcourt, Brace & World, 1962); Richard Hofstadter, *Social Darwinism in American Thought* (New York: G. Braziller, 1965, 1955); Thorstein Veblen, *The Theory of the Leisure Class: An Economic Study of Institutions* (Modern Library, 1934).

The Third Industrial Revolution is addressed by Serge Leontiev's "The New Automation" (*New York Times,* Feb. 8, 1983); John Naisbitt's *Megatrends: Ten New Directions Transforming Our Lives* (Warner Books, 1982); and Daniel Bell's *The Coming of Post-Industrial Society* (Basic Books, 1973).

Those who have raised questions concerning the adequacy of the United States' ability to take advantage of the Third Industrial Revolution include Alfred D. Chandler's *The*

Visible Hand (Belknap Press, 1977) and *Strategy and Structure* (MIT, 1962); and Joseph A. Schumpeter's *Capitalism, Socialism and Democracy*, 3rd ed. (Harper & Row, 1950). For more information on the new and dramatic products, see H. Kahn, W. Brown, and L. Martel's *The Next 200 Years* (William Morrow & Co., 1976); and Robert B. Reich's *The Next American Frontier* (Times Books, 1983).

For more on microprocessing and the microchip, see Dirk Hanson's *The New Alchemists: Silicon Valley and the Microelectronics Revolution* (Little, Brown, 1982).

For information on robotics, see Hearings Before the Subcommittee on Investigations and Oversight of the Committee on Science and Technology, U.S. House of Representatives, Ninety-Seventh Congress, second session, June 2, 23, 1982; and *Robotics: Future Factories, Future Workers,* Robert J. Miller, ed., *The Annals of the American Academy of Political and Social Sciences,* Vol. 470, November 1983. For telecommunications information see, Martin Mayer's "Coming Fast: Services Through the TV Set" (*Fortune,* Nov. 14, 1983). For a quick summary of the biotechnology domain, see "Biotech Comes of Age" (*Business Week,* Jan. 23, 1984).

Peter Drucker discusses new organizational styles in an exciting and imaginative article, "The Coming of the New Organization," *Harvard Business Review,* Feb. 1988, pp. 45–53; cf. T. Pepper, M. Janow, and J. Wheeler's *The Competition: Dealing with Japan* (New York: Praeger, 1985). Arthur Francis summarizes a great deal of the discussion of the impact of new technology on workers in *New Technology of Work* (Oxford: Clarendon, 1986). Harry L. Shipman's *Space 2000: Meeting the Challenge of a New Era* (New York: Plenum, 1987) addresses a theme not treated in this volume, but of inevitable importance, as does James Gleick's *Chaos: Making a New Science* (N.Y.: Viking, 1987), an excellent semipopular treatment of fractals, a new scientific paradigm of enormous scientific and philosophical interest.

No reader can avoid the flood of material, popular and learned, on the Third Industrial Revolution as it transforms our world; this outpouring can only increase as more radical changes occur. A reserved and cautious acceptance is the best guide.

Index

About the Editor

JOSEPH FINKELSTEIN is a Professor of History and Economics and of Industrial Administration and Management at the Graduate Management Institute at Union College. He is co-author of *Economists and Society: The Development of Economic Thought from Aquinas to Keynes.*